CHILD CUSTODY EVALUATION

CHILD CUSTODY EVALUATION

New Theoretical Applications and Research

By

DANIEL J. HYNAN, Ph.D.

CHARLES C THOMAS • PUBLISHER, LTD.
Springfield • Illinois • U.S.A.

Published and Distributed Throughout the World by

CHARLES C THOMAS • PUBLISHER, LTD.
2600 South First Street
Springfield, Illinois 62704

© 2014 by CHARLES C THOMAS • PUBLISHER, LTD.

ISBN 978-0-398-08094-5 (Paper)
ISBN 978-0-398-08095-2 (Ebook)

Library of Congress Catalog Card Number: 2014008339

With THOMAS BOOKS *careful attention is given to all details of manufacturing
and design. It is the Publisher's desire to present books that are satisfactory as to their
physical qualities and artistic possibilities and appropriate for their particular use.*
THOMAS BOOKS *will be true to those laws of quality that assure a good name
and good will.*

Printed in the United States of America
UBC-R-3

Library of Congress Cataloging-in-Publication Data

Hynan, Daniel J.
  Child custody evaluation: new theoretical applications and research / by
Daniel J. Hynan, Ph.D.
    pages cm
  Includes bibliographical references and index.
  ISBN 978-0-398-08094-5 (pbk.) -- ISBN 978-0-398-08095-2 (ebook)
1. Children of divorced parents -- Psychology. 2. Custody of children.
3. Parenting, Part-time. I. Title

  HQ777.5.H96 2014
  346.01'73 -- dc23
                                                      2014008339

PREFACE

Roughly two decades ago, I started carrying out child custody and similar types of evaluations. I had always been focused on integrating scientific evidence into my therapy and assessment practice, and after a fairly short time of doing custody work, it became clear that evaluation methods needed a significant injection of empiricism. That realization started the long run of trying to use some of my limited spare time to write articles focused on combining science and professional experience to promote advancement in the child custody field. At some point, years ago, it occurred to me that I could and should write a book. I aimed for 2015 as a tentative goal.

Along the way, I have gained a lot of knowledge and received a good deal of inspiration from those who wrote pioneering books on child custody evaluation, including Benjamin Schutz and his coauthors (the first one I read), Marc Ackerman, Jon Gould, and Philip Stahl. Although I left behind Barry Bricklin's methodology a long time ago, I still appreciate that his contributions helped to focus the field on making improvements. There are many others whose work I consider to fall in the range between very good and phenomenal, and my more specific views about such matters can largely be seen in my reference citations.

As I was working on the exhaustive task of statistically analyzing test data on hundreds of custody evaluation parents, it occurred to me that the custody evaluation field would benefit most from peer-reviewed articles on tests that did not have such prior publications. Because there had never been any peer-reviewed articles specifically about custody litigants regarding the Personality Assessment Inventory or the Parent-Child Relationship Inventory, I submitted the most fundamental data, including gender comparisons, to the *Open Access Journal of Forensic Psychology*. Two articles on those tests were published in that journal in 2013. I have a great deal of regard for the highly productive way that Editor Greg DeClue manages that journal, and those articles can be downloaded in full at no cost from the journal website. Because there already had been a number of good-quality, peer-reviewed articles on the use of the MMPI-2 in child custody litigation, I concluded it was not necessary to go through the additional work of writing a journal article on that measure.

Anyone who has looked at this book beyond this preface will have noted that each chapter begins with a Practice Checklist. I repeatedly emphasize that evaluators need to engage in careful deliberation, and the checklists can be a highly useful, practical method of doing so. They have been recommended by Nobel laureate Daniel Kahneman and others as a means to promote higher-level deliberation instead of more faulty intuition. I put them at the beginning of chapters to increase the odds that readers will use them.

As I created these checklists, there were repeated quandaries regarding how many points to include. There is an inevitable trade-off between how well checklists grab the reader's attention and their length, and there is no perfect answer for every context. The final ones included here integrate crucial concepts and procedures, with a focus on relative brevity.

In a few places in the book, there is repetition of certain content areas. I think most readers are probably like me in that they do not read this type of book from front to back, but tend to focus on certain chapters or sections, one at a time. Some topics are relevant for more than one chapter, and some material is simply important enough that it deserves to be repeated.

I am grateful to many people, including hundreds of judges and attorneys who have referred evaluations to me over the many years. I greatly appreciate the mainly anonymous reviewers and editors who have read, commented on, and agreed to publish my journal articles.

I am enormously grateful to the team of multidisciplinary professionals who read the manuscript and offered very helpful comments: Sarah Bonkowski, Mary Jean Dolan, and Steven Peskind. I appreciate Bob Emery's suggestion to consider material on early neutral evaluations. Also, I want to thank Marzena Powala and Peter Ji for their great help in assisting me in preparation of parts of this book. I am most thankful for my family for their inspiration and support.

I am lucky for a lot of reasons. One big piece of luck was the genetics lottery where I got the nucleus of cognitive ability to be able to do such work. I was extremely fortunate to have parents who were good models of how to work and interact with other human beings. Also, I was very fortunate to stumble across this area of work that has been both fascinating and a good fit for my set of skills.

There is a saying that individuals who are fortunate enough to have resources have the responsibility to use them well. It is well known that children of divorce are at a very increased risk of experiencing an array of life problems, and the main goal of custody evaluations is to assist those children. It is easy to talk about the importance of helping children of divorce lead positive lives, but in order to carry out actual improvements, many knowledgeable people need to persist through lots of obstacles to do difficult work in multiple areas over a long period of time. The goal is worth the effort.

CONTENTS

CHILD CUSTODY EVALUATION

Chapter 1

WHAT IS IMPORTANT FOR CHILDREN OF DIVORCE?

PRACTICE CHECKLIST

There are negative effects on children of divorce as a result of:

____Exposure to interparental conflict

____Parental psychological dysfunction

____Loss of contact with a parent

____Economic hardship

____Stress

____Multiple family transitions

Other negative effects on children can result from:

____Inadequate affection and nurturance

____Aversive parenting, such as harsh punishment

Positive effects on children of divorce can result from parental:

____Warmth and support

____Active child management

____Relatively close parent-child relationships

____Know relevant state statutes regarding child custody and visitation.

____Know essentials of relevant U. S. Supreme Court decisions.

____Know the common and legal meanings of vocabulary pertaining to child custody.

Note: This form is a guide to promote productive reasoning and good practice. It is not comprehensive or all-inclusive and does not replace adequate training and experience.

Over one and a half million children each year experience the divorce of their parents (Arkowitz & Lilienfeld, 2013). For a significant proportion of these children, there are strong disagreements between the parents about custody, time sharing, and making important decisions about the children. When there are such disagreements, evaluators and other professionals, such as judges, attorneys, and mediators, must try to sort through and make sense of a complex and conflicting array of information to try to reach an accurate idea about what is most important and relevant.

How does anyone decide what is most important and relevant regarding children of divorce? Certainly families are often complex and many people have views of parent-child interactions that are primarily influenced by their own experiences when they grew up. The wide variety of books, television shows, and other media on families and parenting reflect the disparate perspectives and approaches that exist.

My goal in writing this book is to contribute to the advancement of knowledge regarding children of divorce, especially the practice of evaluation as it pertains to child custody, time sharing, and related matters. To work toward this goal, I attempt to integrate scientific findings, relevant theory, and professional experience in such a way as to be both conceptually sound and useful in practice. Also, I strongly consider the perspectives of others who have been very critical of custody evaluation and related concepts (e.g., Emery, Otto, & O'Donohue, 2005; Krauss & Sales, 2000). For example, in chapter 2, I closely examine, from both conceptual and empirical standpoints, the "approximation rule" proposed by the American Law Institute (ALI) (2002) that would change the best-interest-of-the-child legal standard and that includes considerable criticism of custody evaluation.

The reality of custody evaluation work is that there are a plethora of specific circumstances regarding each family that must be taken into consideration. Often, the circumstances and combinations of circumstances are highly challenging. The human reality of divorce is that many evaluations include a very mixed and difficult set of facts, associated with emotionally gut-wrenching experiences for parents and children.

For example, a considerable proportion of custody evaluations include allegations of domestic violence. Such actions are often private events, witnessed by no one, and result in highly conflicting claims by each party. Certain individuals may engage in distortions, purposeful or otherwise, about what actually took place. Some cases involve serious domestic violence. There is a stereotype that domestic violence occurs mainly in lower socioeconomic groups. However, research has found that it affects all realms of society, including those at upper income levels. Upscale women who were victims of domestic violence were the focus of research by Weitzman (2000):

> Living a life perceived to be foreign to the experience of one's peers typically gives rise to emotions like shame. Sally told me, "I was embarrassed by it. When he would hit me, I would become embarrassed. I would be humiliated." Another woman, Alice, strongly asserted, "No, you're married, for better or for worse. You can't tell anybody, and the reason you can't tell anybody is: it's *embarrassing.* It's a very shameful thing." And Jennifer said, "I didn't want anyone to know that

about me; I didn't want them to think that of me. I wanted them to think, 'She's wonderfully happy; she's wonderfully successful; she's a good wife." (p. 26)

A number of other difficult cases include intense emotions and controversies over whether it is good or harmful for a very young child to have overnight visits with the nonresidential parent.

> Consider the young father faced with a court order dictating short visits during the work week, designed to create a relaxed, if brief, parenting experience while not stressing the baby with undue separations from the mother. He may well have a rigidly scheduled, entry-level job that supports not just himself, but his child and his child's mother. Yet, he must find the two, sometimes three, two-hour blocks of parenting time that his employer will allow. His employer will likely have no reason to entertain providing a flexible work schedule to a junior employee. So, the young man leaves work promptly at 5:00 p.m. and speeds to the home of his child's mother. He picks up the baby, who may well be cranky because of hunger or fatigue at that time of day. The child may thus struggle against the transition. He then drives at least a few minutes to his home, arriving there just before six. The baby may now be asleep or frantically hungry. The baby's mood does not improve when she is woken, taken out of her car seat, and fed as fast as the father can, but not as fast as the baby wants. By this time, the father may have only half an hour or so to enjoy his child before the drive and transfer to the mother's home begins. (Ludolph, 2012, pp. 491–492)

It is important for evaluators and others to have empathy with the plight of children and families who are going through a divorce or separation process. However, unlike counseling and psychotherapy, in which empathy can play a direct role as a therapeutic factor, it is not a direct contributor to carrying out a high-quality evaluation. The productive use of empathy in the evaluative process is to provide motivation for evaluators to carry out numerous difficult tasks, including, but not limited to acquiring extensive scientific and professional knowledge, learning and carrying out valid and relevant methodology, using sound reasoning in the analysis of information that is collected, and conveying the probable final product of a written report in a clear and timely manner.

SCIENTIFIC EVIDENCE ABOUT CHILDREN OF DIVORCE

A crucial general principle for custody evaluators is that the most important and relevant area of information in conceptualizing what is best for children is the research evidence that pertains to children of divorce. Dozens of research studies that include tens of thousands of individuals have been analyzed in a number of quantitative and qualitative reviews. In general, this research has found that children of divorce function less well than children from never-divorced families in a number of areas of life, including school achievement, behavior, self-concept, psychological adjustment, marital adjustment, social interactions, and parent-child relationships (e.g., Amato, 2001; Hetherington, Bridges, & Insabella, 1998; Lansford, 2009). Although sources differ about the extent of the negative impact of divorce on children, it is clear that some individuals, but not all, who go through the separation or divorce of their parents experience a significant adverse effect. For example, Kelly (2012) estimated that about 25% of children who go through the separation or divorce of their parents experience significant adjustment problems, compared to about 10% of the general child population. To further examine what it is about divorce that contributes to deleterious outcomes for some individuals, research has looked at a number of factors hypothesized to be harmful to children of divorce.

It is crucial for custody evaluators to have a solid grasp of the empirical bases relevant to child custody matters. In a magisterial review that examined many types of assessments, Garb (1998) emphasized that appropriate reliance on scientific evidence is of central importance in carrying out work that has reasonable accuracy. Also, from a legal risk reduction point of view, it is crucial to have a central focus on empirical evidence and other objective information (Woody, 2013).

A meta-analysis by Amato and Keith (1991) focused on studies that compared children living in single-parent divorced families with those who were living in continuously intact families. In particular, they investigated three hypotheses regarding why children of divorce tended to manifest lower well-being than children from intact families. Those three hypotheses focused on parental absence, economic disadvantage, and family conflict. The authors found that there was statistical support for all three hypotheses, but most strongly for family conflict.

Amato (1993) further investigated hypotheses that might account for the finding that children of divorce generally function less well than children from intact families. In addition to the three hypotheses described above, this study investigated the impact of parental psychological adjustment and the effect of life stress. A primary method involved tracking how many studies supported each hypothesis versus how many studies yielded results that did not support the hypothesis. There were varying levels of support for each hypothesis, but the most robust support was found for the interparental conflict and parental psychological adjustment hypotheses. The author noted that there are important areas of overlap between each of the five hypotheses about what affects children of divorce, and that a model that combines all five is necessary to account well for research findings. In other words, it is clear that numerous factors need to be considered simultaneously in order to develop a good understanding about what influences children of divorce.

FAMILY PROCESSES

Divorce is most productively conceptualized as a process instead of a discrete event. There are numerous individual psychological and interpersonal processes that take place more or less simultaneously during the separation and divorce process. These family processes are influenced by the research-derived factors described above, and in turn can have a significant impact on children of divorce. For example, Davies and Cummings (1994) reviewed considerable research in an investigation of what it is about exposure to interparental conflict that has a negative effect on children of divorce. They concluded that the exposure to such conflict leads to decreased emotional security that plays a central role in the adverse effect on children.

A longitudinal study of a very large sample of adolescents, whose parents had initiated divorce action a number of years previously, investigated factors that had a significant influence on personal adjustment (Buchanan, Maccoby, & Dornbusch, 1996). Parental control and management were strong predictors of adolescent well-being, as was parent-child closeness. In addition, those dimensions were positively correlated with one another. It appeared that the closeness between the parent and the adolescent assisted the parents to better monitor the adolescent's actions, thereby leading to better overall adjustment.

A combination of warm, supportive parenting with active child management and calm limit setting is often referred to as authoritative parenting (Baumrind, 1966). Others have found authoritative parenting to be a positive factor for children's well-being, including children of divorce. For example, in a meta-analysis, Amato and Gilbreath (1999) found that the presence of relatively close parent-child relationships with authoritative parenting by nonresidential fathers was predictive of good child adjustment.

Most research on parent-child relationships following separation and divorce has focused on mothers as parents because they are the more frequent primary caretakers. A close relationship between a child and mother who is both supportive and authoritative has been found to be consistently predictive of better child functioning. In contrast, especially with adolescents, when there is a negative parent-child relationship with limited monitoring, it increases the risk of involvement with dysfunctional peers, and thereby heightens the likelihood of a child developing a variety of problems (Hetherington et al., 1998).

There is consistent evidence that children exposed to numerous family transitions fare worse on a number of outcomes. Such transitions appear to occur more often among cohabitating couples then among parents who form stepfamilies through remarriage. There are questions about the extent to which the negative impact on children is the result of the transitions alone versus being due to relatively general instability on the part of the parents (Anderson & Greene, 2013).

In addition, outside the realm of separation and divorce, considerable research has demonstrated a strong impact of parenting behaviors on later child
functioning. For example, in a longitudinal study that covered hundreds of
individuals from approximately 6 through 33 years of age, there was a focus
on identifying parenting behaviors that placed offspring at risk for personality
disorders during adulthood. Findings included that low parental affection or
nurturing was associated with an elevated risk for numerous types of offspring
personality disorders in adulthood, including antisocial, avoidance, borderline, depressive, paranoid, schizoid, and schizotypal types. Aversive parenting, such as overly harsh punishment, was associated with increased risk for
borderline, paranoid, passive-aggressive, and schizotypal personality disorders in adult offspring (Johnson, Cohen, Chen, Kasen, & Brook, 2006).

It is important to note that the research factors and family processes described here can combine in complex ways. For example, clinical depression
in parents was found to be associated with insecurity in close adult relationships, as well as with conflict between the parents. The interparental conflict
led to perceptions by the children that their parents were rejecting of them.
The children's perceptions that the parents were rejecting in turn were related
to child psychological symptoms (Shelton & Harold, 2008).

Hetherington et al. (1998) proposed a transactional model to try to account
for the numerous interacting factors and processes that affected children's
adjustment following divorce and remarriage. Family processes were one of the
central hubs of the model. Factors such as parental psychological functioning,
stress, economic changes, family composition, and individual child characteristics could have an impact on family processes. Other factors such as social
support and some child characteristics could mediate the effects of family
processes on child adjustment.

STATUTORY FACTORS AND RESEARCH FINDINGS

In addition to these psychosocial variables, it is necessary for custody evaluators to strongly consider legal statutes regarding custody, visitation and
related matters (APA, 2013). A number of states have relied, at least in part,
on the Uniform Marriage and Divorce Act (UMDA) (National Conference of
Commissioners on Uniform State Laws (NCCUSL), 1979), which identifies
that custody and visitation needs to focus on the best interest of the child, and
lists factors to be considered (Elrod & Dale, 2008–2009). Those factors include the wishes of the parents; the wishes of the child; the interactions of the
child with the parents, siblings, and other relevant individuals; the child's
adjustment to home, school and community; the mental and physical health
of all relevant individuals; and other criteria that may be relevant in individual

cases. For example, a number of state statutes describe additional factors to be considered such as the presence or likelihood of domestic violence and child abuse. Some states include what are sometimes known as "friendly parent" statutory factors that examine matters such as the ability and willingness of a parent to facilitate a good relationship between the child and the other parent.

It is crucial to note that there is considerable conceptual overlap between these statutory factors and research findings on children of divorce. For example, the statutory factor that includes the interactions between the child and parents is a relatively broad one that overlaps with research factors such as the loss of a significant relationship with a parent and exposure to interparental conflict. The friendly parent statutory factor overlaps a great deal with a child's exposure to conflict between parents, particularly if one parent is seen to be much better or worse at promoting a good relationship between the child and the other parent. The statutory factor that considers the mental health of all relevant individuals overlaps a great deal with the research finding that shows parental psychological dysfunction that affects parenting functioning to have a negative impact on children. The statutory factors in some states that consider domestic violence and/or child abuse also overlap with the research factor regarding the mental health of all relevant individuals, in large part because such violence and abuse could have a significant negative impact on child mental health; also, perpetrators of domestic violence and/or child abuse often manifest psychological disorders. A number of statutory factors are relevant to the research factor that increased stress can have a negative impact on children of divorce.

OTHER CONCEPTUAL FRAMEWORKS

Although the research factors and the statutory ones are those most important for custody evaluators to consider, other conceptual frameworks have been described as relevant in considering children of divorce. The concept of goodness of fit between a child and parent is one example. In general, this model reasons that custody evaluation should include a search for what might be the optimal fit between a child's individual characteristics and parental features that are relevant for child rearing. The goodness of fit concept is particularly noteworthy because the American Psychological Association (APA) Guidelines for Child Custody Evaluations in Family Law Proceedings (2010) recommends that it be a possible area of focus in evaluation, associated with parenting attributes and children's psychological needs, all within the goal of clarifying the psychological best interest of the child. When there is a child with special needs, the goodness of fit perspective is most likely to be very useful. For example, if a child has special needs such that he or she requires intensive and coordinated healthcare, it would be crucial to consider each parent's ability to be available, organized, emotionally supportive, and proactive about such needs.

In addition, associated with their criticism of child custody evaluation, Krauss and Sales (2000) argued that the legal best interest standard is faulty, and it would be preferable for the legal system and evaluators to adopt the standard of what is the least detrimental alternative to the child. They make a valid point in describing that psychological research and methods are better able to identify what is negative for children of divorce than what is optimal for such children. However, a focus on children's best interest has a great deal of logical overlap with an emphasis on avoiding the least detrimental alternative. On a practical basis, the vast majority of disputed child custody cases referred for evaluation include allegations that at least one possible custody or time-sharing alternative would be very detrimental to a child. When there is no concern about a possible detrimental outcome, such cases are likely to be in the vast majority that are resolved without the need for a custody evaluation.

TYPES OF CUSTODY

The categories or labels characteristically used to describe custody are unfortunately confusing, largely because they can sometimes refer to the amount of time a child spends with each parent, or alternately, to the ability of each parent to make or contribute to major child-rearing decisions. For example, joint custody is often used to describe a legal requirement for both parents to have equal say in making decisions together about major child-rearing areas such as education, healthcare, religion, and extracurricular activities. In this meaning of joint custody, it is contrasted with sole custody. The parent who has sole custody is legally able to make the decisions in such major areas.

However, the term joint custody is sometimes used to refer to the proportion of time children spend with each parent. Because of such multiple meanings, in conversation and in writing, it often is not sufficiently clear what exactly is meant by joint custody.

As a result, joint legal custody is a phrase commonly used among professionals to designate joint decision making. In most of these cases, the children reside with one parent most of the time and visit the other regularly. Joint legal custody is also referred to, at times, as joint parenting.

In addition, the term joint physical custody has been used in multiple ways. Some legal and mental health professionals have used the term to refer to children being with each parent an equal amount of time, or a division of time very close to equal. However, some scholars have used joint physical custody to refer to residential arrangements in which children are spending a good deal of time with each parent, though the time division can vary a good deal between about 50% with each parent to approximately a 25-75% arrangement. In recent years, the term shared parenting has become more common. Among a number of professionals, its initial meaning was essentially a 50-50% time division. However, particularly in research, its meaning has been somewhat more broad and therefore sometimes less clear. That is, among researchers shared parenting has come to generally mean that each parent has the child reside with them between approximately 35% and 65% of the time. (e.g., McIntosh, Smyth, & Kelaher, 2010).

The vagueness of this vocabulary can cloud the reality that it is a much different situation for one set of parents to have a 65-35% time split, as compared to a 50-50% division of time. In the first instance, the child would be with one parent about twice as often as the other parent, whereas in the second example the time is obviously split equally. The divergent realities of life under those different circumstances are considerable. Associated with these factors, the term equally shared parenting has generally come to mean that each parent has the children about equally, between about 48% and 52% of the time.

The lack of precision and clarity in these terms leads to confusion for some parents who are going through the process of splitting up. For example, an attorney may inform the client that the other parent wants sole custody, and the parent who hears that information might erroneously conclude that it means the other wants to have the children all the time.

The vagueness of the terms that pertain to custody can also have a substantially negative impact in terms of people having an accurate understanding of the meaning of research findings. In the social science literature on children of divorce, joint custody is often given a specific definition early in the publication. However, if that definition is not read and clearly understood, the reader can easily misinterpret substantive information that occurs later in the article or book, and thereby miss the meaning of the empirical findings that are reported. In an important example, Maccoby and Mnookin (1992) carried out an exceptional landmark study of families going through divorce. They categorized children as being in dual residences (a term that is conceptualized as meaning essentially the same thing as joint custody) when they spent the equivalent of a minimum of two days out of seven (29%) with the parent who did not have primary residential custody. A number of other researchers (e.g., Cloutier & Jacque, 1997) have followed that definition. However, any reader of this area of research, or anyone who reads references to it, who assumes that dual residences or joint custody means that children are with each parent about the same amount of time would be at risk of making highly incorrect conclusions about children of divorce.

Therefore, in the remainder of this book, for purposes of clarity, to describe children being with each parent an equal amount of time, or very close to it, such as a 52-48% split, I use the phrase equally shared parenting. When each parent has children about an equal amount of time, which appears to occur in a fairly small proportion of cases, it seems to be routinely accompanied by shared decision making. To describe children being primarily with one parent and visiting the other regularly, under conditions of legally determined joint decision making, I use the term joint legal custody. To describe circumstances in which the children are primarily with one parent and visiting the other regularly, but with the primary residential parent having legally determined decision making, I use the term sole custody.

In my decades of experience covering many hundreds of custody and related evaluations, I have never seen a case in which one parent was legally required to have no contact with the child at all. There are cases, of course, in which a parent has highly restricted visits, such as under conditions of supervision only. I specifically describe the relevant circumstances when I refer to such cases. Similarly, I clearly describe when I am referring to a case in which there may be no contact between a child and parent because of the child's refusal.

CONCLUSIONS

There is a strong emphasis all throughout this book on the importance of relying on scientific evidence throughout the custody evaluation process. It is important and relevant that U. S. Supreme Court decisions, relied upon in a number of state courts, indicated that expert testimony must be based on knowledge grounded in the scientific method (*Daubert v. Merrell Dow Pharmaceuticals*, 1993), and there must be a clear basis in scientific evidence for expert opinion to be accepted in court (*General Electric v. Joiner*, 1997). In a subsequent case, *Kumho Tire v. Carmichael* (1999), the U. S. Supreme Court clarified that expert testimony under the *Daubert* standard needs to meet requirements of Federal Rule of Evidence 702, which pertains to scientific, technical, or other specialized knowledge. It states that expert testimony must be based on sufficient facts or data, needs to be the product of reliable methods and principles, and those methods and principles must be applied reliably to the fact of the case. Even in state courts that do not rely on *Daubert* and related decisions, evaluators should be aware of these legal factors because they influence the overall professional environments in which evaluations take place.

Therefore, the field of custody evaluation needs to integrate multiple realms of knowledge. Those areas include scientific findings relevant for children of divorce, the best use of diverse evaluation procedures, relevant statutes, U. S.

Supreme Court decisions, ethical standards, and practice guidelines (see Chapter 15). Also, there must be sound deliberation about all such matters instead of relying on clinical intuition (see Chapter 3). An essential challenge is to integrate such relatively dry, detailed material with very human, messy realities, including anguished emotions inherent in the separation and divorce process. As described earlier, it is important for evaluators to use empathy for the very difficult plight of families to motivate themselves to carry out the challenging steps required to complete high-quality evaluations.

In closing this chapter, I encourage readers to keep firmly in mind the main points made here, some of which are summarized in the Practice Checklist. These points establish a conceptual foundation for subsequent chapters that focus on crucial elements of the evaluation methods and frequent challenges faced by individuals in the field.

Chapter 2

NEW THEORETICAL APPLICATIONS: GAME THEORY

PRACTICE CHECKLIST

____Parents in contested custody cases are likely to have their actions influenced by relevant statutes and case law.

____Proposed legal changes, some adopted, increase consideration of parents' past caretaking of children.

____Parental strategies have expanded to include efforts to spend more time with children, especially in public view, prior to divorce filing, evaluation or trial.

____Parents pay the most attention to their own interactions with their children, and may sincerely disagree, at least in part, on past caretaking.

____Parents contesting custody are very unlikely to agree on past caretaking histories.

____High-conflict parents rarely change into cooperative parents — if they improve they are likely to become disengaged from one another.

____There is no empirical or theoretical support for the concept of *strength* of attachment — what is important is attachment *security*.

____Parental circumstances, especially availability to be directly with the children, often change with separation/divorce.

____Evaluators need to create mechanisms (e.g., checklists) to promote careful deliberation about the assertions of each parent.

Note: This form is a guide to promote productive reasoning. It is not comprehensive or all-inclusive and does not replace adequate training and experience.

Game theory is the study of the strategies used by rational agents in their actions and reactions toward one another (McCain, 2004). A central assumption of game theory is that people act in their own self-interest. A central process in game theory is to determine which are the best responsive strategies to the strategies chosen by others.

Clearly, child custody disputes characteristically involve opposing parties who are likely to engage in various strategies and tactics in order to gain an advantage against the other side, or who are at least seriously considering doing so. Such strategizing is part and parcel of parental efforts within the court system to gain child custody, and can have a heavy influence on interactions with the children and the other parent. It can also play a very large role in how parents present themselves in custody evaluations.

Game theory generally is a broad subject with applications in many fields. For example, game theory has been applied to economics, war, politics, biology, ecology, and social problem-solving. Five game theory scholars have won Nobel prizes and have served as advisors to the Pentagon at some points in their careers (Fisher, 2008).

In this book, however, the focus is limited to those aspects of game theory with clear applicability to child custody disputes. As a result, the quantitative aspects of game theory are not described here, as narrative description adequately conveys the game theory concepts relevant to disputes about time sharing and decision making. More detailed descriptions of game theory, including its quantitative features, can be found in Fisher (2008) and McCain (2004).

This chapter first briefly summarizes the applicability of game theory to child custody, and then describes relevant statutes and proposed legal changes. Next, it describes a number of parental strategies that are carried out in response to current or proposed laws. The following relatively lengthy section integrates relevant research, game theory, and professional considerations with a primary focus on legal policy. The final part of the chapter focuses on applications to evaluation practice.

It should be noted that an entity conceptually related to game theory, called bargaining theory in legal academia, was used to examine the notion that there were trade-offs between obtaining child custody and receiving financial inputs such as child support and/or alimony. In particular, a classic article by Mnookin and Kornhauser (1979) maintained that women, because they tended to be more averse to risk and hypothetically more invested in the children than were fathers, would accept less financial support in order to avoid any possibility of losing custody of the children. There have been numerous empirical investigations, including those reported in the landmark study by Maccoby and Mnookin (1992), and the general conclusion is that there is an absence of evidence that such trade-offs between money and custody regularly take place (Dolan & Hynan, in press). Bargaining theory was not used to focus on the numerous other aspects of the legal process relevant to child custody, including the evaluation of what would be best for children.

Therefore, the current work appears to be the first direct application of game theory to the child custody process. As described later in this chapter, a number of relevant predictions that emanate from game theory were tested in practice-oriented research. Those research findings have been integrated here with existing scientific evidence; together, the theory and research have important implications for legal policy.

Game theory posits that, although self-interest is a primary human motivation, there may also be circumstances that lead people to choose cooperation instead of conflict. One potential objective of game theory is to promote circumstances that facilitate such cooperation. Some individuals may choose to cooperate for the mutual benefit of all, such as parents who recognize that the benefits of a good agreement about their children outweigh the drawbacks. However, others may choose to pursue their own individual self-interest, which can potentially lead to a trap (Fisher, 2008). For example, a trap exists when parents pursue a path of conflict regarding their children which results in the total benefit to both parents being less than the benefits that would have occurred had they cooperated.

Individuals in conflict will sometimes try to determine a strategy that yields a higher payoff than any other one. If one such strategy overpowers the strategy carried out by the other side, it is identified as a dominant strategy. In those instances in which the dominant strategy is different from a cooperative solution, the result is a social dilemma.

These types of strategies are considered by game theory as if they were actual games. Such games are seen as generally having known rules and payoffs, with each side trying to maximize their own benefits. Family law practice regularly includes such strategizing when conflict is present. For example, parents and their attorneys are often described as "positioning" to try to gain the greatest advantage. Survey research found that attorneys highly value preparing their clients for custody evaluations by advising them about how to present themselves well (Bow, Gottlieb, Gould-Saltzman, & Hendershot, 2011), which can be seen as one aspect of positioning.

Conflicts over the relative amounts of time spent with children, and about the extent to which each parent is involved in decision-making, can be understood as examples of constant sum games. In such cases, the total payoff to parents adds up to 100% of residential time with the children, and 100% of decision making about important parenting matters. Perhaps obviously, the larger the proportion gained by one parent, the smaller the proportion remaining for the other.

Game theory, in examining how people pursue their own self-interest in conflict-laden situations, primarily considers rational factors such as each individual weighing the pros and cons of different strategies, and trying to ascertain the intentions and future actions of their opponent. In separation and divorce, powerful emotional factors usually exist alongside rational ones and can serve as strong motivators. Although game theory does not have a primary focus on emotional factors, it is very important to consider them, integrated with rational ones, in efforts to understand what motivates people under conflict-laden circumstances. Many legal and mental health professionals have noted that domestic relations litigants who have particularly strong levels of anger and disdain for their opponents tend to comprise that small proportion of high-conflict cases that consumes a remarkably large portion of the courts' time and energy.

Neuroscience researchers have started to shed light on some of the brain mechanisms involved in both rational and emotional processes that influence decision-making. For example, neuroimaging research has shown correspondence between the area of the brain known as the striatum and social decisions to reciprocate or not reciprocate cooperative behaviors. Other brain areas, the medial prefrontal cortex and anterior paracingulate cortex, appear to be activated when an individual is focused on trying to detect the intentions of other individuals, such as trying to guess their game strategies. Electrophysiological measures of skin conductance have been found to discriminate between levels of acceptance and rejection of offers from others. Perhaps not surprisingly for those familiar with conflict-laden divorces, negative emotional states lead people to reject offers from others more often than those who are in emotionally neutral frames of mind (Sanfey, 2007).

A combination of rational and emotional factors contributes to each divorcing parent's experience of trust in the other party. Trust is a central mechanism necessary to arrive at a settlement of the conflict that is beneficial for both parties (Fisher, 2008).

However, engaging in trust in conflict-laden circumstances involves taking major risks. Those risks have strong emotional elements. If an offer is made to the other side, there is often understandable fear that the other party will reject it or try to take advantage of it, as offers that include gestures of perceived kindness can sometimes be perceived as a weakness. If individuals believe that their trust has been betrayed, it often leads to anger, disgust, and retaliation. Of course, cycles of retaliation between conflicting parties lead to further deteriorations in trust, possible intensification of the battle, and often increased fear. As noted by Fisher (2008), under such conditions it is unfortunately likely that negative emotional factors will override rational attempts at finding beneficial solutions and overcome other positive feelings that might have existed.

In the midst of such emotional distress, rational strategizing, risk-taking, and uncertainties about the future, the law comes into play. Statutes about child residence and decision making in separation and divorce matters are examples of legislators acting as creators of social mechanism designs to try to promote what is best for all involved. Those who create social mechanism designs in the forms of laws and policies need to be concerned that they have generally good results and that the parties do not have incentives to distort information or lie.

As described in Chapter 1, the foundational social mechanisms that have been put into place are state statutes. Most states incorporated the UMDA (NCCUSL, 1979) with additions or other modifications, and eight states adopted it without changes (Elrod & Dale, 2008–2009). The UMDA identifies the best interest of the child as the principle to be followed in custody and visitation. Also, the UMDA describes qualitative factors to be considered in determining the best interest of the child. However, there have been criticisms that the UMDA qualitative best interest factors lead to increased problems for families and the legal system.

ALTERNATIVES TO TRADITIONAL BEST INTEREST STANDARD: APPROXIMATION RULE AND RELATED PROPOSALS

The ALI (2002) proposed an alternative to the UMDA best interest factors in terms of when children should be with each parent after the separation or divorce and how decision-making responsibility should be determined. The ALI described that its primary objective was also the child's best interest, but it emphasized mainly quantitative factors. It stated that a secondary objective is to achieve fairness between the parents. When there is a dispute about time sharing, the ALI approximation rule states that parents should approximate the amount of child caretaking each one carried out prior to the parental separation. More specifically, the ALI maintained that past caretaking provides a relatively concrete point of reference which is allegedly reflective of qualitative factors, including the strength of the emotional ties between the child and each parent, how much each parent puts the child first, and comparative parenting abilities. Therefore, it argued that a past caretaker standard would reduce the need to rely on expensive expert input. The ALI contended that the parent who had been the primary caretaker of the child should continue to be in that role, and that parents who had co-equal roles before their separation should also retain that arrangement. Somewhat similarly, the ALI indicated that decision making about children needs to consider, as a primary factor, the amount of each parent's decision making about children in the past.

In addition, the ALI (2002) listed a number of exceptions to the past caretaker standard. For example, decisions about time sharing would be made in such a way that would avoid harm to a child, such as if there were major disparities in parental ability to meet a child's needs. There were other exceptions, described as limiting factors, such as if a parent engaged in child abuse, neglect or abandonment; carried out or allowed domestic violence; engaged in substance abuse that interfered with parenting; or interfered with the other parent's access to the child.

One of the arguments in favor of adopting the ALI (2002) principles pertains to the significant expense of testimony. That is, adherents maintained that adoption of past caretaking and decision making standards would reduce the need for costly trials and depositions, including testimony by expert witnesses about child custody and related matters. It is important, however, that research indicates only a very small proportion of contested child custody cases go to trial (e.g., Levy, 2006; Maccoby & Mnookin, 1992).

There has been a great deal of dissemination of information about the ALI (2002) proposed changes regarding time sharing and decision making. Scholarly publications include an edited volume with input from many leaders in the legal field (Wilson, 2006), law reviews about its impact (Bernstein & Triger, 2012; Clishman & Wilson, 2008), critique of its use of attachment theory (Riggs, 2005), and reviews of the social science research literature that supported (Kelly & Ward, 2002) and criticized (Warshak, 2007, 2011) the proposal. The ALI principles have led to numerous efforts over the years to change legislation.

West Virginia adopted the approximation rule. Although an academic study (Clishman & Wilson, 2008) that used a key-phrase search in legal databases found little evidence that the ALI (2002) proposals have had an impact on statutes or case law, a more wide-ranging review came to a very different conclusion. Bernstein and Triger (2012) found that a majority of states have included some aspects of the approximation rule to guide allocation of time-sharing responsibility, either by means of statute or case law. More specifically, the law in most states potentially relies, at least in part, on efforts to count and compare how much time each parent has spent with the child prior to separation or divorce action. Therefore, there has been a significant shift in the law regarding child custody to potentially rely on parental assertions regarding how much each parent has carried out caretaking activities in the past, and how much each has been involved in past decision making.

Such efforts to change the law have continued. For example, while this book was being written, there was a bill (HB 1452) before the Illinois General Assembly that included quantitative provisions such as requiring parents to submit an affidavit reporting the amount of time each one had performed child caretaking tasks in the two years before filing a petition. The bill also had a presumption that each parent would have at least 35% of the residential time with the children.

PARENTAL STRATEGIES

According to game theory, individuals who are in conflict will rationally consider relevant facts and circumstances as they plot their strategies to try to obtain an advantage. In child custody disputes, the relevant facts and circumstances include laws and related procedures. Therefore, in attempting to determine the likely benefits and drawbacks of relevant laws and procedures, it is important to consider what strategic behaviors they encourage. Although laws are often successful in changing human behavior in intended ways, it is also quite common to experience unintended consequences.

Traditional UMDA and Related Qualitative Factors

As described in Chapter 1, the UMDA (NCCUSL, 1979) and related statutory factors are generally well grounded in research about children of divorce, and therefore also have a strong moral foundation in terms of working to reduce potential risk of harm for such children. However, in practice they also lend themselves to certain types of manipulative strategies and tactics.

One such general strategy is that parents in contested cases often pursue making themselves appear to be involved in highly positive relationships with their children. The strategy can be associated with efforts to try to make the other parent appear to have negative relationships with the children, or at least much less positive ones, in accordance with what is found in the UMDA and associated statutes. Tactics that emerge from that strategy can include asserting that the other parent is trying to block a good relationship with the children. Other tactics can include claims that the other parent has engaged in domestic violence, child abuse and neglect, and/or manifests mental health problems, perhaps inclusive of substance abuse. Alternate or supplementary tactics can include parental efforts to try to get children on their side, perhaps through behaviors such as buying them excessive material belongings and neglecting to appropriately discipline them. In that manner, a parent who carries out such tactics might hope to have a child actually state a preference to live with her or him. This brief listing of tactics is representative but hardly exhaustive.

ALI Quantitative Factors

As noted earlier, the ALI (2002) principles have a greater focus on quantitative factors, with specific reference to the relevant amounts of time children have spent with each parent prior to the separation or divorce action. In that regard, its putative strength is its greater determinism, which is believed to provide a framework that would greatly reduce the amount of litigation about such child matters, inclusive of lessened expenditures of money, time, and emotional distress for families.

A main strategy of parents guided by statutory changes that rely heavily on reports of prior caretaking, according to game theory, would involve carrying out action to make it appear they had been the primary caretaker, and concurrently working to create a perception that the other parent had been less actively involved with the children. In other words, in this arena, game theory would predict that custody litigants would plan, at times even prior to filing for divorce, to increase the amount of time that they spend with the children and create an impression they were consistently highly involved with them. Similarly, when the other parent had first filed for divorce, a considerable number of parents would have quickly taken steps to increase their times and other types of involvement with the children. In some cases, parents who carried out the strategy would have accomplished spending more time with the children by significantly decreasing the amount of time they spent in their employment. In the years after the ALI (2002) principles had been published and disseminated, I had evaluated numerous cases in which there had been vigorous competition at home between parents about carrying out tasks for children such as making them dinner, helping them with homework, providing transportation, and even putting them to bed. Furthermore, there had been increased parental efforts to provide pleasurable activities for children, such as going on interesting and fun outings more often, or arranging for child play or social activities at times when they otherwise would be with the other parent. Of course, a parent carrying out such behaviors frequently interfered with the time and interactions between the children and the other parent.

The ALI (2002) proposal maintained that parental responsibility regarding decision making should include consideration both of past decision-making routines, as well as what had been the amount of time that a parent spent with a child. Therefore, consistent with game theory, parents who wished to have significant input into child decisions potentially would benefit from following a strategy of increasing their involvement with the children prior to the divorce, as well as injecting more of their own opinions and preferences into decisions, in order to try to establish a foundation beneficial to themselves in upcoming legal conflict. To some extent, however, the ALI presumption of joint decision making has led to less apparent focus on strategies as compared to the future time allocation with children.

As described above, the ALI (2002) proposals include exceptions and limitations that are qualitative in nature, and therefore similar in many respects to a number of the UMDA factors. Because of these ALI exceptions and limitations, litigants may be motivated to try to persuade the court that the other parent is deficient in caretaking skill and/or has engaged in behaviors such as child abuse, neglect, abandonment, or domestic violence. Similarly, litigants might also be motivated to try to demonstrate that the other parent had a substance abuse problem that had a negative impact on the children, and/or was trying to work to limit access to the children.

Therefore, statutes that rely in part on determining the amount of time each parent has spent carrying out caretaking functions, including aspects of the ALI (2002) principles, potentially lead to multiple sets of strategies and tactics to try to gain an upper hand. The first set would involve making changes in one's own parenting behavior to increase involvement with the children, and therefore, if successful, probably reduce the involvement of the other parent. The other type of strategy would be to convince the court that the other parent had engaged in one or more of the problem behaviors covered by the exceptions or limiting factors, while at the same time portraying oneself as entirely free of such dysfunctional actions.

Parental strategies in divorce disputes often have a significantly negative impact on the children, regardless of whether the strategies are aimed at qualitative or quantitative best interest standards and presumptions. It is crucial for all participants in the divorce process, especially those who create statutes and procedures, to have a clear understanding of the effects of divorce on children and the extent to which parents can agree on past caretaking. In addition, it is crucial to have those involved in making and carrying out relevant laws know well the result of past legislative changes pertaining to child custody, findings from in-depth research about the divorce process, and crucial facts about parent-child relationships.

EMPIRICAL EVIDENCE

The results of research studies covering tens of thousands of relevant individuals are described in Chapter 1. The ALI (2002) principles make almost no reference to this considerable and highly relevant body of research, other than very limited and selective comments (pp. 105–106). It is especially noteworthy that one of the most consistent findings about what influences children of divorce is the psychological adjustment of the parents (see Chapter 1). A significant flaw of the ALI Principles is that it does not include consideration of parental psychological functioning in determining the best interest of the child.

As described above, it instead recommended a past caretaking standard to guide future caretaking arrangements, based on the argument that this quantitative method would be superior to the qualitative UMDA best interest factors. As also noted above, many states incorporate an aspect of the amount of caretaking reportedly carried out by each parent prior to the divorce action.

The ALI (2002) principles acknowledged that, in some cases, each parent's proportion of child caretaking in the past may be open to dispute. However, it described optimism that such matters can be clarified by the court without undue difficulty. In terms of trying to assess the relative proportions of past caretaking, the ALI proposed that any person seeking custodial responsibility needs to file a parenting plan that would include a description of what had been the prior pattern of involvement with the children for at least 24 months prior to the filing. There are apparent assumptions that either the reports by the parents regarding past caretaking would be quite consistent with one another, or that fact finding by the court about discrepancies between parental reports would be accomplished comparatively quickly and easily.

However, there is empirical evidence that contradicts these assumptions. In recent years, as part of my regular custody evaluation practice, I have had parents complete a questionnaire that asked them to estimate the proportion of time that common caretaking functions have been carried out by themselves, the other parent, or another individual such as a babysitter.

Parenting Functions Questionnaire

The questionnaire has 16 main items, including tasks such as making meals for children, getting them up in the morning or to bed at night, supervising hygiene, playing with the children, assisting them with education, providing encouragement, helping with peer relationships, and arranging for child care. These tasks are quite similar to what the ALI described as child caretaking functions. In practice, the use of the questionnaire has been to obtain quantified estimates from each parent about their perceptions of each parent's caretaking, because in interview descriptions about such matters, parents frequently have related very different points of view in highly impressionistic and unclear ways. A time frame was used of the prior year, or for one year prior to the physical separation, if one had taken place. Although that time frame of one year differs from the minimum two-year time frame noted in the ALI (2002) principles, it is noteworthy that memory for more recent events tends to be better than recall for activities that occurred further back in the past (Sederberg, Howard, & Kahana, 2008). Therefore, it is reasonable to expect that there would be better agreement between parents with a time frame of one year as compared to two years or longer.

One of the most clear and productive ways of extracting useful information from these data involves examining the proportion of cases that involve parents agreeing with one another on most of the 16 items. The definition I have used for agreement is very broad and theoretically easy to reach. Agreement on any one item (such as "making meals for children") could occur in a number of ways. For example, both Parent A and Parent B could estimate that Parent A made meals for children 80% of the time and Parent B did so 20% of the time. Alternately, they could be in agreement if their specific estimates differed, but both parents estimated that one parent carried out more of that particular task than did the other parent. A specific example of this type would involve Parent A reporting that she or he made meals for the children 90% of the time and that Parent B did so 10% of the time. Parent B might rate that Parent A made meals for the children 45% of the time, that Parent B did so 40% of the time, and that a babysitter did so 15% of the time, and it would be considered agreement for purposes of the current research. Also, on some items both parents might indicate they believed they question to be not applicable, and then it was scored as an agreement. For example, if the couple's children were extremely young, and neither parent had assigned or supervised any chores, both parents might have indicated that the item that asks about "assigning and supervising chores" was not applicable.

Because there were 16 main items that pertain to various caretaking functions, parents in each case were identified as being an overall agreement if they agreed about their estimated percentages on nine or more of those items. Parents were identified as being in disagreement if they agreed on eight or less of those 16 items. There were 110 parents representing 55 couples who completed this questionnaire. Using the relatively broad criteria described here, only 9% of the parents were in agreement with one another and 91% in disagreement (results from a smaller sample were reported in Dolan & Hynan, in press). It is striking that such a remarkably low level of agreement occurred despite the very low threshold for agreement.

An obvious limitation of this research is that it is all drawn from one practice. Also, it is possible that, for research purposes, a more elegant questionnaire could have been created. However, while I would encourage others to collect similar data in order to provide for greater generalization of results, the current findings are so robust that it would be extremely surprising to find substantially different results elsewhere. It is not only that these results are so strikingly strong, but other research also provides very consistent data.

Other Research on Parental Agreement

It should not be surprising that parents have discrepant perceptions of their relative contributions regarding caretaking. Prior research by Ross and Sicoly (1979) found that people in a number of different situations tended to attribute to themselves a greater portion of the work on a common task, as compared to ratings made by others. In one of their studies, they asked husbands and wives who were not going through divorce how much each of them contributed toward common household tasks, including child caretaking. The authors reported that each spouse tended to attribute a higher proportion of such tasks to themselves than his or her spouse had indicated. In fact, Ross and Sicoly stated that, when they had asked each couple to make numerical estimates of the proportion of time they carried out various tasks, and both parents became aware of the estimates of their partner, it frequently caused arguments. The authors labeled this phenomenon an "egocentric bias" (p. 336). It is very important to note that their conclusion was that parents firmly believed in their own estimates of how much they contributed to such common tasks and sincerely disagreed with the estimates of the other parent. Because the spouses in that study were not getting divorced, there would have been no motivation for them to purposely exaggerate the extent of their own individual contributions.

An in-depth study (Hetherington & Clingempeel, 1992) of families in transition, though not actively contesting child custody, yielded similar findings. That is, both men and women reported they had carried out greater proportions of child care and housework, as compared to the spouses' reports of what proportions the respondents had actually carried out.

More recent research yielded similar findings. For example, a 2009 survey indicated that more men than women believed that, in their households, both parents were primarily responsible for taking care of the children ("*Time* poll," 2009).

A uniquely extensive and productive research project on families who were going through the divorce process was carried out by Maccoby and Mnookin (1992). It focused on about 1100 families in California. They studied numerous aspects of the divorce process for this large group through about three and a half years after the marital separation. At their first measurement, which was approximately 6 months after the separation, they asked each parent to give general ratings of each of their respective preseparation involvements with the children. Overall, mothers tended to perceive themselves as having a very high degree of involvement with the children, and they saw the father as having a generally moderate level of involvement the children. In general, fathers tended to report that they perceived both the mothers and themselves to have a moderately high degree of involvement with the children, with very little difference between the genders. The authors further reported that, for couples who showed unusually large discrepancies in their perceptions of involvement in child caretaking, a very substantial proportion exhibited comparatively high levels of overall legal conflict during the divorce process. For those couples whose ratings of preseparation child caretaking were more in agreement with one another, the levels of general conflict manifested in the divorce process was considerably lower. The consistently differing views between mothers and fathers about child caretaking are due, at least in part, to the reality that individuals know more about their own contributions to joint tasks than they know about what was done by others (Kruger, Windschitl,

Burrus, Fessel, & Chambers 2008). As a result, when attorneys provide parents with practical aids, such as charts of parental caretaking roles to record relevant behaviors (Peskind, 2014), honest efforts to complete them may yield very different results for the mother as compared to the father.

Thus, with divorcing couples, there may be an element of each parent having different perceptions and memories of caretaking. These perceptions and memories may be inextricably linked to emotional factors associated with interparental conflict. Of course, consistent with predictions from game theory, parents may also strategically invent reports of past caretaking that are in their own favor.

Results of Past State Law Changes

It has been argued that the past caretaking standard put forth by the ALI (2002) is not the same as a primary caretaking standard (Bartlett, 2002), but there is a great deal of overlap between the two. In brief, essentially any parent who would be seen as the primary caretaker would also be viewed as having been the more active one with the children under a past caretaker standard. Empirical evidence indicates that only a small proportion of children experience equally shared parenting (e.g., Fabricius & Hall, 2000; Fabricius, Sokol, Diaz, & Braver, 2012; McIntosh, Smyth & Kelaher, 2010), and therefore in the vast majority of cases there is a primary caretaking parent.

The experience of the State of Minnesota during the time they had a primary caretaker standard in effect is highly instructive of what might be expected if a past caretaker standard would be the predominant mechanism relied upon to allocate custodial responsibility, as recommended by the ALI (2002).Crippen and Stuhlman (2001–2002) reported that the Minnesota Supreme Court (*Pikula v. Pikula,* 1985) ruled that children needed to be placed with the individual who had been the primary caretaker, unless that individual was shown to be unfit as the residential custodian. The court expected the ruling to reduce litigation and heighten predictability. After that ruling, however, the authors stated there was a "frenzy of litigation" in which "fathers attempted to establish leverage by demonstrating that they were, at a minimum, equally involved in the superficial measures of primary caretaking" (p. 682). As a result, as reported by the authors, four years after that court decision of a primary caretaker presumption, the Minnesota legislature amended the statutory best interest factors to prohibit the court from relying on one factor to the exclusion of the others (Minnesota Laws, 2004); which parent had been the primary caretaker then became just one of numerous factors to be considered.

The ALI (2002) asserted that a past caretaker standard would result in greater predictability of decisions about time sharing and thus less litigation.

The real-world experience of a very similar primary caretaker standard was just the opposite, and consequently there was sharply increased litigation. As described earlier, game theory predicts that individuals, in pursuing their own self-interest, will engage in strategic behavior to try to reach their goals. The Minnesota experience clearly indicates that parents responded to the primary caretaker presumption strategically by claiming that they had actually been the primary caretaker. There was no indication that courts were able to easily investigate and make timely decisions about such competing claims, in stark contrast to the ALI assertions that reliance on quantitative measures of past caretaking would be inevitably superior to efforts at qualitative assessment of the traditional best interest factors.

In addition, the ALI (2002) maintained that there should be a presumption of joint decision-making relevant to each parent who has been reasonably involved in past parenting. A significant aspect of the theory behind such a presumption is that, except in cases that have included negative behaviors such as domestic violence or child abuse, such joint decision-making responsibility would lead to more predictable resolution and less court-related conflict. However, the Oregon experience in making a change to a presumption of joint custody is also in sharp contrast to the theory associated with the ALI principles.

A random sample of over 3800 Oregon divorces over an eight-year period was examined by Allen and Brinig (2005). They compared the public record from the three years prior to the initiation of the joint parenting presumption to the five years after that presumption was put in effect. Some findings were predictable, such as a decrease in the proportion of custody awards only to the mother, though the decrease was rather modest from 66 to 59%. However, the time it took to complete divorces became longer.

In addition, those authors reported that, after the joint parenting presumption had been put in effect, false claims of abuse doubled from 3 to 6%. After the joint parenting presumption had been put into effect, there was also an increase in postdecree disputes over child custody. Somewhat similarly, relitigation rates were found to be higher for joint than sole custody in two states that had court-imposed joint custody orders (Pruett & Barker, 2009).

These negative changes can be productively understood by considering game theory and its focus on strategic behavior. A crucial fact is that the Oregon change to a joint custody presumption had an exception if abuse were present. Therefore, if a parent wished to battle for sole custody and against the joint parenting, one possible legal strategy would be to claim that abuse had occurred, which potentially would overcome the joint custody presumption. As noted above, the frequency of joint parenting outcomes increased after the relevant presumption was put into effect, and it is likely that the increased frequency of joint parenting contributed to heightened conflict over decisions about the children, especially between those parents who may have had a relatively long-term pattern of conflictual interactions. In other words, parents who did not have a history of cooperating well with one another about the children, and who due to the legal presumption were awarded joint custody anyway, probably experienced considerable postdecree conflict with one another, and therefore more frequently ended up in court.

Research on Changes in Interparental Conflict

In their magisterial study of divorce, Maccoby and Mnookin (1992) included an investigation of the patterns of conflict between parents during such disputes. They identified three such patterns of behavior in terms of conflict styles. Cases in which parents showed productive communication and low discord were characterized as Cooperative. Parents who manifested relatively low cooperation and a high level of discord were classified as Conflicted, and those who showed low cooperation and low discord as Disengaged. The authors examined such parental conflict patterns at times that were approximately two years apart.

The most relevant finding pertains to cases that showed Conflicted interactions at the first measurement period. The largest proportion was still in the Conflicted category two years later. There was only a small proportion, less than 9%, who were able to change to the Cooperative interaction pattern well suited to joint parenting. About one third of initially Conflicted couples were able to make improvements, but only to the degree of developing a Disengaged interaction style with one another. Therefore, those couples who showed a consistently high level of conflict with one another were extremely unlikely to make changes necessary for effective cooperation regarding children.

As a result, a legal presumption for joint parenting is likely to have an unfortunate consequence of requiring cooperation between some couples who are simply unable to carry it out. A negative impact on the legal system is that such noncooperative individuals are often the same ones who repeatedly return to court to litigate about the children.

More importantly, an unfortunate consequence of steering all couples, including highly conflictual ones, toward joint parenting is that their children are likely to be exposed to a significant portion of that conflict, and such exposure tends to have a negative effect on children. It is crucial to note that while the ALI (2002) principles include domestic violence as a limiting factor in the allocations of child care and decision-making responsibilities, there is also important empirical evidence that other forms of interparental conflict (such as anger, arguments, and insults, which are in not included as ALI limiting factors) repeatedly have been found to have a major negative impact on children (Jouriles, Norwood, McDonald, Vincent, & Mahoney, 1996; Mc-Donald, Jouriles, Briggs-Gowan, Rosenfield, & Carter, 2007).

Attachment Research

The historical roots of the proposed ALI (2002) past caretaking standard emanate from an article by a law professor (Scott, 1992) who maintained that an approximation standard aimed at replicating past parental involvement with children would be a superior mechanism for determining child custody. That same point of view held that the amount of time a parent spent with the child in the past is a good proxy for the emotional attachment between parent and child. According to the ALI Principles, the strength of child attachment corresponds to the degree of responsibility a parent has had for the past caretaking. However, numerous authorities have criticized this point of view from the perspective of attachment theory and research.

Experts in attachment theory and research who voice differing perspectives on important aspects of that field agree that there is no empirical evidence that the *strength* of attachment is a crucial concern for child development, but instead that attachment *security* is what is important. Somewhat similarly, such experts generally maintain that it is the quality and not amount of parent-child interaction that influences attachment security (e.g., Kelly & Ward, 2002; Lamb, 2007; Riggs, 2005; Sroufe & McIntosh, 2011; Waters & McIntosh, 2011).

It is noteworthy that, in some cases that have involved abused or neglected children, they can appear very attached to the offending parents. More frequently, however, it is relatively common negative parenting, such as emotional rejection or failure to maintain adequate boundaries, which can result in strong but insecure child attachment to dysfunctional parents (Riggs, 2005).

Overall, the amount of past caretaking does not correlate well with attachment security. In addition, even though attachment security is an important developmental phenomenon, it is important to note that it is predictive of only a small proportion of functioning later in life. For example, Sroufe, Egeland, Carlson, and Collins (2005) reported that other areas of childhood experience, such as home environment, parental support, and peer competence predicted a larger proportion of later life functioning than is predicted by attachment security alone. In addition, in a 20-year longitudinal study, negative events, including the divorce of one's parents, were found to have significantly influenced attachment security (Waters, Merrick, Treboux, Crowell, & Albersheim, 2000).

Clearly, the efforts by a number of individuals in the legal profession to tie what is in children's best interest to the quantity of past time spent with parents are not supported by scientific evidence. However, those efforts have had an impact on the on the actions of parents who are disputing custody and practice of the family law.

Relevant Survey Research

Game theory predicts that reliance on a past caretaker standard and a joint custody presumption would lead motivated parents to change their behaviors prior to separation. Such parental changes would include attempts to increase time and activity with the children, and to establish a track record of involvement in decisions about major matters such as education and healthcare.

In order to obtain objective information regarding the accuracy of that prediction, above and beyond informal observations of parental behavior changes after the ALI (2002) principles were disseminated, a brief questionnaire was sent to mental health practitioners listed on two Internet sites, the Professional Academy of Custody Evaluators and individuals in the Attorney Directory of Forensic Psychologists who described child custody, or its equivalent, as an area of expertise. The survey was mailed in 2009 via the U.S. Postal Service to 229 individuals and included informed consent. There were 115 or 116 respondents for the portion of the survey described here, as some individuals did not answer all items. The relatively high response rate was likely influenced by the fact that potential respondents were informed that the entire survey could be completed in five minutes or less. Respondents were informed that the purpose of the survey was to provide information about contested child custody cases, especially regarding the impact of potential or actual legal criteria to decide such cases. The survey did not make any specific reference to the ALI proposals or approximation rule. This part of the survey asked respondents whether they believed there had been changes over the past five years on six areas of parental behavior relevant to the divorce process, prior to any physical separation. That timing of the survey mailing was consistent with allowing ample time for the ALI principles to be disseminated and discussed within the legal community. For example, in 2004 there had been legislative action initiated in Illinois in an attempt to incorporate aspects of the ALI principles into relevant statutes (Thomas, 2004).

More specifically, respondents were asked whether they believed there had been an increase, decrease, or no change in six areas of parental behavior "while the parents still lived together." Also, respondents were asked to consider only parent-initiated changes and not any that resulted from a court Order. The six items were: one or both parents changing (or trying to change) the amount of time they spent with the children; one or both parents changing (or trying to change) the types of interactions or activities with the children; one or both parents decreasing the amount of time they worked for income; parental arguments or fights over time and/or activities with the children; parental conflict over contact with school or healthcare personnel; and parental conflict that resulted in a call to the police. As can be seen in Table 1, for most items, the professionals who responded indicated that the majority of parents increased conflictual behavior that included a high risk of negative impact on their children. On almost all items, the relevant interparental conflict had increased many times more than it had decreased.

Therefore, there was generally strong support in the survey results for the type of behavioral changes predicted by game theory. It is noteworthy that, given the time covered by the survey, the responses to the question of whether parents decreased the amount of time they worked for income may have been affected by the impact of the global recession and understandable worries regarding limited employment opportunities (Dolan & Hynan, in press).

There are limitations regarding this survey research. A primary limitation is that it was retrospective, and did not involve practitioners keeping logs of such changes during the 2004 to 2009 period, as might occur with an approach such as the experience sampling method (Czikszentmihalyi & Larson, 1987). However, despite such limitations, it provides powerful evidence, beyond mere anecdotal reports, that numerous professionals perceived such changes in parental behavior that have a risk of negative impact on children, in accordance with the prediction of game theory.

It is important and relevant that the results of the survey described above are supported by findings from a very different type of research. A qualitative survey of divorce attorneys from three different geographical areas, carried out by legal academic authors, found there were changes in family law practice that likely contributed to heightened interparental conflict. Bernstein and Triger (2012) reported that, in planning for and carrying out child

Table 1
PERCENT CHANGES IN INTERPARENTAL CONFLICT

Interparental Conflict Category	I	D	N
Changing or trying to change time with the children	69	1	30
Changing or trying to change interactions	64	2	34
Parents decreasing time worked for income	48	3	40
Arguments/fights about time/activities with children	59	1	40
Conflict over contact with school/healthcare staff	47	3	51
Conflict resulted in call to police	67	1	32

Note. Interparental Conflict Category descriptions have condensed wording – see text for full wording. I = Increase; D = Decrease; N = No Change; all category percentages do not add to 100 because of rounding error.

custody litigation, divorce attorneys had been coaching their clients to behave in such a manner as to create an appearance of participation in all aspects of the children's lives. Such attorney recommendations included parents working to arrange activities with their children in such a manner as to potentially create seemingly objective evidence of their predominant involvement with the children. More specifically, attorneys had been advising parents to try to create an institutional record by doing things such as taking a child to and/or picking up from a preschool or daycare, especially if it involved a written record of which parent performed the task. Somewhat similarly, parents were being advised to engage in publicly-observed tasks, such as participating in children's organized activities. The authors described that such actions were especially recommended to parents who appeared not to have been the primary caretakers previously.

Returning to the survey of mental health professionals involved with families of divorce, a separate part of it asked individuals about the child-related concerns that led them to be called to testify in court or in a deposition. As described above, one of the arguments in favor of the ALI (2002) proposals is that its standards allegedly would decrease the need to rely on expensive trials and depositions that would include expert witnesses on child custody.

As also described above, the ALI (2002) included a number of exceptions and limiting factors that were similar in content to the UMDA qualitative best interest factors. Therefore, in this portion of the survey, respondents were asked to consider only those child custody cases that had gone to trial, and to estimate in what portion of those cases at least one of the following ALI exceptions or limiting factors had been present (however, no aspect of this survey specifically mentioned the ALI or approximation rule): major disparity in the quality of parent-child emotional attachment; major disparity in parental ability or availability to meet child needs; concern about the child's needs for stability; concern about harm to the child; concern about child abuse or neglect; concern about domestic violence; concern about substance abuse that interfered with parenting; and concern about a parent interfering with the other parent's access to the child.

There were 118 individuals who answered this item. The range of answers by respondents was very broad; many individual stated that 100% of their cases that went to trial included one or more of these features, and the lowest rating was 5%. There was a highly skewed distribution in that 60 respondents gave ratings of either 100% or 98%. In such a skewed distribution, the median is characteristically the best measure of central tendency, and the median here was 98%. The mean was 85%.

During about the same time frame, a similar survey of child custody evaluators was carried out by Warshak (2011). That survey specifically made reference to the ALI (2002) approximation rule, and 100% of respondents stated that their most recent case that had gone to trial included concerns about one of the ALI exceptions or limiting factors. Therefore, both surveys found that ALI past caretaking and decision-making standards would have had very little to no impact on the proportion of cases that went to trial.

To very briefly summarize this relatively lengthy section primarily focused on policy, there is consistent research evidence that efforts to carry out quantitative methods of determining child custody are likely to be unsuccessful. Somewhat similarly, presumptions for primary caregivers, and/or joint legal custody have a risk of resulting in negative unintended consequences. Aspects of relevant research evidence can be usefully conceptualized through reliance on game theory. Other parts of it can be productively understood through the perspective of the egocentricity bias. There will perhaps always be uncertainty about the degree to which parental assertions, and contents of consequent legal pleadings, emanate from the egocentricity bias and how much they are a result of purposeful strategies.

The considerable empirical evidence described here needs to be highlighted to, and strongly considered by, policy makers and others who wish to influence such policy. In particular, outcomes for children and families are likely to be worsened if there is a presumption in favor of apportioning parenting time according to alleged preseparation history or any other method that attempts to rely on a relatively specific marker such as a minimum proportion of time. It is less likely that there would be negative consequences as a result of policy that generally promotes the involvement of both parents and that includes consideration of multiple relevant factors.

GAME THEORY AND THE EVALUATIVE PROCESS

Until this point in the chapter, much of the focus has been on the importance of game theory for legal policy. In this section, the primary focus is on how evaluators can make practical use of game theory principles. An important aspect of the process is to carry out adequate deliberation to try to determine the extent to which a parent is expressing sincere concerns about the children and/or other parent, whether the concerns expressed by a parent may merely be part of a strategy to gain an advantage in the dispute, or whether there are both sincere and strategic features to the parental communication.

The research results described above include areas of parental behavior that are frequently strategic. More specifically, there is considerable evidence that parents have increased the degree to which they attempt to spend time with the children, and have tried to engage in more expansive activities with them in an effort to try to look good in the context of the custody dispute. Not surprisingly, such parental efforts are associated with increased conflict be-tween the parents, including arguments and fights. Of course, children see a lot of this conflict and suffer from exposure to it. The increased frequency of calls to the police over such conflict is undoubtedly highly stressful and em-barrassing for both the children and parents.

None of this evidence should be interpreted to mean that, each time a parent makes a statement critical of his or her partner, it is merely a strategy to create a false impression. Clearly, loss of anger control and domestic vio-lence sometimes occur in custody disputes. It appears that, in a considerably large proportion of cases, children have not been coached to make specific interview statements. Somewhat similarly, in many families, both parents have been actively and positively involved with the children.

The most productive way for evaluators to understand or predict what strategies are likely to be used in child custody disputes is to examine the rel-evant statutory factors and the applicable case law. Although emotions com-monly found in divorce, such as anger, play a role, competent attorneys rely on statutes and case law in assisting their clients to put together the best pos-sible case, including what to emphasize to custody evaluators.

At times, parents present themselves in such a manner that seems not, at first glance, to fit clearly with statutory or case law. For example, parents sometimes maintain that they are more child focused, sensitive, and self-sac-rificing than the other parent. However, such parenting characteristics can easily be seen as falling under the common UMDA (NCCUSL, 1979) factor that refers to the interactions between parents and children. Practical experi-ence indicates that parents who come to evaluation are extremely unlikely to make specific references to statutes or cases.

In certain cases, a parent might be pro bono or have received little attor-ney guidance about how to present in the evaluation. In such cases, they might rely on the advice of family or friends, and/or have read online or other sources of advice and information about the custody evaluation pro-cess. The guidance that parents might get from such sources is likely to be indirectly informed, at least to a considerable extent, by statutory factors that originated from the UMDA (NCCUSL, 1979).

It is important to keep in mind that game theory includes consideration of strategic behaviors that are responsive to strategies adopted by the opposing side. As a result, it is often productive to try to track when the potentially strategic behaviors of each side were initiated, in order to identify the possi-bly back and forth responsive strategies of each parent. Such timing can sometimes be difficult to ascertain. At times, parental interview information is useful, but the research reviewed above indicates that, in a large proportion of cases, the egocentricity bias and/or conscious efforts by parents to present as having been predominately involved with the children may limit the utility of such data. Documents such as pleadings can sometimes be useful sources of information about the timing of strategic efforts to increase child caretaking and/or decision-making, or at least appearances about them.

If a reasonably good history is obtained about such prior parental behaviors, that information can be important because past behavior is often predictive of future behavior, especially if situational factors remain fairly constant. However, it is extremely important to keep in mind that, within the context of separation and/or divorce, there are often very significant changes in relevant circumstances such as parental availability. For example, after parents have split up, it frequently is the case of that one or both parents may need to spend more hours in employment activity and therefore the comparative amounts of parental availability to be directly with the children are changed.

After an evaluator examines the assertions of a parent about the children, the other parent, and related concerns, then what? If the evaluator confidently concludes that these parental assertions fit a pattern of strategic presentation and therefore they must be false, he or she could be making a major error.

As described in more detail in the following chapter, there is an important distinction between intuition and judgment which is highly relevant for custody evaluators. In brief, intuition is defined as a type of thinking that is fast, automatic, and relatively effortless. In contrast, judgment is described as relatively slow, deliberative, and requiring conscious effort (e.g., Kahneman, 2003a). There is extensive research that indicates there is a lack of correspondence between confidence in one's decision making and the accuracy of those decisions. Individuals tend to have a great deal of confidence in their decisions when answers easily come to mind and different aspects of the answers appear to fit together well (Kahneman, 2011).

In order to avoid quickly coming to a possibly mistaken decision, an evaluator reviewing material presented by a parent needs to consider numerous possibilities. One possibility is that the parent made a presentation of his or her perspective based on a strategy rationally guided by legal factors, and at the same time that information might be true, or at least a considerable part is accurate. For any of the central assertions made by a parent in a custody evaluation (such as those that pertain to research findings on children of divorce and/or relevant legal factors), the evaluator needs to look for possible confirmatory and contradictory evidence. Because the confirmatory bias is a particularly powerful form of cognitive distortion and source of judgment error (Garb, 1998), evaluators need to be diligent in attending to information that goes against their initial hypothesis or preferred opinion.

Because evaluations characteristically involve the collection and integration of large amounts of information, usually under at least a moderate degree of time pressure, evaluators need to create a structure to ensure that they attend to and deliberate about information that potentially supports and contradicts working hypotheses. A potentially useful way to do so is to create a type of checklist. This book includes checklists at the beginning of each chapter to promote evaluators specifically attending to the most important facts and concepts.

As one example, a checklist regarding each main parental assertion would include placing that assertion at the top of the page, along with a column for information that supports the assertion, and another column for information that is contradictory to it. Such a checklist would usefully include prompts to consider other sources of data, such as child interview reports, observations of parent-child interactions, statements of the other parent, psychological testing results, and information from collateral sources. Perhaps obviously, the more clearly objective the source of information, the greater reason there would be to give it serious consideration. For example, a child with reasonably well-developed cognitive and verbal abilities who appeared not to have been coached in any way would be a more sound source of information than one with significantly more limited abilities and/or one who presents in such a way as to suggest they had been prompted to report certain material. Somewhat similarly, information that was contemporaneously recorded by health care professional would have more weight than the report of a parental family member or friend.

Put somewhat differently, one of the main tasks for evaluators is to distinguish the reality from the sales pitch. Just as a sales or marketing effort may provide a highly convincingly positive presentation about a poor or mediocre product, or alternately a great demonstration about a truly terrific product, the parental report of reality may have nothing or everything to do with the actual parenting functioning and the parent-child relationships. The evaluator's job is to cut through the smokescreen and shed light on what has taken place in real life, and what is likely to be best for the children in the future.

By itself, game theory will not provide answers about who should be the primary residential custodian or what the time-sharing schedule should be, nor will it necessarily shed accurate light on which parent is being more honest. However, especially when combined with careful deliberation, a good knowledge base, and scientifically supported methodology, game theory can provide a conceptual structure for understanding and making sense of what is often an otherwise dizzying array of competing parental assertions, attorney pleadings, and data from other sources.

The hypothetical cases described here provide examples of using game theory to help make sense of complex material. In order to protect client privacy, the cases are not actual ones but integrate elements from multiple evaluations.

Case A

The mother was a midlevel manager and the father an insurance agent. Both had worked full-time for a number of years. The children were both girls, 8 and 10 years of age. Prior to the separation, both parents had been actively involved with both of the children. It was difficult to clearly ascertain if there had been substantial differences in the overall levels of child caretaking and decision making, though there were consistent data that the mother had been comparatively more involved with preparing meals and laundry-related duties, and the father had been more active in overseeing homework. When the parents separated, a temporary Order was put into effect that had the children with each parent about an equal amount of time.

Both parents were inclined to have the daughters involved in sports, but they had different preferences that led to ongoing time conflicts. The mother wanted both children to play softball. She had played softball through high school and college, and had been a coach for both girls. The father preferred that they both be involved in lacrosse because he believed it was better cardiovascular exercise, and they would have a better chance of making a lacrosse team in high school. Especially in the spring, there were numerous ongoing conflicts between the softball and lacrosse schedules. Each of them had signed up the children for the respective sports at about the same time, and each asserted that the girls most enjoyed playing the sport preferred by the parent.

Somewhat similarly, there was a dispute between the parents over the extent to which the younger child would be involved in other activities. The father wanted her to have a tutor for math. Although she had regularly obtained Bs in that subject, the father preferred that she perform at a higher level in order to get into an advanced math track in school. The mother wanted her to have ongoing involvement in a charity drive associated with her religious education. Although the charity drive was not a direct part of the religious education, the mother maintained that it represented a value strongly associated with religious beliefs and therefore should take precedence over other activities.

Although the children previously had a reasonable level of involvement in activities, their levels of involvement increased substantially with the divorce process and separation. Each parent voiced concern that the children might be overinvolved and therefore often quite tired, and each stated that the other was mainly responsible for the possible overinvolvement.

During the evaluation process, there was consistent information that both parents generally carried out child caretaking duties quite well, and that there were overall positive parent-child relationships. Neither parent manifested significant psychological difficulties other than the transient distress that characteristically accompanies divorce disputes. The children appeared to function reasonably well overall, and had primarily positive adjustments in each parental home. Each parent wanted the children to see the other parent a reasonable amount of time. However, the father somewhat regularly had discussed the mother's actions and statements with the daughters, especially regarding their activities, in a manner that included critical comments about the mother. These discussions included times that he had questioned the children in a leading manner about the mother, giving especially the older child an impression that he was expecting her to have a negative view of some of the mother's behavior and that the child was supposed to agree with him. Understandably, the child voiced discomfort about such discussions, and periodically was anxious that the father would start a new one of that type. Both children stated that the mother had not made comments critical of the father and otherwise did not convey any negative attitudes about him. Both children had voiced that, generally in the past, the father had been much more likely to yell at the mother than vice versa.

It appeared that both parents to some extent were exercising strategic behaviors through their preferences for extracurricular activities, because child involvement in the preferred activity would also increase involvement with the respective parent. It was also clear that there was no good answer to the quandary of the extracurricular activities. That is, there is no clear empirical evidence that involvement in one of these sports versus the other is better for children. There are positive aspects both to activities that involve academic advancement and those related to religious involvement; for an evaluator to endorse one over the other would simply involve exercising a value judgment for which there is no scientific support.

There is considerable scientific evidence that children's exposure to conflict between parents has a negative impact, and in this case, only the father's verbalizations had exposed the children to interparental conflict. The mother had not done so, and this difference between the parents was the primary reason for the recommendation that she have primary residential care of both children.

Case B

Because this case involved potential removal of children from Illinois, additional brief background information is required. Although the relevant statute describes that removal needs to be in the best interest of the child, Illinois Supreme Court case law (*Eckert,* 1988) indicated that the child's best interest needs to be determined on a case-by-case basis. That court case identified a number of factors that need to be considered, including the motives of the parent who wishes to remove the child, the motives of the parent who is resisting removal, the likelihood of the child having a healthy and close relationship with both parents and other family members, the visitation rights of the noncustodial parent, and whether a realistic visitation schedule could be put into effect if the move were to occur. In a more recent Illinois Supreme Court case (*Collingbourne*, 2003), the Eckert case factors were expanded somewhat in that the direct benefit to the parent seeking removal, and therefore the indirect benefit to the child, needs to be considered.

In hypothetical Case B, the parents had been divorced for three years, and had one child, a boy 14 years of age. The son had been in the primary residential care of the father since the divorce. The mother had a severe medical disability with recurrent depression, and the father was a construction worker. He had been unemployed almost completely for over a year aside from having picked up infrequent handyman work. Their parenting agreement included a visitation schedule of the mother having alternate weekends plus one or two evenings per week. However, the mother generally had felt well enough to exercise visitation for only about 10 hours in each two-week period. The father and son shared a one-bedroom apartment, and the dad experienced intermittent difficulty with paying the rent on time.

Assisted by a former coworker, the father obtained a job offer that potentially involved construction work on a very large-scale energy project in a nearby state. The father had an experienced family law attorney who clearly was familiar with the relevant case law. Therefore, the father appeared to strategically collect and present information that followed rather closely the relevant case law factors. For example, he presented evidence which indicated that the construction project was likely to continue for years, as well as a letter from his potential employer about his expected pay and hours. He also presented documents that showed relevant flight schedules and costs, as well as information about travel by car. The father maintained that, if the move out of state were allowed, he would have the financial resources and time to allow the son to fly back every three to four weeks to visit with the mother. In addition, he submitted what he stated was a record of when the son and mother had visited with one another during the most recent year, and asserted that there could actually more total hours of future visitation under his proposed plan. The mother opposed the move, asserting that it would interfere in her relationship with the son.

An important part of the evaluative process was to obtain objective data about the father's assertions, including factual matters such as a job offer, pay, and feasibility of the proposed visitation schedule. Other more common aspects of such evaluations were also carried out, such as child interviews, parent-child observations, and collecting other collateral data. In each case, the father's statements were supported by objective sources of information, and there was considerable evidence that the father for the most part met the

Eckert and *Collingbourne* requirements. Consequently, it appeared that it would be in the child's best interest in this case to permit the move out of state.

CONCLUSIONS

It is clear that game theory is not only useful for considerations about policy pertaining to child custody and related matters, it is perhaps crucial in conceptualizing the impact on children and families of possible changes in legal policy. Keeping in mind, in a deliberative manner, the scientific, factual knowledge about children of divorce, together with the potentially unintended consequences that might be predicted by game theory can help promote policy that is consistent with the best interest of the child.

On the level of individual evaluations, game theory can also be extremely useful in conceptualization. In its most useful current application, it needs to be considered as an additional arena of conceptualization rather than an overarching principle. While game theory will not dictate to evaluators what they should conclude about each case, it can help to provide a conceptual structure for understanding and analyzing what are often dizzying arrays of assertions and other information from parents and their attorneys. It will often be difficult for evaluators to determine the extent to which parental assertions are an integral part of a strategy to gain an advantage in the evaluation.

However, while understanding such strategy can be very helpful, it is much more important to carefully collect and deliberate about information that supports or contradicts each parental assertion. Therefore, the conceptual structure associated with game theory needs to be linked with a consistent focus on sound reasoning about evaluative information that is collected, as described more in Chapter 3.

Almost all new developments such as the application of game theory to child custody evaluation are relatively modest steps forward. It is hoped that the current applications of game theory will help to prompt more concerted attention on this and related areas that may benefit the custody evaluation field and the children of divorce.

Chapter 3

HOW WE THINK ABOUT CHILDREN OF DIVORCE: UNCERTAINTY IN JUDGMENT FROM NOBEL PRIZE-WINNING RESEARCH

PRACTICE CHECKLIST

_____Know the difference between intuition (System 1) and reasoning (System 2).

    _____Intuition is quick, automatic, relatively effortless, guided by habit, and often tied to emotion.

    _____Reasoning is slower, effortful, rule-governed, and deliberate.

Validity in child custody evaluation depends on a number of factors:

_____Focus on the appropriate target attribute: the child's best interest as represented by relevant legal factors integrated with scientific findings about children of separation and divorce.

_____Use of methods that have sound empirical and/or conceptual foundations.

_____Collection of reasonably comprehensive information.

_____Deliberation about the information that is collected, including consideration of alternate hypotheses while remaining cognizant of relevant legal factors and empirical findings.

_____Self-confidence in judgment is not statistically associated with the accuracy of judgment.

_____Stay cognizant of the risk of confirmatory bias and take steps to remain impartial.

_____Avoid factors that can degrade reasoning, such as competing cognitive tasks and excessive time pressures.

_____Use reasoning (System 2) to monitor whether biases (System 1) (e.g., gender, race, attractiveness, etc.) might be influencing judgment processes.

(Continued)

```
┌─────────────────────────────────────────────────────────────────┐
│                  PRACTICE CHECKLIST (Continued)                   │
│                                                                   │
│  ____Recognize that custody evaluation is a cognitive minefield   │
│     and consistently make use of System 2 thinking aids,          │
│     including:                                                    │
│        ____Checklists about relevant legal factors, research      │
│        findings, methodology, and concepts.                       │
│        ____Lists of information collected and analyzed in terms    │
│        of what supports or contradicts relevant assertions or     │
│        hypotheses.                                                │
│                                                                   │
│  Note: This form is a guide to promote productive reasoning and   │
│  good practice. It is not comprehensive or all-inclusive and does │
│  not replace adequate training and experience.                    │
└─────────────────────────────────────────────────────────────────┘
```

Families get referred for child custody evaluations precisely because there is uncertainty about what is best for the children. Daniel Kahneman and his colleagues (e.g., Kahneman, 2003a; 2003b; 2011; Kahneman & Klein, 2009; Tversky & Kahneman, 1974) have spent decades thinking about and researching judgment under conditions of uncertainty. Their work has covered many areas, including financial and economic decision making, politics, and responding to crises. Kahneman, a psychologist, won the Nobel Prize in economics in 2002. This chapter applies insights from his line of work and related research to judgments about children of divorce.

His paradigm provides a conceptual foundation for many of the specific practices recommended in this book. The most distinct practical application is the checklist at the beginning of each chapter.

Kahneman and his colleagues have shown various pathways by which knowledgeable people make mistakes in judgment. In their work, those mistakes are clearly demonstrated because the judgments are largely quantitative, and mathematical proofs show the differences between those judgments and the correct answers (e.g., Tversky & Kahneman, 1974; Kahneman, 2003a).

Obviously, in child custody and related questions, there are no known correct outcomes that can be demonstrated mathematically. However, many of the decision-making processes and principles of the heuristics and biases approach of Kahneman (Kahneman & Klein, 2009) are very applicable to the types of uncertainty inherent in trying to ascertain what is best for children of divorce.

There are no outcome data specifically focused on children who have gone through custody evaluations. More specifically, there are no outcome data regarding children who have been involved in custody evaluations versus those who have not gone through such evaluations, and no data about the outcomes of those who have received one type of recommendation versus another type. A number of scholars (e.g., Kelly & Ramsey, 2009) have called for an increased research focus on judicial system processes related to custody evaluations. However, because it is extremely difficult to imagine any court system randomly assigning child custody cases to evaluation versus no evaluation, or randomly to one type of custody arrangement versus another, there probably never will be any empirical data about these matters based on adequate methodology.

So in the absence of such outcome data, and without the benefit of any mathematical proofs, where would anyone find information relevant to the possible validity of child custody evaluation recommendations? As described in Chapter 1, there is a considerable body of empirical research on children of divorce, based on studies that have included tens of thousands of children. Somewhat similarly, factors such as child abuse and exposure to domestic violence have been found to negatively affect children generally, and thus need to be considered in custody evaluations. Also, there are empirical foundations regarding the most valid use of a number of custody evaluation methods (described later in this book). Furthermore, it is important for the practitioner to consider statutory factors that need to be considered in determining children's best interest, many of which overlap conceptually with empirical findings. Therefore, if sound methods are appropriately used, and steps are taken to adequately consider research findings on what influences children of divorce, or children generally, and if these factors are integrated with relevant legal considerations, then custody evaluation recommendations are likely to have good ecological validity and probably will benefit those children to whom they pertain.

Such a conceptual approach to custody evaluation obviously includes many complicated elements. Families, especially those with children going through contested divorces, are complex systems. Therefore, comprehensive assessment procedures and conceptual processes are needed in order to obtain good quality evaluations on which to base recommendations for children. It is sometimes tempting to take a much simpler approach, but ignoring a comprehensive perspective of families risks evaluation recommendations that are off target in terms of the desired outcome of maximizing children's well-being. As noted by Kahneman (2003b, p. 728) in a different context, "people violate rationality by failing to maintain a comprehensive view of outcomes."

INTUITION AND REASONING

The distinction between intuition and reasoning is crucial to the understanding of findings about judgment under conditions of uncertainty. Briefly, intuition is quick, automatic, and relatively effortless. It is influenced a great deal by habit and can be very tied to emotion. In a number of ways it is similar to perception. In contrast, reasoning is slower, effortful, rule-governed, and deliberate. Similar distinctions about types of thinking have been identified over the centuries, as far back as Aristotle (Sloman, 1996). Intuition has been described as System 1 and reasoning as System 2 cognition by Stanovich and West (2002).

Figure 1 (Kahneman, 2003a) demonstrates the similarities and differences between perception, intuition, and reasoning. As can be seen there, perception and intuition share a number of cognitive processes and differ from reasoning in terms of those processes. Intuition and reasoning are similar in content areas such as conceptual representation and consideration of past and present, as contrasted with perception that pertains to current stimuli. An important feature of this dual process model of cognition is that System 2 is able to monitor cognitive processes and behaviors. However, such self-monitoring, or even more broadly, thinking hard and deliberately, tends not to occur as often as it should in relevant situations.

It should be noted that intuition (System 1) can be accurate and reasoning (System 2) can be incorrect. For intuition to be regularly accurate, there need to be opportunities for learning and extensive practice in environments that give reliable feedback as to the accuracy of judgments (Kahneman, 2003a). That is, with a great deal of practice under optimal conditions, an individual may be able to develop accurate intuition about certain decision areas, which is a type of recognition (Kahneman, 2011; Kahneman & Klein, 2009). A

	PERCEPTION	INTUITION System 1	REASONING System 2
PROCESS		Fast	Slow
		Parallel	Serial
		Automatic	Controlled
		Effortless	Effortful
		Associative	Rule-governed
		Slow-learning	Flexible
		Emotional	Neutral
CONTENT	Percepts	Conceptual representations	
	Current stimulation	Past, present, and future	
	Stimulus bound	Can be evoked by language	

Figure 1. Process and Content in Two Cognitive Systems. Reprinted from Kahneman (2003a, p. 698).

major question is whether the recognition involves valid cues and leads to accurate judgment, or whether invalid cues are recognized, resulting in the erroneous decisions. As stated previously, recognition of valid cues in custody evaluation would potentially include matters such as children's exposure to interparental conflict and parental psychological functioning that influences the children. In contrast, recognition of an invalid cue might involve a parent having a resemblance to a relative the evaluator strongly likes or dislikes.

People sometimes make surprisingly accurate conclusions about others' behaviors based on very brief periods of observation (Ambady & Rosenthal, 1992). Such conclusions can be categorized as intuition. In order for such observations to be accurate, however, the behaviors need to be observable and typically affect-laden. Other characteristics that are less readily observed and expressive, such as conscientiousness and persistence, do not lend themselves so easily to brief but accurate observations by others. Ambady and Rosenthal (1992) described that the ability to accurately detect some types of expressive behavior, such as dominance or fear, may have been highly relevant for survival in human evolution. Perhaps obviously, custody evaluators face the challenging reality of needing to assess numerous types of individual attributes and interpersonal behavior patterns. Many of those attributes and behavior patterns are not readily observable. Also, the research of Ambady and Rosenthal showed that while a surprising proportion of certain types of very brief observations can be accurate, there are major limitations of that accuracy. Therefore, evaluators need to exercise a great deal of caution and deliberate about their own perceptions and thoughts.

For decades, it has been well known that both experts and nonexperts have vast overconfidence in their own judgments (Einhorn & Hogarth, 1978; Kahneman, 2011). A high level of self-confidence in a judgment is related to how easily it comes to mind and how well different pieces of the judgment seem to fit together (Kahneman, 2011). Of course, System 1 itself is characterized by effortlessness. Many times, a belief or judgment can seem quite coherent when we have not bothered to collect comprehensive information and have not retrieved relevant knowledge from memory. Relevant to this tendency to conclude that a judgment is correct because of the appearance of coherence, Kahneman (2011) employs an acronym, WYSIATI, which stands for What You See Is All There Is. In other words, WYSIATI represents a cognitive process in which System 1 jumps to conclusions when information is scarce or inadequate.

In order to avoid erroneous confidence in judgments, custody evaluators need to monitor their own cognitive processes along a number of dimensions. Some of the self-monitoring should be focused on the type and amount of information collected, whether alternate hypotheses are being generated and seriously considered, and whether relevant research-based facts and statutes are relied upon. At the same time, there are additional types of automatic thought processes that can impair judgment quality.

BIASES AND HEURISTICS

There are many types of biases that may have an impact in custody evaluation, and they are best categorized as System 1 thinking. They include but are not limited to biases based on race, gender, cultural background, political preferences, socioeconomic status, and physical attractiveness. Because custody evaluation almost always involves one parent of each gender, bias based on gender is especially relevant.

In addition to biases for or against certain categories of people, bias can involve cognitive processes, independent of the types of people involved in the matter. The confirmatory bias is a particularly relevant and potentially powerful one in custody evaluation. Garb (1998) described the confirmatory bias as seeking, recalling, and using information that confirms a belief or hypothesis, and ignoring or discounting information that refutes it. A similar type of cognitive process has been referred to as biased assimilation (e.g., Kahan, Braman, Cohen, Gastil, & Slovic, 2010) or attitude-based decision process (Sanbonmatsu & Fazio, 1990).

A major conceptual challenge in custody evaluation is for evaluators to collect information in a reasonably comprehensive and impartial manner, and to keep an open mind throughout the process about what is best for the children. That is, evaluators need to avoid any tendency to make quick judgments about the children's best interests. Similarly, they need to avoid focusing data collection and theorizing about the case in a manner that simply confirms any initial intuition. Well-balanced data collection and careful deliberation about relevant information are crucial in order to overcome potential confirmatory bias.

Tversky and Kahneman (1974) described that heuristics are cognitive shortcuts that involve using comparatively simple judgments in place of complex thinking processes. Thus heuristics are a type of System 1 thinking. Heuristics can sometimes be useful but can also lead to serious errors. More recently, Kahneman (2003a) clarified that the general heuristic process is one of attribute substitution:

> A judgment is said to be mediated by a heuristic when the individual assesses a specified *target attribute* of a judgment object by substituting a related *heuristic attribute* that comes more readily to mind. This definition elaborates a theme of the early research, namely, that people who are confronted with a difficult question sometimes answer an easier one instead. The word *heuristic* is used in two senses in the new definition. The noun refers to the cognitive process, and

the adjective in *heuristic attribute* specifies the attribute that is substituted in a particular judgment. (p. 707)

Below, examples are given of a number of types of heuristics and their relevance in the custody evaluation contexts.

In terms of custody evaluation, the target attribute is children's best interest as seen in their well-being, and the factors that have been found in research to influence the well-being of children are of paramount importance. From a legal standpoint, children's best interest is typically defined by statute. As described in Chapter 1, there is considerable overlap between many of the statutory and psychological research factors.

Tversky and Kahneman (1974) listed a number of examples of heuristics. The affect heuristic involves judgments being led by the emotional responses of the individual. There are many potential examples of this heuristic at work in custody evaluation, and some conceptually overlap with the psychodynamic concept of countertransference, in which emotionally important features of a psychotherapy relationship can impact the therapist, at least some of the time in a counterproductive manner. A hypothetical custody evaluation example is an evaluator who grew up in a home with a substance-abusing parent who was emotionally unavailable and sometimes abusive. That evaluator might be overly disinclined to make a recommendation in the favor of a parent who had a substance abuse problem but who nonetheless functioned well as a parent and had a better relationship with the children than the other parent, who was even more dysfunctional.

The availability heuristic involves making a judgment based on the ease that certain attributes come to mind. For example, an evaluator who recently read an article about the importance of social support for single parents and their children might be inclined to excessively weigh that factor in an evaluation case. In strongly considering that social support factor, the evaluator may concurrently give inadequate consideration to statutory factors and important research findings on children of divorce.

The representativeness heuristic involves an evaluator making a judgment based on relatively superficial matters such as appearances, such as which parent most resembles an imagined prototype of a primary residential custodian. For example, an evaluator would be relying on the representativeness heuristic if the recommendation was made for the mother just because most primary residential parents are mothers, without adequate consideration of research and statutory factors that represent the target attribute of children's well-being. It should be noted that there are many well-founded reasons to recommend either gender for primary residential parent, but not because of gender alone.

According to Kahneman (2003a), there is "no finite list of heuristic attributes" (p. 710). He also emphasized that all categories of heuristics are types of attribute substitution. In the custody evaluation examples described above, instead of a deliberative System 2 focus on the target attributes of research-based facts and related statutory factors, the evaluator engaged in an intuitive System 1 judgment that substituted the heuristic attributes of affect, information easily remembered, or superficial appearance.

It is important to note that System 2 cognitive operations are not flawless and can result in errors in judgment. As summarized by Kahneman (2003a), System 2 appears to be facilitated by intelligence, the need for cognition, and statistical thinking ability. In contrast, System 2 operations are degraded by factors such as concurrent involvement in a competing cognitive task, time pressure, and being in a good mood. The last of these is somewhat puzzling but may reflect that thinking hard is often not very fun, and it is much easier just to rely on intuition.

Other research has found that motivation to make a good decision has led people to use relatively deliberative thinking, but there can be interference from factors such as excessive time pressure. For example, when there has been a high level of motivation to make a correct decision, and adequate time allowed to focus on relevant target information, people tend to make reasonable decisions based on the information they have been given. In contrast, when there has been low motivation combined with time pressures, decisions tend to be based more on general attitude, without adequate consideration of the most relevant information (Sanbonmatsu & Fazio, 1990).

As noted above, potential racial bias is a cause for concern and needs to be avoided in any evaluation. Some racial biases have at least partial origins in cultural stereotypes. Individuals who are generally low in racial bias appear to use relatively deliberative thinking to inhibit reliance on such stereotypes. An important feature of System 2 thinking is that it can monitor System 1 thinking. However, when there is interference with the ability to consciously monitor one's own reliance on stereotypes, evaluations of behaviors are more likely to be congruent with such stereotypes (Devine, 1989).

Physical attractiveness can be another source of bias, and there is a general finding that individuals perceived to be physically attractive are also believed to have more positive personality attributes than those low in physical attractiveness. It is noteworthy that those findings are seen more frequently when ratings are made of social competence, but there is essentially no effect for characteristics such as integrity and empathy. It is important and relevant for evaluators that the power of this stereotype is decreased when there is greater additional information given about the individuals who are assessed (Eagly, Ashmore, Makhijani, & Longo, 1999). Presumably, evaluators would avoid being significantly influenced by the physical attractiveness bias if they consciously focus on the appropriate target features of the evaluation.

As described earlier, parental psychological functioning that has an impact on parenting is a significant factor in children's well-being, and thus is an important area of focus for custody evaluators. Parental anxiety is raised as an area of concern in a number of evaluations. Evaluators need to engage System 2 to discern important features of the parental anxiety, especially whether it has any significant role in parenting behavior. Sometimes parents can present as anxious in an evaluation because they are very cognizant of being observed and feel that there is a very high-stakes outcome. That type of anxiety may not extend beyond the circumstances of being evaluated. In contrast, other parents experience more ongoing anxiety that may have a significant and negative effect on their parenting behaviors. Cognitive distractions can potentially lead evaluators to not adequately consider whether the anxiety that they perceive in a parent is generalized or just a temporary response to the circumstances (Gilbert & Osborne, 1989). In addition, even if the anxiety or other dysphoria is ongoing, evaluators need to deliberate about the extent to which it may or may not significantly influence parent-child interactions.

HOW TO IMPROVE JUDGMENT

Kahneman is among the best sources of advice about this matter, and he emphasized that it almost always takes substantial effort to improve judgment. He further described that it is first necessary to recognize the circumstances of required judgment as a cognitive minefield. Next, individuals need to proceed slowly and put into effect steps that require System 2 deliberation (Kahneman, 2011). Kahneman clearly is a world-class intellect and leading scholar in judgment and decision-making, and it is quite striking that he perceives himself as routinely making System 1 errors unless he makes a concerted effort to engage System 2.

Because engaging in System 2 thinking is effortful and time consuming it is easy to skip over it and rely on intuition. Therefore, custody evaluators are likely to improve judgments when they *consistently* use methods that engage System 2.

Over decades, there has been controversy over the accuracy of clinical judgment, with statistical prediction sometimes having been found superior to clinical prediction (e.g., Grove, Zald, Lebow, Snitz, & Nelson, 2000). Kahneman (2011; Kahneman & Klein, 2009) maintained that such findings do not show clinicians to be inept in making important assessments. However, statistical predictions tend to have greater consistency than the clinical ones. A meta-analysis of relevant research showed that a main area of superiority of statistical prediction was that it had greater consistency than judgment by clinicians (Karelaia & Hogarth, 2008).

A useful way to engage in consistent System 2 thinking is to rely on relevant checklists (Kahneman, 2011). Somewhat similarly, Garb (1998) recommended using decision aids as a practical way for evaluators to develop a routine of engaging in System 2 cognitive operations. Garb also emphasized, as his first recommendation to improve psychological assessments, reliance on relevant empirical research.

In an earlier effort to engage System 2 thinking in the custody evaluation process, I compiled a form for use in evaluations that integrated relevant research on children of divorce with statutory factors and other relevant family characteristics. I also created a rating scale and checklist of important individual and interpersonal factors on which to focus during custody evaluation sessions that involve children interacting with parents (Hynan, 2003a). Those forms have been useful in prompting me to consistently think in a deliberative manner, both within certain evaluation sessions and when integrating information prior to writing the report.

More recently, Gawande (2009), a surgeon, has championed the use of checklists, especially in medicine, construction, airline flight, and other potentially high-risk or complex circumstances. He has pointed out that, especially in complex situations, the amount of information available has overwhelmed human abilities to process it accurately and consistently. According to Gawande, specialization and what he refers to as superspecialization have been methods that medical fields have tried to use to cope with such complexity. Those methods have their benefits but also limitations, as can be seen in part in excessively high levels of medical failures such as those due to infections. In many ways, custody evaluators need to function well both as generalists and specialists in certain areas. That reality is one of the many challenges of the field.

Gawande (2009) described that there are distinctions between simple, complicated, and complex problems. An example of a complicated problem is sending a rocket to the moon. He stated that carrying out assessments and interventions with people are more difficult, and are categorized as complex problems, in large part because each individual is unique. Individual differences between people are magnified in complexity when considering human interactions, an integral aspect of every custody evaluation.

Checklists have been found to lead to significant improvements, including substantial decreases in death and other major complications for surgical patients. In a very different complex field, venture capital, those who used a checklist type of approach to investment decisions had a much better rate of success than those who took a more intuitive approach (Gawande, 2009).

When steps had been taken to initiate the use of checklists in medicine, many staff tended to resist at first. However, there is a tendency for users of the checklist to become convinced of their usefulness over time, especially when there is an opportunity to directly observe the prevention of operating room errors. When Gawande (2009) asked surgical staff if they would want a relevant checklist used if they were the ones undergoing surgery, 93% replied yes.

There is certainly nothing magical about checklists. In fact, their relative simplicity is probably one of the reasons many professionals resist using them. Many of us would prefer to believe that our thinking processes are sound enough that checklists are not needed. Also, discipline is required to consistently use decision aids such as checklists. As described above, System 1 thinking is easy, and System 2 thinking is considerably harder. Humans generally prefer easier to harder. Completion of a custody evaluation tends to be a long and difficult process, and greater reliance on System 2 makes it even more long and difficult.

The Practice Checklists in this book are aimed at facilitating the use of System 2 in custody and related evaluations. They are influenced by the work of Gawande (2009), but differ in a number of ways from his examples of airline emergency or surgical checklists because the tasks and circumstances of custody evaluations are quite different.

Recently, Drozd, Olesen, and Saini (2013) focused on other means to assist cognitive processing of information by evaluators. They emphasized the use of decision trees to facilitate productive steps and reduce the likelihood of errors.

If the goal is the accurate evaluation of what is in a child's best interest, then checklists and related decision aids are highly relevant. Their presence and use remind us that we are in that cognitive minefield (Kahneman, 2011). Checklists prompt us to use important principles, necessary methods, and crucial concepts. Potentially, they can even help guide us to manage time pressures well, avoid competing tasks as we carry out our work, limit the influence of bias and stereotypes, and prompt us to carry out at least minimally necessary steps to do competent work. They are well worth the effort.

Chapter 4

TIME SHARING

PRACTICE CHECKLIST

Time-sharing plans need to consider:
_____Almost all children benefit from regular contact with both parents
_____Restrictions on contact with a parent should be limited to cases in
    which unrestricted access would be a potential danger to the child
_____Histories of contact and interaction between the child and each
    parent
_____Any special child needs
_____Parenting skills and deficits
_____Parental psychological functioning
_____Present and past conflict between parents
_____Abilities of the parents to promote a good relationship with the other
    parent
_____Abilities of the parents to cooperate well about the children
_____Histories of parental family structure and stability
_____Parental availabilities
_____Distance between parental residences
_____Very young children need frequent contact with both parents
_____Relevant factors need to be considered for each case on an individual
    basis

Note: This form is a guide to promote productive reasoning. It is not comprehensive or all-inclusive and does not replace adequate training and experience.

One of the main challenges for evaluators often involves making recommendations about when children should be with each parent. Although there is no consensus that a noncustodial parent should have at least a minimum amount of time, it is clear that almost all children will benefit from regular contact with both parents. There are many different types of potential schedules and many factors to consider in recommending one. It is not possible to cover all considerations, but a number of frequently relevant factors are described in this chapter. Also, although time sharing and decision making are somewhat separate entities, they sometimes overlap. For example, it is rare to find a case in which parents have equally shared custody yet only one of them is legally able to make major decisions about the child. Therefore, in certain instances, considerations regarding decision making are integrated with time sharing in this chapter.

Although time sharing and decision making essentially comprise the totality of the child custody arena, there is no attempt to summarize all relevant material in this chapter. Instead, there is a distillation of empirical and practice-oriented material with the primary focus on time-sharing considerations.

During the remainder of this chapter, there is first a discussion of evidence about parenting in which each parent has the child about the same amount of time, identified as equally shared parenting, and regarding more broadly defined joint custody. Second, there is a focus on individual child and parental characteristics, situational factors, and types of interactions. The third section provides an overview of the highly controversial area of possible overnight visits for very young children. Fourth, there is an examination of controversies centered on interparental conflict and visits between children and nonresidential parents. Fifth, there is a focus on unusual situations that may require limitations on visits. The final section includes a number of practice-oriented considerations aimed at facilitating children having a reasonable balance of good-quality time with each parent.

EQUALLY SHARED PARENTING AND JOINT CUSTODY

One potential time-sharing arrangement is for each parent to have the children an equal amount of time, or very close to equal, identified as equally shared parenting. At first glance this arrangement may seem like the most fair for each parent. In practice, a substantial proportion of children state that they would prefer such an arrangement, largely because it appears fair. In addition, a survey of the general population found that most adults favored equally shared parenting (Braver, Ellman, Votruba, & Fabricius, 2011). However, deliberation about this matter yields more complex considerations that need to be taken into effect to promote children's best interest.

Although equally shared parenting certainly creates regular contact with both parents, which usually is very positive, there are questions about whether it is feasible for children to go back and forth equally between two households, in part because it can lead to reduced stability and increased stress, especially when children have to juggle the challenges of school, extracurricular activities, and social lives. Judges at times voice skepticism about equally shared parenting because there is no primary home base, but they may consider such an arrangement in the interests of reaching parental agreement (Peskind, 2014). If equally shared parenting was a good, easy answer, it would be reasonable to expect it to take place a fairly large proportion of the time.

Although there are unfortunately very few sources of empirical information about the frequency of equally shared parenting, the data sources that are present indicate that it occurs infrequently. A study by Fabricius and Hall (2000) asked university students who grew up in divorced families to report their relevant past experiences. Only 8% reported that they had lived an equal amount of time with each parent. In that sample, 80% said they had lived primarily with their mother, and 12% mainly with her father. More recently, using data collected in 2005–2006, 9% of university students reported that they had spent about an equal number of days with their mothers and fathers. More specifically, that proportion was with their fathers about 45 to 55% of the time in a typical 28-date period (Fabricius et al., 2012). An extensive investigation of time-sharing patterns that involved very young children from the Longitudinal Study of Australian Children (McIntosh, Smyth, & Kelleher, 2010) was generally consistent with these data reported by Fabricius and his colleagues.

It appears reasonable to assume that when equally shared parenting does work successfully, the parents are able to cooperate with one another in an effective manner and have minimal, manageable conflict about the children. Such parents therefore may be particularly unlikely to present for custody evaluation, which takes place when there is conflict about significant areas such as parenting time and/or decision-making.

It is also important to consider longitudinal research that has gathered evidence about the residential circumstances of children in joint custody or dual residences arrangements. As noted earlier, Maccoby and Mnookin (1992) studied families of divorce over number of years. Their first measurement occurred about six months after the marital separation, and their third data collection was about three and a half years post-separation. Their dual residences or joint custody group was defined as spending time with the non-custodial parent at least two of seven days (29%) on the average. They did not identify any group of children who had equally shared parenting, perhaps because it occurred so infrequently. At their first measurement time, 15% of children were living in the dual residential circumstances. Over the approximately three years between the first and third measurements, only 54% of dual residence children remained in that arrangement. In contrast, 84% of those who lived mainly with the mother during the first measurement and 70% who lived primarily with the father during that measurement time continued to live in those circumstances three years later.

Cloutier and Jacque (1997) conducted longitudinal research of a similar type in Canada, but their first measurement time was an average of 5.8 years after the separation, and therefore was much later than the first measurement period of Maccoby and Mnookin (1992). Their second data-gathering time took place two years after the first one. Their definition of joint custody or dual residence was essentially the same as that used by Maccoby and Mnookin. During their first measurement time, 35% of the children were in joint custody residential circumstances. Of the joint custody children, 54% made no residential change over the two years. In contrast, 81% of those living mostly with the mother and 75% of those primarily with the father made no residential change.

More recent longitudinal research was conducted on a high-conflict mediation sample in Australia (McIntosh, Smyth, Wells, & Long, 2010). Data were collected over four years after mediation. The authors reported that there was greater residential stability and fewer changes in the sole custody group than the shared care group. Not surprisingly, the shared care parents who were able to be cooperative with one another manifested higher levels of sustaining that residential arrangement over time than did parents with relatively high levels of conflict with one another.

Therefore, these longitudinal studies that examined joint custody (or broadly defined shared care) arrangements found much higher levels of residential change for those children in joint custody or dual residence, as compared to other residential arrangements. In the first two studies described here, despite relatively short time frames of only two to three years, almost half the children changed residences. In other words, even with joint custody or dual residences that involve the child being with the noncustodial parent as few as nine days per month, there was a significant change to one primary residence. It seems reasonable to conclude that it may be even more difficult to sustain an equally shared parenting residential arrangement, and therefore residential instability might be even greater in such circumstances.

It is possible, however, that there are societal changes taking place, especially since the two longitudinal studies were conducted, in the direction of children of separation and divorce spending a larger proportion of time with the noncustodial parent. Fabricius et al. (2012) maintained that there has been a trend for children, at least in some states, to spend larger proportions of time with their fathers, who usually are not the primary residential parents. Similarly, McIntosh and Smyth (2012) reported that shared care (defined more broadly than equally shared parenting) in Australia is unusual but appears to be getting more common.

It is clear that most children of separation and divorce primarily live in one home and see the nonresidential parent on a regular basis. Therefore, it seems quite appropriate to use the term visitation schedule to describe when a child sees the nonresidential parent. However, it is understandable that some parents who do not have primary residential custody prefer not to consider their time "visitation." Also, a number of professionals have voiced a hope that the use of a term such as parenting time instead of visitation would facilitate reaching agreements about children; at this point, there are no clear indications whether such wording has improved, or has the capacity to improve, the frequencies of positive agreements between parents.

A main objective of a good visitation schedule would be to allow adequate contact with each parent, and therefore provide a foundation for the types of quality interactions that promote healthy parent-child relationships. Accordingly, positive visitation schedules would promote parent-child interactions that benefit children and would limit factors that would provide risks for children's well-being.

INDIVIDUAL CHARACTERISTICS, SITUATIONAL FACTORS, AND TYPES OF INTERACTIONS

As noted in Chapter 1, there are a number of factors found to affect children of divorce, as well as statutes that identify legal criteria to be considered in evaluations. These empirical findings and statutes need to be considered when recommending visitation schedules. For example, because the loss of a parent increases the risk of negative outcomes for children, having regular contact with the noncustodial parent is crucial except in the most extraordinary of circumstances. The level of conflict between parents, parental psychological adjustment, and the general levels of child stress also need to be considered in schedule planning.

Well-adjusted parents who do a good job cooperating with one another may be able to successfully execute a schedule in which both have a considerable amount of time, with many exchanges of the children between the two. In contrast, high conflict parents, who may have significant psychological dysfunction, tend to create a great deal of stress for children, and are more likely to require a schedule that includes decreased contact between parents, including fewer transitions. Transitions that include interparental conflict can unfortunately expose the children to those conflicts and consequently contribute to experiences of child stress.

It is also important to consider a broad array of parent characteristics and child needs in visitation planning. There can be a wide variety of such features to consider. It is not possible to identify all such parent and child characteristics, and each case needs to be considered in terms of its unique and relevant features.

In general, parenting is so complex and multifaceted that it can be extremely challenging to identify what are the most important and relevant aspects of it beyond those factors found to affect children of divorce. Consequently, a number of authorities have worked to identify the most frequently important and relevant dimensions of parenting. Those dimensions include affection, support, reinforcement, informal education, limit setting, clear communication, adequate though not excessive amounts of structure, family cohesion, and maintaining an appropriately authoritative role (e.g., Baumrind, 1966; Beavers & Hampson, 1990; Budd, Clark, & Connell, 2011; Darling & Steinberg, 1993; Epstein, Baldwin, & Bishop, 1983). Of course, there are a number of differences in specific parenting behaviors required with different child ages and stages of development, as well as with different child temperaments, needs and strengths.

In terms of visitation recommendations, a child who is inattentive and disorganized may do better with a schedule that promotes organization and focus, such as one with fewer transitions, at least during the week while school is in session. Somewhat similarly, it is likely to be helpful for such a child to spend time during the school week with the parent who is able and willing to provide external structure to provide adjustments for the child's neuropsychological deficits that impact organization and time management. A very different circumstance would involve a sensitive child prone to emotional distress who may benefit from relatively frequent contact with a noncustodial parent who is especially emotionally available and communicative. In another example, a child who is isolated from peers in the home of the residential parent may especially benefit from time with the nonresidential parent that includes many opportunities to be with positive peers.

Especially when parents are off work on weekends and there are school-age children, weekday and weekend visits provide very different opportunities for parent-child interaction. Many school-age children, especially those who are beyond the very early grades, are involved in extracurricular activities, have routine homework responsibilities, and also frequently socialize with peers. As a result, weekdays are often a hectic combination of many activities with limited time for relatively extended parent-child interactions, even with full-time, stay-at-home parents. In contrast, weekends characteristically involve less rush and more opportunities for children and parents to interact. Depending upon parental availability and competency, there may be benefits for children of experiencing each parent carrying out a mix of task-oriented behaviors such as supervising homework and making dinner, as well as leisure activities such as going on outings, playing with electronics, or simply talking. At the same time, parental histories, abilities, and interests need to be considered in these matters so that the parenting time that takes place is of good quality. In many cases, considerations of relative deficits in parental or family functioning are most relevant in recommendations for the primary residential custodian, but they may also be important in trying to identify parenting time for the nonresidential custodian.

For instance, some parents may sincerely love their children and want what is best for them, but may not be sufficiently active in crucial aspects of parenting. Low levels of parental monitoring and household management have been found to lead to negative outcomes for postdivorce teens (Buchanan et al., 1996).

Somewhat similarly, a parent may have a lifestyle that has involved, or that would be expected to include numerous relationship transitions. Such transitions occur more frequently among nonmarried parents, and a greater number of relationship transitions is associated with decreased well-being for children; in general, married stepfamilies show better child outcomes than cohabiting families (Anderson & Greene, 2013). Although there are questions about the extent to which relationship transitions cause child dysfunction versus being a result of individual parental instability (Fomby & Cherlin, 2006; Sweeney, 2010), it is reasonable for evaluators to consider household stability when making recommendations about visitation schedules.

Also, perhaps obviously, on the severe end of the spectrum, evaluators need to keep in mind that parenting deficits such as inadequate nurturance and excessive punishment have been found to place children at risk for serious adulthood psychological disturbance (e.g., Johnson et al., 2006). Therefore, such dysfunctional parenting must be considered in parenting schedules even if present only in the nonresidential parental family.

In many cases, situational factors such as parental availability, distance between households, and distances between homes and schools need to be considered in making schedule recommendations. A large proportion of traditional visitation schedules have had parents alternate weekends with the children. In many cases, such a split of weekend time makes a great deal of sense. However, the changing world of employment results in a requirement for a number of parents that they need to work on weekends, and such factors cannot be ignored. If a noncustodial parent is available to directly care for the children at particular times, it is logical to try to schedule visits when they are directly available.

In some cases, there is an important interface between children's needs and circumstances and parental availability. For example, some noncustodial parents need to leave for work so early in the morning that they would need to wake up the children at an hour that requires them to lose substantial sleep. In such circumstances, it would be important to consider a visit that involves only an evening and not an overnight.

In recent years, there has been increased focus on the use of online communication tools such as Skype in maintaining contact between children and parents. For example, Wolman and Pomerance (2012) surveyed parents and children about their experiences with such communication after separation and/or divorce. In general, both parents and children were very positive about the use of tools such as Skype to maintain parent-child interactions (though no parents in that sample said that they used it to maintain communication with their ex-spouses). More specifically, the respondents stated that the visual contact with the other individual was much more engaging than just using the telephone. However, direct in-person contact was reported to be superior to online communication. The authors noted that a number of states have begun to directly address online parent-child communication in relevant statutes.

Perhaps not surprisingly, given the newness of the technology, there has been only limited research on the topic, including a lack of relevant outcome data on the use of such technology (Saini, Mishna, Barnes, & Polak, 2013). There are numerous individual child and family circumstances that need to be considered. Saini et al. (2013) summarized the general potential benefits and limitations of such virtual contact between children and parents. On the positive side, because the visual communication is more engaging than just talking on the telephone, there potentially can be increased parent-child interaction quality. Especially when relocation occurs, communication tools such as Skype can facilitate relationships when the frequency of direct contact is relatively low. Related online technologies can provide activities for parents and children to do together that potentially are enjoyable and/or educational. However, a potential limitation of such virtual contact is the risk that it could be used to limit more optimal in-person contact between a child and parent. There is a potential for significantly less privacy for a child and parent when using a tool such as Skype, though such concerns need to be balanced with general safety considerations for children online. High-conflict parents might interfere with the virtual contact between the child and the other parent, and some families might not have access to the required technology. Presumably, as there are more experiences with the use of such online communication tools, there will be a more comprehensive picture of benefits, drawbacks, and important considerations regarding specific family circumstances.

VERY YOUNG CHILDREN

Over a considerable period of time, there has been a good deal of controversy about appropriate time-sharing arrangements for very young children. In large part, this controversy represents a conflict between a wish to promote good quality relationships between very young children, especially infants and toddlers, and primarily fathers, while at the same time protecting the children from potentially undue stress associated with what some individuals fear to be inappropriate visitation with the nonresidential parent. The question of overnight visits for very young children is at the very center of this controversy.

The question about overnight visits for very young children is especially important because they constitute a large proportion of children of divorce. Associated with the fact that many divorces take place when children are young, most children whose parents have gone through a divorce have experienced it by the time they were six years of age. Of that group of children, most are under three years old (Emery, 1988).

Previously, a number of authorities, writing from a theoretical perspective, maintained that, in general, overnight visits with the nonresidential parent should not occur for children who were under three years of age (e.g., Goldstein, Freud, & Solnit, 1973; Hodges, 1986). Others contended that even the youngest of children, given appropriate circumstances, would generally benefit from overnight visits (e.g., Kelly & Lamb, 2000; Warshak, 2000).

A central conceptual issue pertains to parent-child attachment. One view emphasizes that very young children tend to become attached to a primary caregiver, usually the mother, and that undue interruptions in that attachment lead to very negative experiences for the child. An alternate view emphasizes that children tend to become attached to both parents when very young, attachment can change in important ways over the lifespan, and that there are other important interpersonal experiences that influence child and adult development.

Research

Likely associated with the difficulties of carrying out research in this area, there has been all too little of it. The main empirical research is briefly summarized here. It is crucial to note that, by necessity, none of this research is experimental, as there is no random assignment of participants to experimental conditions. That is, in all such research, parents were self-selected to each visitation condition according to what had been their pattern of child visitation prior to entrance into each study. Accordingly, between-group differences could be due, at least in part, to factors other than the visitation schedules that were investigated.

An early relevant research project compared infants who had only daytime visits, infants who had overnights with the father, and infants whose parents were in intact marriages (Solomon & George, 1999). Infants who had regular overnight visits with the father were classified less frequently as securely attached as compared to those whose parents were in intact marriages. There was no statistically significant difference between infants who had overnight visits and those who had daytime visits only, though that difference approached the conventional level of statistical significance. For the group of children who experienced overnights, dysfunctional attachment to mothers was associated with high levels of conflict and relatively poor communication between parents. In addition, as pointed out by Lamb and Kelly (2001), the infants who had overnights, in a number of cases, had never lived together with both parents and/or had experienced extended separations from their fathers.

More recently, McIntosh, Smyth, and Kelleher (2010) investigated visitation patterns in a large sample of very young children, through age 5, in Australia. The classification of children into different overnight visitation groups differed somewhat depending upon child age. For all age groups, rare overnights were defined as occurring less than once per year. For children under the age of 2, primary care was identified as ranging from one overnight per month up to just under once per week, and shared care was defined as one or more overnights per week. For children in the older two age categories, 2 to 3 years of age, and 4 to 5 years old, primary care was defined as at least one overnight per month but less than five in a two-week period, and shared care was defined as five or more overnights in each two-week period of time. In general, for the youngest age group, those in shared care had lower parent ratings of health than those in the rare overnights group. For the 2- to 3-year-olds, children who had shared care had lower ratings of persistence than those with rare overnights. For the oldest group, those in shared care showed less conflict with teachers or other caregivers than those in the rare overnights group.

A very recent study (Tornello, Emery, Rowen, Potter, Ocker, et al., 2013) investigated a large, geographically diverse but low socioeconomic status United States sample. Only about 25% of parents were married. The research investigated associations between overnight visits, attachment security, and young child adjustment. Findings were similar to McIntosh et al. (2010) in that frequent overnights were associated with attachment insecurity in infants from birth through age 1. However, that correlation was not evident for children ages 1 through 3. In addition, frequent overnights were not associated with adjustment problems in children ages 3 through 5, and frequent contact at age 3 actually predicted more positive behavior at age 5.

Pruett et al. (2004) investigated children of 132 couples, through the age of 6, in Connecticut. They compared children who did not have overnight visits with those who had one or more overnights per week. There was an overall main effect for overnight visits such that children who had overnights tended to function better, though that main effect was entirely due to better functioning only in children ages 4 through 6. In other words, the overnights did not make a difference in functioning in the younger children.

Applying Research to Individual Cases

It may be that differences in parental histories and backgrounds accounted for the divergent research findings (Hynan, 2012). As noted above, it appears that a significant number of parents in the Solomon and George (1999) study had problematic histories with one another, and many of the infants had not had consistent contact with their fathers prior to the research data having been collected. Somewhat similarly, in the Australian study, relatively small proportions of parents had ever been married to one another, and many had never cohabitated. For example, for children less than 2 years of age, only about 10% of primary parents had ever been married to the nonresidential parent. That proportion was higher, at roughly 40%, for the 4- to 5-year-old children. As noted above, only 25% of parents in the Tornello et al. (2013) study were married. In addition, in McIntosh et al. (2010), a very large proportion of the parents studied were mainly relying on government financial support. In contrast, in the Pruett et al. (2004) sample, 77% of couples had been married, and the average duration of marriages was eight years. Of the 31 unmarried couples, 90% had cohabitated at some point. Prior to the start of the study, 75% of the families had already been carrying out overnight visits, typically more than once per week. In addition, that sample may have been particularly inclined to cooperate well with one another by virtue of having volunteered to participate in a research project on collaborative divorce. That United States sample was described as having come from economically diverse backgrounds, though there was no description of the proportion primarily reliant on government financial support.

Overall, characteristics of the families may have played a major role in the divergent findings of these research projects. In the Solomon and George (1999) and McIntosh, Smyth, and Kelleher (2010) studies, the children generally appear to have had very limited opportunities to have considerable contact with both parents prior to the research data having been collected, and the parents had little to no history of having learned to cooperate adequately about the children. In contrast, in the Pruett et al. (2004) research, most parents had significant histories of having been married to one another or having lived together, as well as a majority of them having had regular overnight visits in effect. It may also be that the differences in general socioeconomic status between the two more recent studies played a role because parents who have greater financial stability may have greater personal resources generally, including better capability to successfully carry out cooperation about overnight visits (Hynan, 2012).

At this point, there is no empirical evidence to support or refute the hypothesis that parental characteristics and childcare histories play a major role in the impact of overnight visits on children. However, as future research might be carried out, it will be important to determine if such a pattern is supported or disconfirmed by the data.

In evaluation practice, it is important to have a solid knowledge base about such matters. At the same time, it is crucial to look at the individual circumstances and facts of each case. Such circumstances and facts would include the histories each parent has with the children, and with one another.

Gould and Stahl (2001) have described other parenting skills and behaviors that need to be examined when considering the question of overnight visits for very young children. In addition, AFCC (2010) has published a pamphlet of helpful considerations for parenting plans across a number of age groups.

Aside from the controversy about overnight visits for very young children, there appears to be a degree of consensus about frequency of contact with each parent. For the youngest of children, up through about the age of three, frequent contact appears to be preferable. A combination of research-based information and practical experience indicates that, within this age range, contact with the parent should in most cases occur at least three times each week, without any very extended times away from either parent to promote positive attachment. Such visits do not have to be very lengthy, however.

INTERPARENTAL CONFLICT AND PARENTING PLANS

As research evidence and practical experience has accumulated over time, authorities have voiced conflicting points of view about how much inter-parental conflict should be taken into consideration in the creation of time-sharing schedules. As noted previously, exposure to interparental conflict has been found to be perhaps the most robust factor that predicts a negative out-come for children of divorce. Therefore, there has been concern that schedules which include considerable contact between high-conflict parents increase the risk of children exposure to excessive conflict. There is good deal of empirical support for that concern, though it is a complicated matter. It is very challenging to conduct high-quality research in this area, especially longitudinal studies that would potentially shed light on the experience of interparental conflict and cooperation over time. In addition, the presence of interparental conflict is less important than children's exposure to it, and such patterns of conflict can change over time. For example, Booth and Amato (1991) found that predivorce conflict levels are not always accurately predictive of postdivorce conflict.

Practical experience reveals that a couple might have been characterized as low conflict prior to the separation and divorce, but if that divorce was largely a result of unexpected marital infidelity, the parent who had remained faithful could easily have experienced it as a traumatic betrayal and responded in part through actions that initiated a great deal of conflict. In a different type of change in conflict level, research by Maccoby and Mnookin (1992) found that a significant proportion of originally high-conflict parents decreased their level of conflict over time by having disengaged from one another.

Furthermore, research studies have used a number of different methods to try to measure interparental conflict. Understandably, many methods to measure parental conflict are retrospective in nature, and therefore memory limitations come into play. Some studies have used pre-existing research measures whereas others have created their own questionnaires (Bauserman, 2002).

Because postdivorce joint custody families are diverse, and include parents with varying levels of conflict with their former spouses, a simple examination of joint versus sole custody is an inadequate method of examining this matter. Instead, research needs to compare high-conflict groups with others who manifest lower levels of conflict.

Cummings and Davies (1994) described the numerous negative effects on children of exposure to interparental conflict, including problems with emotional regulation and inadequate learning of appropriate social skills. Interparental conflict has also been found to have a negative impact on parenting behaviors, especially parental acceptance of children and appropriate discipline, and low levels of these behaviors have a very negative impact on children (Krishnakumar & Buehler, 2000). Children from joint custody families who nonetheless were engaged in high levels of ongoing conflict were found to experience considerable distress, especially at transitions, including withdrawal, tension, and somatization (Johnston & Campbell, 1988). Similarly, with high-conflict post-divorce couples, frequent visits with the noncustodial parent appeared to increase both the frequency of conflicts and the extent of child problems (Tschann et al., 1989).

Other authorities have maintained that concern about the level of conflict between parents has often inappropriately functioned to decrease the amount of time that children spend with their fathers (who are predominantly the nonresidential parents) after separation or divorce, to the detriment of the children's well-being. For example, a frequently cited study reported that children in joint custody arrangements had better overall adjustment than those in sole custody, even when there were statistical controls for pre-existing levels of interparental conflict (Gunnoe & Braver, 2001).

More broadly, a meta-analysis by Bauserman (2002) found that children in joint physical or legal custody manifested better adjustment in a number of areas than those in sole custody. Joint custody groups reported less interparental conflict than the sole custody group, though the level of conflict did not predict child adjustment. The author noted that only a small proportion of studies in his analysis provided usable data on group differences in conflict. He also noted that the studies were all correlational in nature, could not demonstrate that joint custody caused improved adjustment in children, and the results could also represent support for the argument that there is a self-selection process such that relatively low-conflict couples both have better adjusted children and tend to enter into joint custody arrangements.

Fabricius and his colleagues have also reported data that indicate increased time children spend with fathers after divorce is related both to better relationships with fathers and better health status. For example, Fabricius and Luecken (2007) asked a university students sample about their experiences when their parents had divorced. Those experiences included past living arrangements with each parent, patterns of interparental conflict, and physical health. Overall, they found that increased time with the father was positively correlated with a good relationship with the father and better health. Interparental conflict was associated with a less positive relationship with the father and more somatic symptoms. Because there was no interaction between exposure to interparental conflict and time with the father, the authors concluded that increased time with the father was beneficial in both low- and high-conflict families. The authors noted that the positive correlation between time with the father and a good relationship quality with the father could be due to factors such as good-quality fathers having chosen to spend more time with their children.

Fabricius et al. (2012) reported more recent data on the amount of parenting time and parent-child relationships. Their large sample of university students, whose parents had divorced prior to them turning 16 years of age, reported on the amount of time they had spent with their fathers postdivorce and the degree of emotional security with their fathers that they experienced as young adults. The authors described that there was a significant positive correlation between the percentage of time (up through 50%) the respondents spent with their fathers and the emotional security experienced with them, and that the mother-child relationship did not manifest any decrement in quality up through 50% of time having been spent with the father. On the relevant graph (Fabricius et al., 2012, p. 195), the steepest part of the curve, representing the strongest portion of the overall correlation, was the section between 0 days with the father and 1 through 3 days with him in a 28-day period. The next steepest portion of the curve was between 1 through 3 days and 4 through 6 days. Therefore, it appears that the greatest magnitude of this positive correlation can be attributed to the relatively low emotional security with fathers of individuals who had contact with their fathers less than once per week. Fabricius and his colleagues noted that their findings are not applicable to families that have experienced domestic violence or abuse.

At my request, William Fabricius kindly sent me more detailed data on the individuals represented in the 2012 report. Just under 38% of respondents saw their fathers less than once per week, and approximately 18% did not see them at all. Although there is no further information available about these respondents or their fathers, it is reasonable to wonder about them. What might lead a father-child relationship to be nonexistent, or so meager that there is not even contact once per week? Although it is possible that some of these cases were the result of highly misguided legal action that left good fathers with little or no time with their children, there are also other possible explanations.

It is reasonable to hypothesize that in some of the zero contact cases, the father essentially left the child, or there was such a negative father-child interaction pattern that the child chose no contact. In either case, it is likely that a significant proportion of these fathers had considerable psychological and/or interpersonal problems. In a somewhat different vein, if a significant portion of the positive correlation between time spent with the father and emotional security with him is due to dysfunctional fathers causing these no- or very low-contact cases, to what extent can these data be practically applicable for custody evaluators or policymakers? Of course, there is periodic concern expressed that negative maternal gatekeeping (e.g., Pruett, Arthur, & Ebling, 2007) can so discourage fathers that they give up efforts to have a relationship with their children or settle for seeing them infrequently. Clearly, more detailed, solid information is needed about such cases, including data about levels of family conflict and gatekeeping.

Of course, correlational findings are not causal ones, and yet the fact that this applied field of work generally does not allow for random assignments of individuals or families to experimental conditions leads to frequent questions about the most appropriate interpretation of findings. In oversimplified terms, the question is to what extent increased time with the nonresidential parent leads to improved functioning, or to what degree better-functioning families promote more frequent time-sharing arrangements that includes a considerable amount of contact with the noncustodial parent. Of course, other relevant factors that are not directly measured in the research can also play an important role.

However, certain research methodologies are helpful in this regard, though challenging and expensive to conduct. A longitudinal study of a high-conflict Australian mediation sample reported that, over four years, a better father-child relationship early in the time frame led to more contact later on; more contact by itself reportedly did not lead to an improved father-child interaction pattern (McIntosh, Smyth, Wells, & Long, 2010).

In trying to sort out and understand these finding, some authorities (e.g., Pruett & Barker, 2009) have concluded that only a high level of conflict between parents provides a risk in terms of children's exposure to it. Unfortunately, there are no clear delineations in the divorce field of high versus moderate versus low levels of such conflict. Although the greatest risk may be from exposure to severe physical violence between parents, it is also crucial for relevant professionals to be aware that exposure to verbal and psychological aggression has a negative impact on children. For example, exposure to nonphysical aggression between parents such as loud arguments, insults, and swearing contributed to child behavior problems independent of the presence or absence of parental physical violence (Jouriles, et al., 1996; McDonald et al., 2007).

LIMITS ON VISITATION

In relatively rare circumstances, the court system gives serious consideration to placing unusual limitations on a parent's visitation time. Because there is often considerable disagreement about any limitation, it appears that a significant proportion of such cases are referred for evaluation.

The only appropriate reason to consider restrictions on visitation is the risk that a child might be endangered if unrestricted visitation took place. Such potential endangerment could be physical or psychological (broadly defined) in nature.

When restricted visitation occurs, much of the time it takes the form of legally required supervision of the visits. Because there are often significant financial and time costs to visitation supervision, when it occurs, there frequently is a consequent reduction in the amount of visitation time that otherwise would likely have taken place. On other occasions, sometimes due to the reality that there is no available supervisor, the restriction may take the form of specific time limitations. For example, if a nonresidential parent has a demonstrated pattern of excessive alcohol use in the evening and late-night hours, visits might be restricted to blocks of time during the day.

Once again, evaluators considering possible visitation restrictions need to be well informed by relevant scientific and professional information, and apply such data to the specific circumstances of each case. One of the frequent practical challenges of evaluating limitations on visits is the question of how long they should occur. That is, when restricted visitation takes place, there are typically efforts to improve the parenting of the individual with the restricted visits, and/or to enhance the quality of the relevant parent-child interactions. At times, therapy is involved for the parent and/or the family. In some such cases, the supervision is designated to have a therapeutic component to it.

While it is very difficult to make predictions as to how long it might take for significant improvements in parenting and parent-child interactions, a reasonable option is to recommend that there be a re-evaluation of such matters within a period of time such as three or six months. It may be useful for an evaluator who recommends a future re-evaluation to specifically state that the future evaluator could be a different individual, in order to dispel any concerns that a re-evaluation may be recommended mainly to generate more work and revenue for the evaluator.

When there is a decision that it might be appropriate to discontinue the supervision or other restriction, doing so gradually can provide a reasonable trial basis. For example, depending on the particular case circumstances, it may be useful to consider first trying a nonsupervised hour or two of visitation, followed immediately by supervised time so that the supervisor may gain at least a degree of helpful perspective about how interactions proceeded during the nonsupervised time. If things seem to go well with such initial steps, a gradual reduction and eventual discontinuation of the restriction on a step-by-step basis is often useful. The specific timing required to attempt a gradual discontinuation of supervision or other restriction will depend a great deal on the specific facts and circumstances of the case. In general, more serious and long-term concerns about the parent who has restricted visitation should lead to a slower phase out of restrictions in order to give greater opportunity to cautiously assess safety considerations.

CONCLUSIONS

When making recommendations about time-sharing plans, it is once again crucial for evaluators to be fully cognizant of the scientific and professional knowledge base, and to apply relevant principles to the specific facts and circumstances of each case. As well described in greater detail by McIntosh and Smyth (2012), the complexities and inevitable limitations of the relevant research mean that it is not reasonable to expect that any specific parenting time schedule will inevitably result in a desired outcome. Of particular importance is that it has not been possible to randomly assigned cases to different time-sharing schedules, and that in much research there is inadequate information about crucial features such as preseparation parent-child interactions and interparental conflict levels.

No exhaustive list of relevant considerations about time-sharing plans is possible. However, as noted above, the numerous factors that need to be considered include the clear benefits of good relationships with both parents, the preseparation relationship (including attachment) with each parent, the ability of parents to cooperate with one another and minimize conflict, parental availability, child age and stage of development, child needs, parental psychological functioning, other parental strengths and deficits, and the distance between parental residences.

Other factors of both practical importance and emotional significance frequently come into play in evaluations. Especially as there may be gradual movement toward children spending a good deal of time with each parent, there are questions of balance between consecutive days in one household and seeing each parent with sufficient frequency that the child does not miss him or her excessively.

For example, there are a number of positive characteristics associated with children spending consecutive days in one household, with relatively fewer transitions, especially when they are of school age. Such positive features include greater residential stability, greater ease in keeping track of school materials and personal belongings, and often a feeling of life being less hectic and stressful. A drawback of such a schedule is that there is an increased risk of the children excessively missing the parent in the other household. In contrast, a schedule with more frequent transitions between households reduces the risk of children being separated for too long from any one parent. On the other hand, more frequent changes between residences can be accompanied by experiences of increased stress and hassle associated with the transitions. Also, if parents do not consistently shield the children from whatever conflict take place, a greater number of transitions may expose the children to higher levels of conflict. Other factors need to be considered as well. For example, a child with attentional and organizational challenges may be especially burdened by more frequent transitions, whereas an emotionally sensitive child with strong ties with each parent may feel greater stress with fewer transitions. Perhaps obviously, there are likely to be relatively fewer practical barriers to transitions when parents live quite close to one another, and potentially increased difficulties the further away from one another they live.

Understandably, judges often have case settlement as a priority, and evaluation frequently are ordered in part as a potential settlement tool. Therefore, it is reasonable for evaluators to consider time-sharing schedules that might help cases to settle, as long as they mainly consider the overall goal of what would be in a child's best interest. Most frequently, the parental battle is focused on time sharing. Sometimes, creative thinking by an evaluator can promote a settlement that is very positive for the children and acceptable to both parents.

It frequently occurs that one parent wishes to be the primary residential custodian, at least most of the time such as during the school year. Often, the other parent also voices a wish to be the primary residential custodian, and yet also notes that they would be open to equally shared parenting. In some cases of this type, it can be productive to consider the school year and the summer vacation calendar to be very different in terms of the parenting schedule. In a hypothetical example, while school is in session, the children may primarily be assigned to be with Parent A most of the time, and to visit with Parent B about 11 to 13 days per month. During summer vacation, they would be with Parent B a solid majority of the time, and visit with Parent A periodically. In a large proportion of cases, parents equally divide major holidays, relevant birthdays, and other vacation times. In such an overall arrangement, the parents may have contact with the children approximately an equal number of days over the course of a calendar year, while Parent A maintains the desired status as the primary residential parent during the academic year. A similar arrangement was described by Ackerman (1995).

Of course, in considering such a potential problem-solving recommendation, the children's well being needs to be the priority. In the example above, if one or more of the children experience serious academic challenges, and Parent B clearly is more able and active assisting with school matters, that potential time-sharing solution probably is not the best. Focused deliberation about all relevant facts is needed in each case.

Chapter 5

COLLECTING INFORMATION FROM PARENTS AND COLLATERALS

PRACTICE CHECKLIST

___Focus information collection on the child's best interest as represented by an integration of scientific findings on children of divorce with relevant legal criteria.

___Have parents complete relevant substantive background information forms in the office, without input from others.

___Interview parents individually.

___Interview other adults who are living with the child, or who will be living with the child for more than just a very temporary time.

___Routinely include structured clinical interviews of parents about common psychological disorders, substance use, and the domestic violence.

___Consider the credibility of each collateral informant.

___Emphasize to all collaterals that they need to describe direct observations of interactions between children and parents, and/or relevant individual behaviors.

___Ask collaterals for descriptions of relevant behaviors and verbalizations — do not accept their inferences at face value.

Note: This form is a guide to promote productive reasoning and good practice. It is not comprehensive or all-inclusive and does not replace adequate training and experience.

Custody evaluations characteristically begin with parent interviews. In many cases, there are also adults other than the legal parents who provide information. Some of these adults are stepparents or live-in parents, and others are individuals identified by a parent as potentially useful sources of information and perspective. At times, there are aspects of relevant information that are difficult for parents to encapsulate and describe in a productive manner during an interview.

This chapter first focuses on primarily verbally related information described by parents. Second, the focus is on the Parenting Functions questionnaire, which was designed to assist parents in communicating an estimate of the proportions of common parenting tasks carried out by themselves, the other parent, or a third party. The third section summarizes the collection of information from collateral sources. Some of the most relevant collaterals are individuals who live in the same home as a parent, and who therefore are functionally part of the family unit. Other collaterals outside the family unit are individual such as extended family or friends. Collateral information can also come from institutional sources such as schools or healthcare providers, and/or individuals who work in such locations.

When collecting such information from any of these sources, it is paramount for evaluators to keep in mind the main objective of the evaluation, which is to clarify what is in the child's best interest. As described in Chapter 1, a child's best interest is most accurately and productively represented by research findings about children of divorce, integrated with relevant legal criteria.

While considering these priority scientific and legal factors regarding children of divorce, evaluators also need to recognize the reality that there can often be practical limitations to the time and financial expense of conducting evaluations. Therefore, because there is almost always a considerable amount of information to collect, integrate, and cognitively process, it may not be productive or even possible in all cases to cover each and every area of information that theoretically could be at least indirectly relevant. For example, I have read evaluation reports that included pages of detail about arguments the parents had with one another when they were dating, prior to ever having had children, and others that included a great deal of information about parental retirement funds. Those reports did not indicate how such areas of information were relevant for the children's best interest. Although it is possible that, in some cases, such information may theoretically shed light on how parents historically have handled conflict with one another, or relevant aspects of personality functioning, in general, practical limitations contribute to the necessity of focusing on what are the most important and relevant areas of information to help clarify a child's best interest.

Prior to a first appointment, it is common for evaluators to have parents complete forms of relevant background information. In part, it is a productive way of gathering basic background information. Such forms often include basic family data, health problem history, whether there is current medical treatment, current medications, history of mental health services, family medical and mental health (including substance misuse) histories, and whether the individual had ever been arrested or convicted for any crimes. Evaluators can then follow up, as needed, about such reported information in interviews.

As described in Chapter 2, parents generally are motivated to present information in a way that will maximize the likelihood of reaching a desired outcome, which usually includes primary residential custody. In many cases, parents discuss with their attorneys, prior to a first interview, what and how to present to the evaluator.

A number of evaluators have forms to submit background information available for parents prior to the first interview. Sometimes, these forms include extensive questionnaires about very substantive items, including perceptions of child functioning and relationships, histories of parental interactions with one another, individual adult and child health histories, and related content areas. Although it is understandable that parents often receive input from their attorneys about how to present in evaluations, a main drawback to having substantive background information forms available for parents to complete prior to coming into the office is that they can potentially receive very specific input from their attorneys about how to complete them. In doing so, a parent can make it more difficult for the evaluator to disentangle objective factual information from whatever impression the parent and attorney wished to create. Therefore, I recommend that parents do not have access to such paperwork prior to the relevant appointment.

INTERVIEWING PARENTS

Understandably, parents frequently begin custody evaluations feeling nervous and badly wanting to persuade the evaluator that their preferences actually are what are best for the children. Many parents will have had prior meetings with their attorneys that focused on what should be said in the first interview and how to say it. Different individuals will have different communication and persuasion styles. Some will try very hard to "sell" their points of view whereas others will be more focused on trying to frankly portray their concerns and family circumstances. Evaluators need to keep an attitude of open-mindedness about what each parent is relating to them. At the same time, each parent is likely to bring at least elements of the egocentricity bias and motivation to present their information and perspective in such a manner that will have a positive payoff for themselves (see Chapter 2).

Each parent needs to have an opportunity to tell his or her story and describe what is believed to be relevant and important. Over the decades of conducting custody and related evaluations, I have had numerous opportunities to talk with attorneys about their criticisms of evaluations and reports. One of the most common criticisms that attorneys hear from their clients is that the evaluator did not pay attention to, or at least did not include in the report what parents felt to be important.

At the same time, as noted above, evaluators need to have firmly in mind the types of information that characteristically are the most important. In other words, evaluators need to integrate giving parents ample opportunity to describe what they believe is important, and perhaps in doing so allow clients to follow attorney advice of what to emphasize, while also ensuring collection of data that are relevant and important from psychosocial and legal perspectives. Therefore, parent interviews need to have a semistructured format, and evaluators need to be skilled in smoothly shifting between what parents seem intent on describing and the areas of information that are usually highly relevant for a competent evaluation. Of course, a well-prepared parent will describe information that includes a good deal of what evaluators appropriately perceive to be important and relevant.

Although it may be impossible to definitively state what areas of information should always be collected from parents, in general, it is crucial to obtain parental perspectives on child functioning, including needs, strengths, and relative deficits. Similarly, it is essential to acquire perceptions of the relationships between the children and each of the parents. It is very important to inquire about parental histories of interaction with one another, including how they have related to one another in their dealings with the children, and how they have managed conflict with one another. In addition, it is useful to regularly obtain parental perspectives about the emotional atmosphere in the home, anticipated living situations, and child care routines and plans.

Because the mental health functioning of parents regularly has a significant impact on the well being of children of divorce, it is important to routinely interview about this area. The use of a format such as a structured clinical interview has been found to be among the most accurate methods of attaining a diagnosis (Garb, 1998), and therefore its use is warranted in custody evaluation interviewing, at least about the more frequently-experienced Axis I symptoms.

Such interviewing focused on mental health functioning should include routine questioning about alcohol use. Although there is no interview methodology that will always lead individuals to be truthful about this matter, I have found that it is routinely necessary to ask a number of focused questions. For example, I regularly ask individuals to give an estimate of how often they might have anything to drink in an average week, month, or whatever might be the applicable length of time. I also inquire about the range of drinks an individual would likely have on such occasion. I have found that such questions usually result in more useful detail than the very vague answers typically given to initial questions about alcohol use. It is also advisable to ask each parent whether their alcohol use had ever been at a different level, at any time in the past, as compared to what they described. If there has ever been a period of substantial alcohol misuse, it is necessary to obtain details of the pattern of alcohol ingestion and consequences in relevant areas of life functioning.

Similarly, it is essential to routinely ask parents if they have ever used any drugs other than alcohol at any time in their lives. If there is an affirmative answer, there must be more detailed questioning. Those inquiries include earliest and most recent use, frequency of use and typical amount used each occasion, and details of drug use during the heaviest period of use. Regardless of the type of substances that have been used, it is important to ask if the parent has ever experienced any negative physical, psychological, occupational, and/or family consequences.

In addition, it is important to routinely ask parents whether they smoke. The Uniform Marriage and Divorce Act (NCCUSL, 1979), relied upon by many states in relevant statutes, includes the physical health of all involved parties as a factor that needs to be considered in custody determinations. As described in more length elsewhere (Hynan, 2002) it is well established that child exposure to environmental tobacco smoke significantly increases the risk of a number of childhood illnesses, some of them quite serious, especially if a child may already have a physical vulnerability (e.g., DiFranza & Lew, 1996). The effects can persist into adulthood; recent research has shown that childhood exposure to environmental tobacco smoke can lead to increased signs of early emphysema in adult nonsmokers (Lovasi, Diez Roux, Hoffman, Kawut, Jacobs, et al., 2009). It is also well-established that parental smoking is likely to contribute to heightened adolescent cigarette use (e.g., Doherty & Allen, 1994), and that smoking at a relatively young age is predictive of a higher risk of illegal drug use and related problems (Newcomb & Bentler (1989).

Recently, there has been increased focus on what a number of authorities have called thirdhand tobacco smoke, which is the residual tobacco smoke contamination that remains after the cigarette has been extinguished. A powerful tobacco-specific lung carcinogen was found much more frequently and at higher concentrations in homes of smokers than nonsmokers (Thomas, Hecht, Luo, Ming, Ahluwalia et al., 2014). Children are uniquely sensitive to the effects of thirdhand smoke, and bans on home smoking may be among the best methods to protect them (Winnickoff, Friebely, Tanski, Sherrod, Matt et al., 2009).

It is very difficult to obtain useful information as to whether a personality disorder is present, for a number of reasons, even though there are structured clinical interviews focused on personality disorders. Individuals who have personality disorders tend to have very limited insight about their own dysfunction and much of the time do not experience acute symptoms that allow for more clear identification and description.

A common part of structured clinical interviews is whether the individual has ever received any mental health services of any type. If any parent has received mental health services, I ask them to sign a release so that I might obtain records. See the section below on Collateral Information for greater detail about this area.

Allegations of domestic violence occur in a substantial portion of custody evaluations, as described in more detail elsewhere this book, and it is frequently hidden (Weitzman, 2000). Therefore, it is advisable to routinely ask about whether there has ever been domestic violence between the parents, including physical altercations, threats of harm, and/or controlling intimidation.

There is a broad variety of other information that may be very relevant to the facts, circumstances, and/or allegations of some cases but not others. Although there is no finite list of such topics, such content areas can include relationship (including marriage) histories, information about families of origin, work history, residential history, how household tasks are handled, how parents met and developed their relationships with one another, social networks, and leisure time.

As described previously, in a large proportion of cases it is not practically useful to carry out detailed interviewing about all possible areas. A key consideration is whether a topic or content area has relevance for what is in a child's best interest.

Above, I described a report written by another evaluator that included a lot of detail about financial information, without indication of relevance for the children. In most cases, I have found financial matters to play no direct role in the child custody dispute. However, in a very different set of circumstances, a parent might describe that the children have been negatively affected by the alleged poor financial management of the other parent, to the extent that their stability and emotional security has been challenged. In such circumstances, comparatively detailed interviewing of each parent about that matter, accompanied by efforts to gather other relevant data would be very important to carry out.

An argument is made by some individuals that parents should routinely go through a joint interview, unless concerns about matters such as domestic violence point in the direction that they should not be required to be together. The usual main reason given for a joint parental interview is that it supposedly would provide the evaluator useful information about whether any type of joint custody would be successful. However, there are considerable reasons for concern that a joint interview may not in fact actually accomplish that objective.

The most important factors to consider in assessing the likelihood that joint parenting would be successful are the parental track record of cooperation and managing conflict with one another, especially about the children; whether there are sound reasons to believe that any circumstances would change the likely accuracy of expectations based on such a track record; and the extent to which parents agree or disagree about major areas of relevant decision making about the children. How parents act in a joint interview, for number of reasons, may shed little light on their likelihood of success in joint parenting.

For example, a parent may be very aware that one of the legal factors to be considered by the evaluator (in a number of states) is the extent to which each parent would promote a positive relationship between the child and the other parent. Therefore, that individual may purposely act, in a joint parental interview, in an especially cooperative and understanding manner that does not accurately represent how she or he characteristically behaves toward the other parent. Somewhat similarly, a parent may try to make the other parent look bad in front of the evaluator by making a statement known to have repeatedly upset that individual.

A reader might wonder why it is not crucial to observe parents interacting with one another, whereas it is necessary to observe parents and children together, as described more in the next chapter. There are important differences between the two methods. First, the objectives are different. In parent-child observations, the goal is to obtain a reasonable sample of a number of important parent-child interaction dimensions. Because parents may have limited insight about their own interaction patterns with the children, and/or might be motivated to report on them inaccurately when other methods are used, there really is no good substitute for observing children and parents together. As noted above, a main goal of the joint parental interview is to assess the likely success of future joint parenting. Parents are much more likely to be able to create desired impressions about themselves, as they can almost always exert much greater control over their own actions and statements, as compared to their abilities to control the actions and responses of children. In addition, there are other means of gathering information about the likely success of joint parenting that in most cases would provide a more ecologically valid database, such as examining the content areas described above.

PARENTING FUNCTIONS QUESTIONNAIRE

Many cases include disputes about parental histories of child caretaking, and it is quite common for a parent to maintain that he or she has carried out a wide range of parenting duties over the years that the marriage has been in effect. Such assertions are frequently associated with the stated belief by a parent that he or she has been the primary parent throughout a child's life. Such histories are often seen as very relevant. For example, the UMDA (NCCUSL, 1979) factor that includes the relationships between the child and the parents can accurately be viewed as encompassing childcare histories as one of its elements. Also, as described in Chapter 2, relatively recent efforts at modifying custody law have included reliance on proportions of past child caretaking.

In evaluation practice covering about two decades, I have routinely found it very difficult for parents to productively describe what has been the characteristic division of labor in terms of interacting with the children. In general, parents can take a great deal of time trying to describe such matters, typically with limited clarity. At the same time, many parents and attorneys have emphasized that they believe such matters to be quite important, likely associated with a perception that it is important to the court.

In order to address this dilemma, I created the Parenting Functions questionnaire for parents to complete in custody evaluation cases (its use in a research study is noted in Chapter 2). The main part of the questionnaire includes 16 items that represent common parenting functions. Some items pertain to relatively physical parenting tasks, such as making meals for children and doing their laundry. Others ask about more interpersonal behaviors such as providing encouragement and discipline. The parent is asked to estimate the proportion of time each of those parenting functions was carried out by themselves, the other parent, or another individual. The time frame given is the past year if parents are still residing together, or the one year prior to the parental separation, if they are no longer living together. The time frame of one year was used because the most recent year may be the most relevant for circumstances in effect at the time of the evaluation, and memory for more recent events tends to be more accurate than for older ones (Sederberg et al., 2008).

In practice, I have found that the use of this questionnaire provides a useful summary of parental perspectives. The primary and initial use of the questionnaire was to assist in collecting this type of perceived information. Parents can add narrative descriptions they feel would assist in their reporting of relevant information. In some cases, the questionnaire responses may lead to additional evaluator inquiries in interviews.

COLLATERAL INFORMATION

Collateral information generally comes from individuals identified by the parents, sources of potentially relevant information such as schools and healthcare providers, and/or other information from sources generally seen as external to the custody evaluation matter. Information in this section has mostly been derived from practical experience. The initial focus is on individuals as collateral informants. Then, I describe collateral information largely based on documentary sources.

Individuals

I frequently talk with collaterals identified by each parent, and those individuals almost inevitably described the parent who asked them to talk with me in glowing terms, such as wonderful, loving, and supportive. Simultaneously, they tended to describe the other parent negatively, and often used terms such as absent, controlling, and hostile. That is, unless assertively guided otherwise, such collaterals are likely to offer opinions and inferences, and sometimes even confidently voice a preference about who should be the primary residential parent. The bases of many such statements are comments directed to the collateral informants by others, instead of reliance on direct observations. Those types of information are not productive for evaluators, and as noted by Bricklin (1995), can be iatrogenic for the family because they often increase the divisiveness inherent in custody disputes.

As a result, it is crucial to set the stage appropriately before any substantive discussion with a collateral informant. As described by Woody (2000), it is important to educate any potential collateral informants that there is no privacy or confidentiality in their statements because the evaluation procedure does not constitute healthcare, and a signed informed consent form that covers such information should be obtained before a session takes place, at least for individuals who meet with the evaluator in person. The evaluator should emphasize to each individual that they should describe only information that they have directly seen or heard, and leave out any secondhand information or hearsay. A number of collateral informants will need to be reminded of that during the interview.

When I verbally educate collateral informants about our conversation, I emphasize that what is generally most productive is for me to learn what they have directly observed in terms of interactions between children and each parent. Also, I tell them that it would be important to let me know if they have observations of any child or parent as an individual that might help to shed light on what is best for the child.

If there is another adult, such as a stepparent, live-in parent, or other individual who is in the same home as the child, or who will be there in the future, for anything but a very short time, they are routinely included in the evaluation. Their involvement includes an individual interview.

When collateral individuals describe perspectives that are largely opinions or inferences about what they have seen, I ask them to describe the behavior they have directly observed that had led them to their conclusions. It is not unusual that the conclusions I draw from such descriptions of behaviors are quite different from the collaterals' opinions about such actions. If collaterals do not offer much in the way of specific behavioral descriptions, I characteristically prompt them to tell me what else they have directly seen in terms of parent-child interactions.

I find it important to specifically ask collaterals approximately how frequently they have an opportunity to observe the relevant children together with each parent, as well as what had been the most recent occasion. Although collaterals frequently described an average frequency of contact that would give them a good sample of interactions to see, on other numerous occasions I have learned that there have been very few opportunities for direct contact, and the most recent one had been over a year ago or longer.

Austin (2002) espoused many of the same views described above. However, Austin indicated that he selectively identifies collaterals with whom to have contact. In the geographical area where I practice, it appears commonplace to agree to have contact with whomever the parent identifies, within a reasonable number. In other words, to be highly selective in choosing collaterals might result in a complaint from a parent or an attorney. However, evaluation parents are always informed that collaterals such as family and friends, who would be expected to side with them, generally have their information and perspectives given much less weight than data from those who would be expected to be relatively objective.

In other words, the greater the objectivity of the collateral, the stronger is the credibility of the information. Nonetheless, parents often propose their own family members and close friends as collaterals, and even though that information needs to be taken with many grains of salt, their participation might provide support and assurance for parents as they go through the anxiety-arousing ordeal of the evaluation.

In very rare instances, a family member offers information that is contrary to the position taken by the relevant parent. Although it is important to examine whether that family member may hold a grudge against the parent, and therefore wish to portray them in an inaccurately negative manner, I have found that such reports generally represent sincere concern for the child or children on the part of the collateral family member. Under such circumstances, that type of collateral information needs to be taken quite seriously.

Evaluators need to be wary especially when it appears there may be competition between the parents in terms of how many collaterals to identify. Just as it is important to keep in mind that past caretaking histories are not determinative of what might be the best future parenting plan, the mere number of collateral sources identified may only shed light on the breadth of an individual's social network, and/or how assertive that parent was in asking people to participate in the evaluation.

Documents

Another type of collateral information involves the collection and review of documents. Often, parents ask what type of documents they should submit to me. In such cases, I assure them that it is a good question and one asked by many evaluation clients. I encourage them to focus on the principle of the child's best interest as a guide to determine what would be useful to give me. In other words, as parents go through documents they have available, they should ask themselves whether the information contained in such documents potentially sheds light on what is in the child's best interest. If the answer is yes, they should submit the documents. If it appears the material they are considering just pertains to interactions only between the parents, or about some other topic, and is not relevant for the child, it is probably not productive to submit it for review. I usually also advise parents to consult with their attorneys about such matters.

In recent years, it has become more common for parents to submit narrative descriptions of their perceptions and/or regarding events that have taken place. Sometimes these descriptions are in journal form. Although I always review them if they are submitted to me, the utility of such information is very spotty. In some very productive instances, such reports may contain highly relevant information that might otherwise have been overlooked by parents, and sometimes they can be corroborated by objective sources. Much of the time, however, most of the narratives created by parents do not contain information or perspectives that are uniquely useful in clarifying the child's best interest.

Documents from presumably more objective sources such as schools and healthcare providers are often more useful, and probably need to be routinely requested, given the apparent expectations of many attorneys and court systems, even when there are not significant controversies about school or healthcare. For most children, requesting healthcare information from a primary care physician is adequate, though in some cases, if there is a specialty medical provider, other health provider, and/or mental health practitioner, such records may need to be requested depending upon the circumstances. It is optimal, though not always possible, to obtain such records directly from the relevant sources, with appropriate release forms completed by the parents, and where applicable, the child. It is important to try to obtain such information directly, because on a few occasions, a parent has directly handed me such information after having removed pages that contain information contrary to their preferences. In many cases, however, schools, healthcare providers, or other agencies can be very slow to respond to requests for information, and a parent is the only possible source of obtaining the data prior to completion of the evaluation.

Over the years of carrying out custody evaluation, I have found that a high proportion of mental health providers respond by sending a largely retrospective summary letter. If the therapist's client is an adult, such letters frequently function as an advocacy document for that individual, sometimes with an opinion stated by the therapist that their client should have custody of the child. In other cases, when the child has been the primary client, but only one parent has been substantively involved in the therapy, the letter from the therapist tends to act as an advocacy piece for the parent who has been involved.

Other healthcare providers, especially larger clinics and hospitals, require providers to make a contemporaneous record of the assessment and treatment, often typed, and therefore such information is much more useful. In recent years, especially when sending signed releases with requests of information to mental health providers, I specifically requested a copy of a contemporaneously made record that includes content areas such as presenting problems, other intake information, diagnoses, treatment, response to treatment, and plans. Such information tends to be much more objective, detailed, and informative.

Although it is most common to request documentary information from sources such as schools, healthcare providers, and other relevant agencies, there is likely no finite list that can be identified. Decisions about what information to request need to follow the facts and circumstances of each case, including child needs and the reports of the parents. Additional perspectives can be found in articles by Austin (2002) and Bow (2010).

CONCLUSIONS

Collecting accurate and reasonably comprehensive information from parents is a considerable challenge for number of reasons. Any parent may be significantly influenced by an egocentric bias that contributes to cognitively processing a wide range of information in such a manner that favors his or her own position. In addition, parents are understandably motivated and often encouraged to relate information in a manner that will shed favorable light on themselves. Typically, information received from parents is a first step in the evaluation process. At that time, evaluators get a first look at the reality of the children and family from the perspective of the relevant parent. Accordingly, it is a good time for evaluators to begin to record the main positions of each parent, a process that should continue throughout the evaluation in terms of making note especially of objective evidence that supports or contradicts each such position.

Chapter 6

OBSERVING PARENTS INTERACT WITH CHILDREN

PRACTICE CHECKLIST

____Base conclusions about parent-child interactions on applicable science/theory and not on intuition or value judgments.

____Know the most important facets of parent-child interaction.

____Rely mainly on office observations.

____Conduct home visits or obtain visual information about child residences if there are concerns about safety or other residential features.

____Start observation sessions with pleasant warm-up activities.

____After the warm up, assign family tasks that are mildly to moderately stressful, including requirements that family members work together.

____Use a problem-solving or similar task that is moderately challenging and requires families to talk about real-life concerns (if child age is appropriate).

____Observe all children together with each parent.

____Record relevant behavioral examples.

____Use a summary sheet of important interactions to maintain appropriate focus and contemporaneously record inferences.

Note: This form is a guide to promote productive reasoning and good practice. It is not comprehensive or all-inclusive and does not replace adequate training and experience.

The most powerful criticism of custody evaluation is that it is a vehicle for mere evaluator value judgments disguised as a blend of scientific and professional wisdom (Emery et al., 2005; Krauss & Sales, 2000). Nowhere in the array of custody evaluation methodology is the risk of reliance on personal value judgment higher than in observing children interact with their parents.

A major part of the problem is that a large proportion of professionals, including custody evaluators, rely on intuitive notions of how a family is supposed to act. Undoubtedly, much of this intuition has its origins in our experiences in our own families as we grew up, good, bad, or otherwise. As described in Chapter 3, while intuitive judgments sometimes can be accurate, comparatively deliberate reasoning is more likely to result in accurate conclusions and is especially important to carry out in cognitive mine fields (Kahneman, 2011) such as observing parent-child interactions in custody evaluations. Perhaps obviously, people often disagree in their intuitive judgments about what is truly important for children, parents and their interactions. Bookshelves, whether wooden ones in brick and mortar stores or virtual one in the online world, are full of works that emphasize the alleged primacy of different aspects of parents-child interactions.

For good reasons, custody evaluations typically include watching children interact with their parents. Other main custody evaluation methodology, including the self-report of parents and children, psychological testing, and the perspectives of collaterals are all crucial, but can only cover certain realms of important information. Because individuals often interact in ways that are different from their self-perceptions and/or self-reports, evaluators need to complement these methods by seeing parents and children interact together, and relevant APA (2010) guidelines state that such observations should take place.

However, crucial questions arise. As alluded to above, what behaviors are really most important in the arena of parent-child interactions? Also, what are the best structures and methods to employ in observing children and parents interact?

I have heard different custody evaluators assert very divergent perspectives about what it takes to assess well how parents and children interact. An evaluator with decades of experience argued that observing a family play a board game together for 15 to 20 minutes provided a sufficient sample of behavior to make clear conclusions about important parent-child interaction patterns. In contrast, another highly accomplished evaluator asserted that it was crucial to directly observe everything possible about how children interacted with their family, including seeing them in their home and viewing their bedrooms, with each family member (including siblings) individually, and whenever possible, to extend the observations to view each child in neighborhood surroundings and with friends.

Of course, it is necessary to go well beyond evaluator anecdotes and rely on sources such as relevant research and professional writing about such matters. Survey research about custody evaluation practice is very relevant, though they have varied in the levels of detail collected about evaluation practices. The most recent survey (Ackerman & Pritzl, 2011) indicated that custody evaluators generally carry out observations of parents and children together, and the mean time spent was 3.7 hours, but it did not report more detail of how such observations are carried out.

An earlier survey by Bow and Quinell (2001) described more detail about what evaluators reported in terms of parent-child interactions. The mean total observation time reported was 1.59 hours. According to that survey, evaluators generally stated that they observed each child with each parent and also observed all the children together with each parent. As described in the three chapters in this book that include psychological test data specific to custody evaluation, the average number of children per custody evaluation family is two. Therefore, according to the Bow and Quinell data, in the typical family with two biological parents and two children, there would characteristically be a total of six observation sessions, with an average of about 16 minutes per session.

These results raise important questions. Clinical researchers such as Marc Ackerman and James Bow and their colleagues have carried out an important service to the custody evaluation field by collecting and reporting such information about what evaluators stated that they do in practice, though others (Hagen & Castagna, 2001; Martindale, Tippins, Ben-Porath, Wittman, & Austin, 2012) have voiced criticism of certain aspects of such surveys. Inevitably, such surveys rely on retrospective evaluator self-report. I have used the same research methodology to collect important data reported in Chapter 2. However, sometimes there are significant limitations to retrospective self-report. The reality is that, in many important research endeavors, retrospective self-report is the only method that can be used, and other means such as the experience sampling method (e.g., Csikszentmihalyi & Larson, 1987) cannot be practically carried out because the survey was not prospectively planned and/or it is extremely unlikely that enough cooperative respondents could be found.

Regarding parent-child observations, while the survey data are valuable, the main question is to what extent those reported data (especially the more detailed data of Bow & Quinell, 2001) are truly representative of what evaluators tend to do in practice. In the decades that I have worked in the custody evaluation field, I have had reason to review many evaluation reports, and I cannot recall having read any that described the number, type, and brevity of sessions that would be suggested by the mean data presented in that survey research. However, the survey research raises useful questions. For example, is it necessary for each parent to be observed both with all children together and with each child separately (assuming there is more than one child in the family)? What inferences should be drawn if the quality of parent-child and child interaction is very different for one child versus another, if they are observed separately? What is a useful length of time for each observation session? How many such sessions should occur?

It is also useful to consider the assertions of authors of previous books on custody evaluation. An early book (Schutz et al., 1989) offered among the most detailed recommendations for parent-child observations. In terms of the structure of observation sessions, those authors recommended unusually extensive and time-consuming observational methodology. Specifically, each parent would be observed twice in the office with each child separately and once in the home with all children together. Therefore, if it is a relatively typical family with two parents, two children, and no stepparent, they recommend 10 observation sessions. Perhaps obviously, the number of observation sessions would expand if there were more than two children or any stepparents.

More recent books on custody evaluation, while all containing useful information and perspectives, tend to focus less extensively on direct parent-child observations than on other areas. In contrast to the survey results and recommendations of Schutz et al. (1989), Ackerman (1995) wrote that it is most productive to observe each parent separately with all the children together, because such an arrangement would most resemble the reality of life after the separation or divorce. Gould and Martindale (2007) recommended systematic observation, recording examples of relevant behaviors, and proposed a list of quality-focused questions evaluators can ask themselves about their observational procedures. Rohrbaugh (2008) suggested a number of in-session tasks for such observations and relied a good deal on recommendations of previous authors, such as Hynan (2003b) and Schutz et al. (1989). Somewhat similarly, Fuhrmann and Zibbell (2012) described rather brief material based primarily on the work of prior authors. Stahl (2011) offered a perspective based on his experiences carrying out such observations, and reported that he sometimes uses a variety of different methods depending upon circumstances such as child age, including observing children as he interviews them with parents present. He added that, whereas he formerly (Stahl, 1994) used symbolic play as a means of understanding especially young children, he no longer uses such techniques because they lack scientific validity. Tolle and O'Donohue (2012) described the possible use of the Home Observation for Measurement of the Environment (Caldwell & Bradley, 1984). That instrument reportedly has reliability and validity data available primarily through 2 years of age.

Because the information from research and professional sources is comparatively brief, the likelihood of reliance on faulty intuition and personal value judgment is unfortunately high. The more there is a solid foundation of research-based facts, the more an evaluator has an opportunity to engage in higher-level reasoning to facilitate drawing accurate inferences.

FAMILY INTERACTION THEORY AND RESEARCH

Family interactions can generate huge amounts of information in a short period of time, so that it can become confusing and overwhelming in terms of what realms of behavior are worth focusing upon (Epstein, Baldwin, & Bishop, 1983). In addition to the sheer volume of potential data, it would appear that, conceptually and empirically, some behaviors are more relevant and important than others for children's well-being. It is necessary to draw on information outside the custody evaluation field to identify the most crucial dimensions of parent-child interaction.

Theoretical models of family functioning were informed, to some extent, by observing child and parent behavior, whether or not it occurred in a structured setting. It is important that early theories of parenting, while often based in very different general theoretical frameworks, tended to emphasize the importance of dimensions such as affection, control, hostility, and involvement (Darling & Steinberg, 1993). There is also considerable convergence between more recent, yet long-standing models of authorities such as Beavers (Beavers & Hampson, 1990), the McMaster group (Epstein et al., 1983) and Marschak (McKay, Pickens, & Stewart, 1996) in terms of which parent-child interactions were believed to be the most important. Although those conceptual models have their differences from one another, all emphasized family emotional expressions, behavioral control, and the management of conflict.

Much of the research that has included direct observations of children interacting with parents has taken place in the arena of minimal parental competence, including whether any parental abuse or neglect has taken place. More specifically, a good deal of the research has attempted to identify different behavior patterns between abusive and/or neglectful parents as compared to normally functioning ones. When considering these findings, it is important to keep in mind that relevant behavioral differences found in the studies do not necessarily accurately predict whether a parent might engage in highly negative actions such as neglect or abuse. It is also important to keep in mind that, despite considerable research of varied types focused on families, there is a good argument that there is no universally agreed upon, complete model of parental competence (Azar, Lauretti, & Loding, 1998).

At the same time, there are consistent research findings, based on observations of parents and children together, that abusive families manifest more negative emotionality, more inappropriate parental response to positive child behavior, and more prominent child problem behavior as compared to families of nonabusive parents (e.g., Bousha & Twentyman, 1984; Cerezo, D'Ocon, & Dolz, 1996). It is noteworthy that abusers manifested lower levels of positive behaviors such as praise and reasoning as compared to nonabusive parents (Oldershaw, Walters, & Hall, 1989). Outside the realm of parental abuse, Patterson (1982) found that the frequency of positive and negative actions by a parent or child was correlated with measures of child and family adjustment.

In a study of neglectful parents, such individuals were found to manifest less positive and more negative emotion than families in which neglect did not occur. That research also found neglectful families to be generally more chaotic and less verbally expressive and organized, as compared to non-neglectful families (Gaudin, Polansky, Kilpatrick, & Shilton, 1996).

An important question for parent-child observations in custody evaluation is what types of parent and child interaction to observe. In that regard, a crucial research study found that accurate classification of families as abusive versus not abusive, based only on parent-child observation, was accomplished when families were assigned a moderately stressful tasks to complete together. Prior research had not been able to successfully distinguish between abusive and nonabusive parents when a very low-stress activity was used, such as unstructured free play (Deitrich-MacLean & Walden, 1988).

It is also important to be aware that observations of parent-child interaction can be predictive of interaction patterns years later. Weinfield, Ogawa, and Egeland (2002) found that observations made at preschool age could significantly predict observed interaction patterns four years later.

Although a good deal of the focus of the studies described above pertain to negative parental and family behavior, it is also extremely important to pay considerable attention to positive parental actions directed toward children. Reviews of research and conceptual considerations in minimal parental competency assessments emphasized that effective parents tend to manifest strong levels of positive reinforcement, sensitivity to children's distress, informal teaching, age-appropriate language, reasonable reciprocity in interactions with children, and appropriate explanations when setting limits (Azar et al., 1998; Budd et al., 2011).

A meta-analysis investigated differences in parental communication patterns between physically abusive, neglectful, and normal parents during interactions with their children. Parental behaviors were organized into categories of positivity, aversiveness, and involvement. When normal parents were compared to abusive or neglectful ones, there were significant differences in all three areas that had approximately medium effect sizes, with normal parents showing superior behavior patterns, as expected (Wilson, Rack, Shi, & Norris, 2008).

General categories of parenting style have been described and focused upon by a number of scholars, clinicians, and evaluators. Parenting styles involve clusters of related parenting behaviors.. The main categories that have been identified are authoritarian, authoritative, and permissive, following the work of Baumrind (1966). Authoritarian parenting is generally characterized by relatively strict parental control, with limited opportunities for child input and autonomous decision-making. An authoritative style includes more democratic interaction within families, including give-and-take communication patterns, parents being open to input from children, and relative acceptance of psychological autonomy, while parents maintain executive roles through supervision and child management. Permissive or lax parenting is characterized by relatively little supervision and children having a great deal of freedom.

The Baumrind (1966) conceptualization of parenting styles was followed a number of years later by a proposed revision. Maccoby and Martin (1983) maintained that parenting styles were most usefully and productively conceptualized as being a function of two intersecting dimensions, responsiveness and demandingness. Authoritarian parents were described as highly demanding but low in responsiveness. Authoritative parents were seen as both highly demanding and high in responsiveness. Maccoby and Martin divided the permissive category into two different patterns of parenting. They identified neglectful parents as low in both responsiveness and demandingness, and indulgent ones as low in demandingness and high in responsiveness. In a review of the parenting style literature, Darling and Steinberg (1993) posited that parenting style is best conceptualized as providing a psychologically important context for more specific parenting dimensions or behaviors.

In general, at least in the mainstream of United States families, authoritative parenting has been found to result in better outcomes than the other parenting styles. For example, Steinberg, Lamborn, Dornbusch, and Darling (1992) studied a very large sample of families with high school students and found that authoritative parenting led to better school performance. At the same time, there appear to be exceptions to the superiority of authoritative parenting. For example, there is research evidence that, at least for some African-American girls from relatively low socioeconomic backgrounds, authoritarian parenting resulted in better assertiveness, though it led to more timid interpersonal behavior among children from European-American backgrounds (Baumrind, 1972). Research on a large sample of teenagers in Spain found that an indulgent parenting style generally led to superior outcomes in areas such as self-esteem, psychosocial adjustment, school performance and problem behaviors (Garcia & Gracia, 2009). In addition, children from Chinese-American backgrounds have been found to perform comparatively well academically, and the predominant parenting style includes an aspect of training that is quite different from authoritative parenting (Chao, 1994).

FAMILY OBSERVATIONAL CODING RESEARCH

Another relevant source of research data regarding parent-child interaction has emerged from family behavior rating systems. A number of coding systems have been developed. The ones that are practically useful for custody evaluators combine a focus on a reasonably broad realm of parent-child interaction, and have a moderate number of specific rating dimensions or categories.

Perhaps the most useful one is the System for Coding Interactions and Family Functioning (SCIFF) (Lindahl & Malik, 1996). It is based on observations of discussions of recent family problems or arguments. The SCIFF includes rating dimensions for parental behaviors such as parental emotional support and withdrawal. It provides dimensions for child features such as positive affect and defiance. Also, it includes ratings for dimensions that pertain to the family as a whole, such as cohesiveness and conflict. The SCIFF shows evidence of good interrater reliability and has been used effectively in clinical research (Lindahl, 1998; Lindahl & Malik, 1996, 1998).

Another rating system that can be useful for custody evaluators is the Family Problem Solving Code (FAMPROS) (Forbes, Vuchinich, & Kneedler, 2001). In part, the ratings focus on positive and negative behavior from one person to another. Perhaps the most useful aspect of the FAMPROS for custody evaluators is the focus on the problem-solving process. In this procedure, the family is told to identify one or more concerns or problems and to discuss them during the session. The most pertinent ratings for custody evaluators are the definition of the problem, the extent of the resolution, the quality of proposed solutions, and the overall problem solving quality. In general, it is useful with children at least eight years of age, although if a younger child is also present it can be employed productively. In order to gain useful observational information and to avoid discussing content that would be inappropriate for children, evaluators should inform participants that there should be no discussion of court-related matters and no reference to other family members who were not in that observation session. There are indications of adequate to good FAMPROS reliability, as well as evidence of external validity (Forbes et al., 2001; Vuchinich, Angelleli, & Gatherum, 1996).

OBSERVATIONS AND EVALUATION PRACTICE

As described above, it is important to try to identify a research-based and professional consensus of what are the most important dimensions or categories of parent and child interaction. The behaviors described here may be open to some debate, as there is no universally agreed upon model of complete parental competence. It is necessary to consider family-level interaction, as well as individual behaviors manifested by each child and parent.

For the family as a whole, it is important to focus on levels of positive and negative expressed emotion, conflict, cohesiveness, and the clarity of communication. The degree of responsiveness between the parent and each child is crucial, also. As described above, for families that have a child at least eight years of age, a problem-solving task potentially is very useful. Specific attention should be paid to how well the family defines each problem, the quality of proposed solutions, the extent of problem resolution, and the overall process of problem-solving. Although the ratings of the problem-solving task pertain to the family as a whole, because parents would be expected to take a leadership role, the focus is somewhat stronger on the parents that the children in this task.

Overall, for each child, there needs to be close attention paid to the level of positive affect, defiance of the parent, withdrawal, sadness, and frustration or anger. For each parent, there needs to be focus on the overall level of emotional support they provide, praise and verbal reinforcement, informal education, and how well they spread attention between the children. There needs to be attention to how well parents balance providing appropriate structure for the children while allowing reasonable initiative given the children's ages and stages of development. How well parents carry out limit setting, if needed, is a necessary area of focus. In addition, there should be attention to possible negative behaviors by parents, such as coercion, withdrawal, and rejection or invalidation of children. Although it is rare to observe highly negative parental or family-level behaviors in observation sessions, they do occur on occasion and need to be addressed. For example, there needs to be clear focus on and recording of any parental harsh control, reinforcement of oppositional behavior, denigration of prosocial behavior, or chaotic family interactions.

As an aspect of observing parents and children interact, there should be attention to the overall parenting style, also. It is very likely that a large proportion of families will primarily manifest behaviors consistent with authoritative parenting, combining reciprocal give-and-take with the parent maintaining a clear executive role. It is necessary to examine more specific differences that may occur in interaction patterns between the children's interactions with one parent versus the other. For example, one parent may be considerably stronger than the other in terms of manifesting appropriate praise and verbal reinforcement. In another family, a child may be relatively withdrawn from one parent and yet actively engaged with and responsive toward the other parent. A previously published worksheet (Hynan, 2003a) provides an outline to record relevant individual behaviors and family interactions.

An important empirical and conceptual question is how much observed parent-child interactions are truly representative of the real world, and an aspect of this issue is how much families may change their behaviors when they know they are being observed. For example, families may act in a self-conscious manner and/or attempt to behave in an artificially positive way (Kerig, 2001). Even though the reality of being observed leads families to likely make some changes in aspects of their interactions, important information about the family behavior patterns usually emerge anyway (Budd et al., 2011), and families appear to manifest significant difficulties in faking their behaviors in a positive direction (Kerig, 2001). Therefore, it is very likely that direct observations of parents and children together can contribute valuable information for evaluators.

There are questions about whether it is best to observe parents and children interact in an office setting or at home. Considerations about this matter are described in the later section about home visits. The material directly below about how to structure observations can apply either to office or home visits.

The type of instructions and tasks given to families is important. Because it is very important to have children and families feel comfortable, observation sessions, especially those that include young children, should start with free play or another task that is likely to be experienced as pleasant. In some sessions, important information can be obtained even during this initial warm-up. As described above, however, it is crucial to have more structured tasks that place a mild to moderate level of demand and stress on the family, which can be particularly useful if they include directions for the family to work together. Within such an instructional context, there are more requirements for parents to engage in functions such as prompting, reinforcing, educating, and setting limits. Similarly, such tasks place requirements on children that have important similarities to the requirements of real life, including being reasonably responsive to parents, taking initiative, and managing emotions. When children and parents focus on a relatively structured task, especially after they have previously engaged in a pleasant warm-up time, there is a tendency for the participants to become less self-conscious, and ecologically valid interactions are more likely to emerge. However, very highly structured tasks, which allow little to no spontaneity or initiative on the part of the participants, are unlikely to be useful because they minimize opportunities to observe representative samples of family interaction (Wilson et al., 2008). It is crucial to note that it would be unethical to include any highly stressful tasks or circumstances in parent-child observations.

Helpful suggestions have been made by Rorbaugh (2008) and Schutz et al. (1989) for tasks to be used in observation sessions. Also, as described above, when families contain a child who is at least eight years of age, assigning a problem-solving task (Forbes et al., 2001) can be particularly useful.

As noted above, there have been questions about how much parent-child interaction to observe. Brief observation sessions are unfortunately likely to not include a representative sample of behavior. Also, if only a single observation session is used with each parent, there is a considerable risk of not obtaining a representative sample, especially if a child or a parent might happen to be in a negative frame of mind on that occasion that has nothing to do with the focus of the evaluation. It is very relevant that, in clinical research, one observation session alone has not been found adequate in terms of generating valid conclusions about family interactions (McKenzie, Klien, Epstein, & McCurley, 1993; Vuchinich et al., 1996).

As also described above, there have been questions about whether to observe each child separately with each parent, or to observe all the children together with each parent separately. Some evaluators have stated that they routinely observe children, either separately or together, interact with both parents simultaneously. In general, the position that it is optimal to observe all the children together with each parent separately (Ackerman, 1995) appears to have the most sound conceptual basis. If there is a step-parent or live-in parent, it would be important to include that individual, perhaps most productively in one of the observation sessions, so that there is an opportunity to observe the legal parent alone with the children, as well as the legal parent and the partner together with the children. After parents split up, assuming there is more than one child, a consistent parental challenge is to manifest good parenting skills with more than one child at a time. There are major challenges of simultaneously parenting a number of very young children, such as twin three-year-olds and a one-year-old. Similarly, there are challenges in parenting multiple teenagers, as well as children of very different ages such as 4 and 14.

At the same time, there may be specific circumstances that make it important to observe a child separately with each parent. For example, in a family with multiple children, if one of them has serious special needs such as autism or severe attentional problems, and there are questions about parental competency in caring for such needs, it may be productive to observe the child individually with each parent. However, it would also be important to have the child together with siblings in other observation sessions. There does not appear to be compelling reason to have both competing parents together during an observation session; the potential stress for children of having to interact with parents who are in conflict with each other appears to outweigh the possible benefits.

Some authorities have maintained that, especially with young children, formal assessments of attachment, such as the Strange Situation procedure, should be used in custody evaluation (e.g., Main et al., 2011). However, there are numerous problems associated with such an approach, including multiple concerns about validity, expense, and ethics (e.g., Hynan, 2012).

There is no clear answer from research or the professional literature regarding the assertion of some evaluators that it is best to have very extensive opportunities to observe children interact with parents. A natural practical limitation is that most custody evaluations include a considerable expense, and a very large number of observation sessions are not financially feasible for many families. It is reasonable to wonder whether individuals who carry out a large number of observation sessions would be especially likely to rely excessively on their own intuition. However, there is a significant risk of relying excessively on intuitive judgments whether the number of observations is very small, very large, or in between.

As with other evaluation procedures, it is crucial to keep a record. Of course, it is necessary to record family members present in each session. One of the benefits of having identified the most important dimensions or types of parent-child interaction, as summarized above, is that it helps the evaluator to focus on the most crucial behaviors during the observation sessions. Concurrently, such a focus assists the evaluator in recording the most important interactions. As emphasized by Gould and Martindale (2007), evaluators need to record instances of specific relevant behaviors. Such behavior should be associated with the type or dimension of interaction that is represented. For example, if a child appears to be relatively withdrawn from a parent, it is important to make a note of it, and yet the record should include what withdrawn behavior the child manifested, such as facing away from the parent, not making eye contact, and/or offering minimal verbal replies to parental statements. Somewhat similarly, if a parent is directing positive reinforcement toward a child, the record should include instances of such behaviors such as telling the child "good job," or giving the child a high five.

In addition to keeping a narrative record of such behaviors, the use of a summary rating sheet (e.g., Hynan, 2003a) can be useful in a number of ways. It helps not only to keep a productive, contemporaneous record for each observation session, but the centrally important parent, child, and family-level behaviors contained on the summary form can prompt the evaluator to keep the focus on actions that are most important within the steady stream of often multiple family interactions. It is crucial to keep in mind that a summary rating form, including numerical ratings, does not constitute a test of any type.

Home Visits

Clear empirical data are lacking as to whether it is better to conduct observations of parents and children together in an office setting or in the home. In terms of what evaluators stated that they actually do, Bow & Quinnell (2001) reported that home visits were used by about one third of evaluators, and a more recent survey (Ackerman & Pritzl, 2011) did not report on the use of that procedure.

When considering the question of research observations at home or in a laboratory/office setting, Kerig (2001) maintained that strategic choices need to be made based on numerous factors, including the purpose of the observations. She voiced a belief that studies of potentially dysfunctional family processes would better occur in an office or clinic because that setting may make it easier to have the desired impact on the levels of family stress experienced during the sessions.

It potentially is important for evaluators to keep in mind that they may be less likely to have the type of control they would like in a home setting as compared to an office. For example, it may be easier in a home setting for children to simply walk away from the family if they are bored, upset, or simply insist on watching their favorite television show. There may be unexpected visitors, and a greater likelihood of competing tasks such as a family member feeling that they need to check their computer or take a telephone call. Unless an evaluator has arranged in advance for the family to carry out certain tasks during the home visit, she or he may be less likely to observe behaviors that are of central importance than in an office setting.

Of course, there can be a number of objectives of home visits, and observing the family interact there is only one potential goal. A home visit is necessary if there is a need to see the physical residence.

For example, a very legitimate concern may be that there are important safety considerations about one or both residences that are crucial for evaluators to assess (Hynan, 2002). Unintentional child injury results in a large number of emergency department visits and hospital admissions. Also, it is the single leading cause of death among children.

At other times, one parent may assert that the quality of their home and/or neighborhood is superior to that of the other parent, completely apart from any safety considerations. Although it is extremely important to try to protect the child from unsafe or otherwise truly inadequate environmental circumstances, it should be kept in mind that there is no evidence that children benefit more from a very upscale physical environment as compared to a more moderate yet adequate one.

In most cases, the main practical consideration regarding whether or not to include a home visit is cost. Because there routinely are charges for travel to and from a family residence, home visits tend to be costly and sometimes logistically difficult to carry out. As I stated previously (Hynan, 2003b), it is important to try to determine whether a potential home visit would add unique and relevant information, regarding factors such as safety or other facets of the physical residence, to the overall evaluation. If a home visit occurs, and there are very young children who live at the residence, the evaluator should make note of the presence or absence of appropriate childproofing (Hynan, 2002).

If a home visit takes place to one residence, it should occur for both, unless there is compelling reason not to do so. For example, in some cases Parent A has voiced considerable concern about the residence of Parent B, but Parent B thought there was no good reason that a visit needed to occur at the home of Parent A.

Under some circumstances, an evaluator may be able to obtain a reasonable view of a physical residence without having to carry out a time-consuming and costly home visit. For example, sometimes, photographic or video evidence can capture well the interior and exterior of a home and surroundings.

Also, if there are questions raised about the relative safety of different neighborhoods, publicly available crime data are likely more informative than an actual visit to the home.

CONCLUSIONS

The main way to have parent-child observations be productive and contribute toward shedding light on what is in children's best interest is to carry them out with a consistent focus on the most important dimensions or types of interactions, and steady attention to the methods most likely to result in behavior samples representative of real-life family functioning. Reliance on scientifically-based information and well-founded professional principles will increase the likelihood of careful deliberation about parent-child interactions. Similarly, such reliance will decrease the risk of intuitive value judgments taking the place of a high level of competency in the evaluative procedures.

Chapter 7

INTERVIEWING CHILDREN

PRACTICE CHECKLIST

_____Know essential research findings about interviewing children.

_____Review chart and prepare for the interview.

_____Consider the child's age and verbal development, and use easily understandable statements, questions, and words.

_____Build comfortable rapport with the child.

_____Educate the child that it is most important for her/him to describe true experiences, feelings, and thoughts.

_____Instruct the child to tell you if she/he does not understand a question, statement, or word.

_____Educate the child that if she/he does not know an answer to just say "I don't know."

_____Tell the child to correct you if you say anything wrong.

_____Ask the child to promise to tell the truth.

_____Conduct a practice interview about pleasant and/or recent events.

_____Attend to the child's comfort level.

_____Begin the substantive portions of interviews with relatively easy questions about low-stress content areas.

_____Open-ended questions generally lead to the most informative and accurate answers.

_____Use open-ended questions as much as possible.

_____Have appropriate variations of open-ended questions readily available.

_____Use more focused (wh-type) questions when open-ended ones have not led to adequately informative responses.

_____Use relatively specific questions as sparingly as possible.

_____Use relatively specific questions only after open-ended and focused ones have been unproductive.

_____Make generally supportive statements without reinforcing specific answers.

Note: This form is a guide to promote productive reasoning and good practice. It is not comprehensive or all-inclusive and does not replace adequate training and experience.

Child interviews play a central role in custody evaluations. The main purpose of interviewing children is to ascertain their feelings and thoughts about their relationship with each parent and regarding relevant experiences within the family.

There are many possible questions to ask children. The most important principles to use as guides for questions are those represented by relevant statutes integrated with the factors found to be most influential in affecting children of divorce. Those areas are covered in Chapter 1.

For a considerable period of time, accuracy in child interview statements has been raised as an issue both in practitioner-oriented books (e.g., Ackerman, 1995; Bricklin, 1995; Gould & Martindale, 2007; Stahl, 1994, 2011) and in a great deal of research. In general, it is taken for granted that child interviews need to occur, as long as the child in question has adequate cognitive and verbal capacities. An exception is the view of Bricklin (1995), who described interviews as iatrogenic because they can encourage family members to make critical statements about others that may worsen conflicts.

The preponderance of evidence is that, under many circumstances, children can and will be reasonably good reporters of accurate and relevant information. However, there has also been considerable controversy about this matter, fueled in large part by questions about the accuracy of children's statements that took place in investigations of child sexual abuse. In particular, the complexities of interviewing about possible child abuse have led to volumes of research. For more than a decade, there has been extensive multidisciplinary collaboration to identify what factors are most important in child interviews, with a goal of providing guidelines for interviewers who ask children about events that they have experienced or witnessed. This collaboration has resulted in the Investigative Interview Protocol of the National Institute of Child Health and Human Development (NICHD) (Lamb, Hershkowitz, Orbach, & Esplin, 2008). Such research is highly relevant to child custody interviewing because the studies generally have focused on children's statements in a variety of forensic contexts, and are not limited to sexual abuse only.

Within the context of child custody evaluations, there are frequent allegations of domestic violence, substance abuse, child abuse, and/or psychological disorders. For example, Johnston and Campbell (1988) stated that 64% of their research sample had personality disorders and almost 25% manifested substance abuse. In two separate samples, a strong majority of women and men reported that they had been the recipients of abuse during the marriage or separation (Newmark, Harrell, & Salem, 1995). As described in more detail later in this book, custody evaluation parents who were the focus of my psychological test research manifested frequent allegations of child abuse, domestic violence, and/or substance abuse. All such allegations provide high levels of challenge for custody evaluators, including interviewing children to try to obtain valid information about such events.

Therefore, it is essential for custody evaluators to have a solid grasp of the most relevant empirical research on factors that influence the accuracy of children's interview statements. It is also extremely important for custody evaluators to integrate such research findings into the practical realities of carrying out sensitive and productive interviews with children.

Below, the most relevant aspects of the research literature on interviewing children are summarized first. Afterward, the focus is on integrating research, professional literature, and close to two decades of practical experience to outline an approach to conducting child interviews within the context of custody and related evaluations.

RESEARCH

When a child is interviewed, a number of cognitive, emotional, language, and other behavioral factors are in operation simultaneously. For example when asked a question, a child must understand it, recall relevant information accurately, have motivation to be honest, and have the capacity to explain oneself to the interviewer. Also, a child must be able to distinguish reality from fantasy and be sufficiently free from social pressure to give an accurate answer. It is also very helpful for the child to be comfortable with the interviewer. Therefore, research has needed to focus on multiple, interrelated factors. In order to gain a greater understanding of how these factors operate in child interviews, a good deal of relevant research has needed to focus on just one, or at most, very few of these factors at one time. Much of the applied research has endeavored to apply results of comparatively basic research findings in such a manner as to facilitate the best possible interview methods with children.

Age

Although it is a relatively superficial characteristic, age is a crucial variable to consider because there are far greater challenges in interviews with younger children as compared to older ones. There are numerous developmental factors that contribute to this reality. For example, the most powerful predictor of a child's memory capacity is age (La Rooy, Malloy, & Lamb, 2011). Also, language development characteristically is highly dependent on age. Children's word acquisition normally develops extremely rapidly starting at about the age of two, and with increasing age there is continued development of word knowledge and numerous other aspects of language (e.g., Landauer &

Dumais, 1997) such that a few years of difference in age has a huge impact on a child's practical language usage.

In general, younger children are less informative than older ones, and have less patience for relatively longer interviews. At the same time, there can be a great deal of variability in language competence for children of the same age. Adjustments need to be made by interviewers to assist particularly young children to participate in a reasonably competent manner (Goodman, Quas, & Ogle, 2010; Lamb et al., 2008).

Memory

Memory in children overlaps with other factors such as age, repetition, social influence, and cognitive abilities such as abstract reasoning. In general, younger children encode memory traces that are weaker than those of the more meaning-laden and interpretive memories of older individuals. As a result, children forget more quickly than do adults. Because their memory traces are comparatively weak, young children in particular are more susceptible than others to recalling and believing fictitious events (Ceci & Friedman, 2000; Poole & Lamb, 1998).

However, it is extremely important to be aware that even very young children can accurately recall and answer questions about events that they experienced. Their responses tend to be very brief and therefore typically incomplete. For example, if children are asked about experienced events and the questioning occurs on different occasions, each time they tend to give accurate yet incomplete descriptions of what had taken place (Fivush & Shukat, 1995), as long as they have not been subjected to coaching or other forms of suggestibility.

As a result, there needs to be a great deal of caution when faced with inconsistencies in the details that are related by children (Hynan, 1998). Within the legal system, there is often skepticism about the veracity of an individual's statements that differ in significant respects when related at one time versus another. However, especially for young children, an evaluator may find significant differences in statements made about the same event on two different occasions. The differences in those statements may be due to a child giving accurate yet incomplete information on one occasion, and also giving accurate but incomplete information during the other interview. The phenomenon of individuals simply recalling somewhat different yet all accurate information about events at Time 1 versus Time 2 is called reminiscence, and it also frequently occurs in adults (La Rooy et al., 2011).

In contrast, a very different phenomenon, called infantile amnesia, involves relatively older children and adults having an inability to recall most everything about their lives when they were extremely young, approximately under the age of three. For example, in one study, children were interviewed between 1 and 5 years after having experienced a highly uncomfortable medical procedure. That procedure took place when the children were between 2 and 7 years of age. None of the children who had been 2 years old at the time of the procedure recalled what had occurred, half who had been 3 years old recalled the procedure, and most of the children who were 5 and older at the time of the procedure remembered some aspects of it (Quas, 1999). There are numerous other examples of well-established findings for infantile amnesia (Hayne, 2004).

It is noteworthy that a significant proportion of people are unaware of the infantile amnesia phenomenon. For example, a study found that a majority of adults, including jurors, indicated agreement with the belief that if a child had been subjected to repeated and painful sexual abuse as an infant, that individual would later be able to recall those experiences (Quas, Thompson, & Clarke-Stewart, 2005).

There are inconsistent findings regarding the effects of stress on memory. In particular, there are uncertainties about how stress affects memory at the time of encoding. Stress at the time of memory retrieval appears to have a generally negative impact for children (La Rooy et al., 2011). Therefore, evaluators need to make a number of efforts to help children feel as comfortable as possible during interviews.

Lying

Over the years, there have been questions about whether children, especially very young ones, would lie. It is clear that children of any age may do so, as long as they have developed adequate verbal and cognitive capacities. Some of the most common motivations for children telling lies involve protecting themselves or others, personal gain, or to avoid embarrassment (Hynan, 1998).

The legal system considers whether a child manifests competency to distinguish truth from falsehood. As a result, it has become a recommended practice for interviewers of children to ask questions to try to establish the extent that they understand the difference between truth and lies. Protocols that state investigative interviewers of children should ask such questions have largely been based on the fact that the legal system places value on such procedures. However, there is little evidence that children's accuracy in distinguishing between truth and lies is predictive of them giving accurate answers in the more substantive portion of the interview. Despite this finding, researchers also have found that child interviewees who promised to tell the truth during interviews, or who went through a discussion about the importance of telling the truth, tended to give more accurate responses during the substantive portion of the interview (London & Nuñez, 2002; Lyon & Dorado, 2008; Talwar, Lee, Bala, & Lindsay, 2002, 2004).

Suggestibility

The issue of suggestibility in children's interview statements came into increased focus for professionals and researchers following allegations that large numbers of young children had been subjected to various forms of abuse at daycare or preschool centers. The research literature in this area is extensive and has been reviewed in sources such as Ceci and Friedman (2000), Lamb et al. (2008), and Poole and Lamb (1998). The focus here is to summarize the main findings of this body of work, represented by high-quality research studies.

When children have been subjected to repeated, suggestive interview questions, typically over a number of interviews, a significant minority of especially very young children make inaccurate statements. For example, fictitious events were recalled by over one-third of 3- and 4-year-olds and one-fourth of the 5- and 6-year-olds when they were asked repeated and insistent questions over multiple interviews (Ceci, Huffman, Smith, & Loftus, 1994). Similarly, repeated yes-or-no questions and inquiries about details that a child could not possibly know led to increased incorrect statements (Poole & White, 1991, 1993). Based primarily on reviews of actual investigative transcripts in which children were subjected to insistent questions across multiple interviews, Ceci and Bruck (1995) warned about the risks of repeated questions over more than one interview session.

In addition, research found that very young children made high levels of inaccurate statements in a single interview when interviewing techniques combined a number of features to pressure children into making misleading statements. Specifically, when suggestive questions were combined with reinforcement for specific answers, social influence, and encouragement for children to speculate about what might have occurred, most 3-to-6-year-olds gave incorrect "yes" answers to misleading questions (Garven, Wood, Malpass, & Shaw, 1998).

The research in this area generally shows that younger children are more susceptible to such suggestive and misleading techniques as compared to older children. However, the effects of such techniques on the accuracy of children statements can be seen in numerous child age ranges. In particular, young children have a tendency to acquiesce (that is, say yes) to leading questions, especially repeated ones asked in an insistent manner. In part, the comparatively weaker memory traces of younger children likely play a role in this phenomenon. However, social influence may also play a larger role with younger children as compared to older ones.

Numerous efforts have been made to try to identify individual differences other than age that have an impact on suggestibility in interviews. With a few exceptions, such efforts have not been successful. The exceptions include that children who are below the normal range of intelligence are generally more suggestible than others of the same age who are within the normal range of intelligence. If only individuals with normal-range intellectual ability are considered, intelligence is not a good predictor of suggestibility. For younger children, if language ability is measured by means of a comprehensive assessment (instead of just a single measure of vocabulary ability), those with a higher language competency level tend to be less suggestible than those with lower language ability. When the focus was on a type of suggestibility that involves the invention of a story about an entire event that never actually occurred, highly creative children in the 5 to 8-year-old age range were found to be more suggestible than less creative children in that age range (Bruck & Melnyk, 2004).

Use Of Language

In recent years, much of the applied research regarding investigative interviewing of children has had a goal of identifying interviewer language and behavior that would maximize the chances of accurate and thorough verbal reports by children. A very striking and relevant research study found that even when mental health professionals had training in interviewing children, they tended to use interview questions that were not easily understood by children (Korkman, Santtila, Drzewiecki, & Sandnabba, 2008). Often, young children tend not to ask for clarification because they do not fully realize that they do not accurately comprehend the question.

There is considerable evidence that children give the most accurate information when they make comparatively open-ended narrative statements. Also, there tends to be more detailed information that is offered in such open-ended statements, in contrast to the more brief replies that tend to be given to relatively focused and narrow questions. Therefore, efforts need to be made very early in child interviews to guide interviewees into a conversational style that includes as many open-ended narratives as possible. The more an interviewer is able to elicit substantive open-ended statements, there is less of a need to rely on more specific and potentially leading questions that have a higher likelihood of resulting in inaccurate replies (Lamb et al., 2008; Poole & Lamb, 1998).

In order to encourage open-ended statements by children, it is very useful to conduct what amounts to a practice interview prior to the more substantive part of the interview. In the practice interview, the child is asked to relate as much as they can about a relatively meaningful and/or recent event. For example, a child may have experienced a fairly recent holiday or birthday, and the interviewer can ask the child to describe whatever he or she can recall about the event. Questions need to primarily be asked in an open-ended manner, such as "Tell me everything you remember about your birthday." Prompts also need to be as open-ended as possible, such as "tell me everything else you can remember about it." In general, research has found that using such a practice interview promotes children of all ages to make relatively lengthy and detailed narrative statements (Lamb et al., 2008; Roberts, Brubacher, Powell, & Price, 2011). Also, open-ended questions have generally been found in both laboratory and field research to result in more accurate child statements (e.g., Hutcheson, Baxter, Telfer, & Warden, 1995; Lamb et al., 2003).

At the same time, sometimes especially very young children tend not to give very substantive answers to open-ended questions. There is often a need for more focused and specific questions. Perhaps obviously, the specific nature of these follow-up questions will rely in part on the prior statements by the child interviewee. A research study that examined investigative interviews with children aged 4 through 14 years found that open-ended questions were most effective with 12-to-14-year-olds. Younger children reportedly gave more information in response to relatively specific questions that were not leading. It is noteworthy that only an extremely small proportion of questions in this study (Davies, Wescott, & Horan, 2000) were asked in an open-ended manner, a finding also reported elsewhere (Lamb et al., 2008), but it illustrates that younger children are more likely than older ones to require prompts through relatively focused and specific questions.

Rapport

A number of studies have demonstrated the benefits of establishing rapport with children in terms of the productivity of the substantive part of the interview. While rapport development is a very useful clinical technique in almost any type of interview, researchers found that the specific type of rapport building techniques used with children in investigative interviews matters a great deal. For example, relatively brief rapport building has been found to be more effective than longer rapport building in facilitating the amount of relevant information later related by children (Davies et al., 2000; Hershkowitz, 2009). The authors hypothesized that the longer efforts at rapport building may have taxed children's attention levels, or may have contributed to decreased effort by interviewers in the substantive part of the interview. In the Hershkowitz (2009) study, it was found that longer rapport building was associated with a lower proportion of open-ended interview questions.

The use of open-ended questions during rapport building was found to lead to children offering generally greater amounts of information in the substantive portion of interviews (Hershkowitz, 2009). Somewhat similarly, more accurate child statements in the substantive parts of interviews followed open-ended rapport building with children (Roberts, Lamb, & Sternberg, 2004).

Beyond an initial rapport building phase that takes place before the more substantive part of the interview, offering support to children by means of nonsuggestive statements can facilitate the productivity of interviews. There are numerous examples of nonsuggestive support, including checking on children's comfort level, asking if they need something to drink, commenting that they have done well in persisting through the interview, and thanking children for their participation at the end of the interview. For young children, it is often helpful to comment to the parent as the child is returned to the waiting area that he or she has done very well in the interview. It is extremely important to make such supportive comments in a manner that does not selectively reinforce certain types of statements, as such selective reinforcement has a risk of leading to inaccuracies in child statements (Hershkowitz, 2011).

Supplementary Techniques

Because especially very young children often respond with very short, noninformative answers to interview questions, a number of supplementary techniques have been tried that involved props such as dolls, toys, and human figure diagrams. The intent of such efforts has been to facilitate accurate communication by children about relevant experiences. Although such techniques have sometimes been found to increase the total amount of communication by children, Boat and Everson (1996) reported that, when anatomical dolls were employed, children did not relate more relevant detail than when they were not used. Also, with the use of such supplementary techniques, there is a significantly increased risk of inaccurate statements (Brown, 2011). For example, when children were asked to report on the experience of having been touched by another individual, the use of human figure drawings during interviews led to decreased accuracy (Bruck, 2009).

There is also a significant risk of using props with young children during the substantive parts of interviews because there may not be a clear differentiation between the need to report on what they actually experienced and the fantasy aspects inherent with playing with such material. At times, especially with very young children, it may be necessary to provide toys for play or drawing material prior to the substantive part of the interview in order to help a child feel at ease (Brown, 2011). However, it is important for the interviewer to put such materials aside prior to the start of the substantive interview, and to state that questions about real experiences are starting, in order to clearly indicate to the child that they are to talk about reality and not fantasy.

CONDUCTING AN INTERVIEW

The research summarized above has largely been done within the context of investigations regarding specific incidents such as child abuse, and having witnessed significant events such as domestic violence. Again, this research is not limited to child statements in the courtroom, and it is highly relevant to child custody interviewing. At the same time, in custody evaluations, children need to be interviewed about a broader range of experiences than such specific events. Therefore, there needs to be an integration of findings from the scientific research with the practical realities of ascertaining relevant perspectives from children within the child custody context.

During interviews, evaluators need to keep a primary focus on information that is relevant to the best interest of children, and in doing so, keep in mind relevant statutory factors and research findings about what most influences children of divorce. There are content areas that are important to try to cover in almost every child interview, whereas other content areas will be relevant for only some families. Also, there need to be adjustments in the specifics of each interview according to the child's age and level of verbal abilities. It is crucial that evaluators consistently use language that can be clearly understood by the child being interviewed.

Also, it is important to have reasonable expectations for each child in terms of the length of time that they can be productively interviewed. For the youngest children, their focus and patience very rarely extends beyond a half-hour, and sometimes is less than that. Most children 12 years of age and older do reasonably well with an interview length of one hour. Many children between the ages of approximately 8 and 11 appear to tolerate well an interview length of about 45 minutes. Of course, these are estimates, and there are many individual differences between children.

Because of past concerns that there was an increased potential for suggestive and leading questions to have a negative impact on the accuracy of children's interview statements if repeated interviews took place (Ceci & Bruck, 1995), there had been controversy over whether was advisable to have more than one interview. More recently, there has been recognition that repeated interviews may be more effective as long as guidelines are followed that emphasize the importance of open-ended questions and that direct interviewers away from potentially misleading ones (La Rooy, Katz, Malloy, & Lamb, 2010). In addition, because child custody interviews need to cover a broader range of content areas than those focused primarily on whether the child has experienced or witnessed a particular event, they often require more time (Hynan, 1998). In general, two separate interviews for each child often allow ample time to collect relevant information and perspectives from them. It is optimal for each parent to equally share the task of transporting a child to the interviews. That is, each parent would bring the child on one of the two occasions, in order to keep such matters even between the parents, and potentially to allay parental fears that the other parent would have an opportunity to thoroughly coach the child's interview statements.

I strongly believe that each child needs to be interviewed individually, without the presence of any parent, sibling or other individual. Such a structure increases the likelihood that the interviewee will feel free of any social influence and therefore facilitates the collection of accurate information, feelings, and related perspectives. Poole and Lamb (1998) described that most authorities recommend interviews without a parent or other support person present, both because of concern that the adult may detract from the quality of the interview and a lack of research evidence that the presence of such a support person is positive for the child interviewee.

At least a brief period of planning is likely to facilitate a high quality interview. A review of relevant parts of the client file can be a reminder about the characteristics of the individual to be interviewed, as well as regarding content that may be particularly important for the child and family. Allegations may be brought up in some cases, but not others, that need to inform the contents of some interview questions. For example, children in some cases will need to be asked whether they have observed matters such as domestic violence and/or parental substance misuse. Other possible topics specific to just some interviews include interactions with controversial babysitters, experiences with stepparents or other relatives, and feelings about certain extracurricular activities.

It can be useful for evaluators to conceptualize child interviews as semi-structured. In other words, a number of aspects of the structure and contents of interviews are largely the same for each child, whereas other characteristics differ in accordance with the circumstances of the case.

When the interview itself begins, the main focus needs to be on helping the child feel at ease and building rapport. As noted in Chapter 6, it is very useful to conduct parent-child observation sessions prior to child interviews in order to promote the child feeling at ease in the office and with the evaluator. Still, in a few cases, a very young child may be somewhat anxious and reluctant to leave the parent in the waiting area and come into the office alone. In such cases, it frequently helps to have the parent accompany the child into the office, help get them settled, and then depart to the waiting area, with repeated assurances to the child that the parent will be in close proximity and that they can take a break from the interview to check on the parent. In the vast majority of cases, such an approach will be successful. For a very small number of young children, it may be necessary to engage them first in a play task in the office to help them feel comfortable enough to allow the parent to go back to the waiting area. Once they appear to be more comfortable after a short period of play, it is important to set aside the play material and convey to the child, in word and action, that the evaluator needs to ask them questions about things that are real and not play or pretend. Assurances that the period of time for questions will be relatively short, with a return to the parent directly afterward are useful in these circumstances.

For the vast majority of children such steps are not necessary because they do not show distress at the beginning of the interview. However, all children need to experience a presubstantive interview process that helps to build rapport, provides basic education about the interview, and promotes productive responses to primarily open-ended questions.

One of the very first steps in the presubstantive part of the interview involves brief education that integrates relevant research findings with the necessities of questioning about content areas relevant for child custody, time sharing, and related matters. It is crucial to inform children that a main goal of the questions they will answer is to let the interviewers know their true experiences, feelings, and thoughts. Perhaps obviously, for young children, the vocabulary used in such brief education would need to be at a more basic level, such as "the most important thing is for you to tell me what you have really seen and heard. Also, say what you really feel and think." Children need to be specifically told that they should tell the interviewer whenever there are any interviewer questions, statements, or words that the child does not completely understand. Children also need to be specifically told that it is perfectly fine for them to tell the interviewer "I don't know" in response to any question to which the child actually does not know the answer. It can be useful to emphasize and clarify this matter by pointing out that the interview is very different from how things often appear to be in school. That is, in school children are frequently under the impression that they are supposed to know the answers to questions, and are supposed to know the meanings of all words used by teachers, and therefore will often pretend that they know something when they actually do not. In contrast, in the interview the child needs to feel very assured that it is completely acceptable for them to indicate there is something they do not know. In fact, if the child states that they do not understand something the interviewer said, praising the child for having brought that up is productive in terms of facilitating accurate communication and is appropriately supportive. It can also be useful to inform children that if they believe they know an answer to a question, but are not completely certain, they should feel free to say whatever their idea happens to be, and simply inform the interviewer that they are not entirely sure about it.

It is extremely important to inform children that the interviewer sometimes makes mistakes, and if the child notices that the interviewer has said something wrong, it should be pointed out to the interviewer. It can be useful to tell children that pointing out such a mistake actually helps the interviewer.

To further educate children about accurately stating that they do not know something, and about pointing out erroneous statements made by the interviewer, it can be very useful to ask relevant practice questions. As described in relevant interview protocols (e.g., Lamb et al., 2008), a child who is five years old can be asked "so you're eight years old, right?" If the child happens to incorrectly acquiesce to that question, the interviewer needs to point out the child's correct age, and the importance of the child making that type of correction. Somewhat similarly, an interviewer can ask the child "what's the name of my dog?" If the child guesses or otherwise offers a name, the interviewer needs to point out that the child does not have any information of that type, and therefore needs to respond "I don't know."

In the presubstantive part of the interview, it is customary to have a discussion about telling the truth. In order to obtain basic information about a child's grasp of truth versus lies, or reality versus fantasy, it is useful to ask a few questions about factual matters that are mostly obvious just within the office. For example, children can be asked if it is truth or a lie whether they are in a room/car, standing/sitting, whether the lights are on/off, and whether the interviewer's shoes are black/white. More importantly, any child needs to be asked to promise to tell the truth. In the extremely unlikely event that a child replies that she or he will not make such a promise, relevant follow-up questions should be asked, and consideration given to whether or not it would make sense to continue with the interview.

As described above, it is crucial to conduct a practice interview in the presubstantive section in order to establish the routine of starting each content area with relatively open-ended questions, and even more importantly, to promote open-ended narrative responses by children.

As part of the planning process before the interview, it can be useful to determine whether there had been any special events that may have taken place a fairly short time prior to the interview, in order to have a focus for the practice interview. Even if no such special events have occurred recently, it can often be productive to ask children what had taken place during the weekend prior to the interview. On some occasions, depending upon the circumstances, it can be productive to ask children what they had done during the day prior to coming to the office for the interview. It is crucial that the questions initially be open-ended, such as "tell me everything you did this past weekend." If the reply is relatively brief, at least the first few prompts should also be open-ended, such as "please tell me everything else you remember about what happened that weekend." Perhaps obviously, children can differ a great deal in levels of responsiveness. If the child has given relatively little relevant information, the interviewer can use part of what the child said as a prompt for further questioning. For example, regarding a birthday, an interviewer might state "you said you opened presents, tell me everything that happened after that." If a child gives a reasonably substantive response, given the child's age and stage of verbal development, it can be useful to verbally reinforce their reply, with a statement such as "that's great, you did really well filling me in about all those things."

After having covered the material described above, there can be a change to collect more substantive information. The material covered below summarizes much of the most useful contents for questioning. However, it is not possible or productive to cover all material of potential relevance for child interviews because there is almost an infinite variety of topic areas for questioning, depending upon the individual circumstances of each case.

It is useful to begin the substantive portion of interviews with questions about relatively easy and noncontroversial content areas. Most children will be in school (even if school happens to be out of session at that particular time) and can be asked for information about it initially in an open-ended manner, such as "so tell me about your school." It may be necessary to ask more specific, focused questions, such as the school name and grade. It can also be helpful to ask for such information such as things the child most the likes about school, features of the school that are disliked, and the type and amount of homework typically assigned. Such information is potentially relevant background for the interviewer and is useful for purposes of helping a child feel comfortable. Also, that information is generally easy to talk about and relatively free of conflict or controversy. The more a child experiences relative comfort and ease in reporting information in the earlier portions of interviews, the more they are likely to respond productively and with adequate resilience to questions about potentially more difficult content areas later on.

Other typically lower-stress content areas for the earlier portions of the first interview include favorite activities, friends, extracurricular activities, and usual activities both before and after school and on weekends. Although they are relatively easy areas for a child to discuss, they provide useful information about the essentials of a child's daily life. Obtaining information about routine activities also provides a forum for more specific questions about when each parent is home and available to the child, and therefore gives relevant information about relationships with each parent and adjustment at home.

In general, teenagers are able to give relatively substantive, meaningful responses when asked to describe, separately, their relationships with each parent. In my experience, when children below the age of approximately 12 are asked about their relationships with each parent, they tend to give extremely brief and nonproductive answers. Because one of the common uses of the term relationship refers to romantic attachments, it is very helpful for purposes of clarity to give a more comprehensive working definition of relationship that includes how any two individuals feel and think about one another, how they perceive one another, what their communication is like, and what they do together. As is the case with almost all content areas, it is best to use an open-ended question when starting to ask about relationships with each parent.

Because younger children do not appear to have the capacities to respond productively to such a question about relationships with each parent, it is useful to obtain their experiences about such matters through a series of more specific questions (Shutz et al., 1989). For example, it is frequently productive to ask questions such as what are a child's favorite activities with each parent, what each parent does that is helpful for the child, what each parent does best as a parent, and whether there are any things that the child would like the parent to do differently. These more specific questions permit the evaluator to collect basic yet important information about parent-child relationships from the child's perspective.

It can be useful to gather information about the child's view regarding how the parent tries to manage them, including regularly used positive and negative consequences (which are important aspects of relationships between parents and children). Somewhat similarly, it can be helpful to ask children about their interactions with parents regarding routine rules and chores at home. Questioning children about with whom they prefer to talk if they feel worried or under stress can shed light about emotional comfort levels with each parent.

How parents handle conflict is important in multiple ways in terms of the impact on the children. Therefore, it is productive to routinely ask children what they hear each parent say about the other parent. Because children frequently assume this question means whether they have heard each parent say something negative about the other, it can also be very worthwhile to ask if they have heard each parent make any positive comments about the other. It is important to ask children how much they have heard each parent yell at the other parent, and how much each parent yells at them. Somewhat similarly, children routinely should be asked if they have ever observed each parent to have engaged in action such as hitting or pushing the other parent. Questions regarding whether either parent has hit or physically hurt them in any way are also important to ask, especially to protect the child from actual or potential harm.

As noted above, some areas for inquiry are going to be relevant for only certain children. For example, if a child has been identified as having significant educational difficulties, it is important to ask a series of questions about how that child interacts with each parent regarding school matters.

Although all children should be asked about whether they have observed any type of domestic violence or experienced any physical aggression from a parent, based on information collected earlier in the evaluation, as well as during the child interview, some individuals will need to be asked questions about such matters at greater length. If interviewing is focused on the possible presence of child abuse, some type of electronic recording of at least that portion of the interview is highly recommended. If high-quality interviewing has already taken place about the potential abuse, it may be best to review an available recording instead of subjecting the child to additional questioning.

39-b

As described above, it is crucial that initial questions about matters such as domestic violence and child abuse be asked in an open-ended manner. Also, when children are being asked about specific events, it can be useful to prompt them to picture themselves in the circumstances that were in effect at the time. Such mental reconstruction by children has been found to assist in the retrieval of information (Brown, 2011), as long as children work to mentally reconstruct the context of the event by themselves and are not given leading or suggestive prompts.

To the extent that open-ended questions lead to productive answers, the interviewer should continue to use them. With many interviewees, however, the response productivity declines after a number of open-ended questions. Then, if more detail is needed, a change to more focused questions, such as asking more about what specific actions occurred, where the event took place, and when they happened (i.e., wh-type questions) is necessary. As a last means of attempting to get further information and clarification, it may be necessary to ask specific questions of the multiple-choice or yes-no variety. However, it is important for interviewers to remain diligent and rely on open-ended questions as much as possible because specific questions hold a greater risk of being leading and resulting in inaccurate responses. Unfortunately, it is all too easy for interviewers to carry out styles of questioning that do not promote productive and accurate responses (Lamb, Sternberg, Orbach, Esplin, & Mitchell, 2002).

When a child is asked what they have observed in the behaviors of others, it is necessary to emphasize, sometimes repeatedly, that the interviewer is interested only in what he or she has directly seen and heard, as opposed to any other information that has been learned secondhand. For example, in addition to making such a statement to the child before asking relevant questions, it may be necessary after the child has finished the response to double check that all such information was directly observed and was not told to them, even in part, by another individual, such as a parent or sibling. Such double checking needs to be done in a manner that does not inadvertently use leading questions.

When children are asked questions especially about controversial areas, it is crucial that it be carried out in a balanced manner, consistent with a scientific hypothesis-testing approach. For example, if the child volunteers that Parent A has been physically aggressive toward him or her, it is crucial that the interviewer asked whether Parent B has also been physically aggressive toward the child. Somewhat similarly, if a child states that Parent A has said mean things about the other parent, in addition to asking whether Parent B has made such statements, it would be important to ask, separately regarding each parent, whether that individual has said nice things about the other parent.

When there are allegations of parental alienation, evaluators need to question children in such a way as to potentially shed light on the matter. Unfortunately, the nature of parental alienation, and allegations about it, is such that there is considerable difficulty in gathering good-quality research information about it (Saini, Johnston, Fidler, & Bala, 2012). Therefore, evaluators sometimes must rely a good deal on sources such as the professional experience of others and learning experiences from prior cases. There are a number of child interview characteristics that suggest parental alienation could be taking place. For example, there is cause for concern when the child makes spontaneously negative statements about a parent that are not in response to questions and are otherwise out of context. Child statements about a parent that are vigorously and overwhelmingly negative are also causes for concern, especially if the child is not able to describe parental behavior that would give good reason for such estrangement, and when they are paired with extremely positive views regarding the other parent.

When the child voices an opinion that a parent is mean and awful, it is necessary for the evaluator to prompt the child to say more about that matter, initially in an open-ended manner. If such questions do not result in descriptions of actions or statements that give clear examples, the next step would be to ask more focused questions, such as what that parent has done and/or said that shows he or she is mean and awful. Similarly, if a parent is described as thoroughly wonderful, initially open-ended and then perhaps focused questions need to be asked so that the child gives examples in terms of actions and/or statements by the parent. Perhaps obviously, if a child is able to identify relevant behaviors and statements that provide good evidence for their opinion about the parent, and there are clear indications that their reports are accurate, it is very likely that they are simply reporting on their actual experiences.

A child may acknowledge that one parent prompted him or her to report negative material about the other parent. It is important to keep in mind that although such parental behavior is not optimal, it does not, by itself, indicate that parental alienation is taking place. For example, that parent may have prompted the child to accurately report that the other parent regularly drinks excessively and becomes angry.

In contrast, if a strongly negative opinion about a parent exists in the absence of relevant examples of parental behavior, there is cause for concern about potential alienation. At times, a child may use language to describe negative attitudes about a parent that strongly resembles the language used by the other parent, and may not fit well with the child's own level of verbal development. In such instances, an evaluator needs to be open to the possibility that parental alienation is taking place. In a number of cases, there may be allegations of parental alienation, but during the interview the child voices generally positive attitudes about both parents, which suggests that the allegations do not have substance. It is also important for the evaluator to consider whether the degree of negative feelings and opinions a child might have about a parent are proportional to any reports they may make about negative parental actions or statements. In that regard, in a number of cases in which parental alienation is alleged, the supposedly alienated parent may have engaged in negative behaviors, but ones that are relatively modest in extent and severity in comparison to the fiercely negative attitude voiced by the child. While there are no definitive empirical data about the matter, a number of parental alienation allegation cases appear to take the form of one parent amplifying or exaggerating the relatively moderate deficits of the other parent and exposing the child to such attitudes.

However, it is crucial that evaluators keep in mind that there are no certain signs of parental alienation in child interview statements. Also, all such information needs to be integrated with other aspects of the evaluation process. See Chapter 13 for further detail about the challenges of assessing allegations regarding parental alienation.

As described earlier in this book, a common statutory factor considered in the legal system is the wishes of the child regarding custody. However, directly asking children with whom they would primarily like to live can create an inappropriate emotional burden to choose between parents. Consequently, it is important to look for ways that children can express their feelings and thoughts about this matter if they would like to do so, while also allowing a clear avenue for the child to avoid making any statements about a preferred parent. It is useful to ask children what they think or expect it would be like to live mostly with each parent, while still seeing the other one regularly (assuming that regular contact with both parents would likely take place). Also, if equally shared parenting is within the realm of possibilities for that case, children can be asked what they think it would be like to spend an equal amount of time with each parent.

At the end of each child interview, it is important to spend a brief time talking about neutral or relatively positive matters to help decrease whatever tension or stress the child may have experienced during the interview. I recommend thanking each child for participating. As described above, especially for young children, it can be helpful to mention to them and the parent who brought them that they did very well during the interview.

Chapter 8

THE PERSONALITY ASSESSMENT INVENTORY (PAI): EXPANDED RESEARCH

PRACTICE CHECKLIST

In the current custody evaluation sample:

_____The mean score on the defensiveness scale (PIM) was moderately elevated.

_____Using the cutoff score of PIM 68 T for profile invalidity, 22% had elevated scores.

_____Using the cutoff score of PIM 57 T for need of caution about possible defensiveness, 74% had elevated scores.

_____Clinical scale scores were generally below average.

_____Interpersonal scales showed modest elevations.

_____Gender differences were generally small and consistent with research on the prevalence of psychological disorders.

_____Exception is that the manic scale (MAN) had a moderately higher mean score for men, but significant elevations on MAN are unlikely to occur for either gender.

_____It is essential to integrate PAI results with other types of evaluative information.

Note: This form is a guide to promote productive reasoning and good practice. It is not comprehensive or all-inclusive and does not replace adequate training and experience.

As described earlier in Chapter 1, one of the factors consistently identified as a significant risk for a negative outcome is parental psychological dysfunction that impacts parenting behavior (Amato, 1993, 2001; Amato & Keith, 1991a, 1991b; Hetherington, Bridges, & Insabella, 1998; Lansford, 2009). Also, the UMDA (NCCUSL, 1970) indicates that the mental health of all relevant parties is a factor to be considered in custody determination.

Therefore, in child custody evaluations, psychological testing is routinely used to try to objectively assess psychological maladjustment. It is important to use well-validated psychological tests to increase reliance on scientific data, and thereby augment more subjective clinical impressions, the latter of which appear more likely to reflect judgment errors (Garb, 1998).

It is crucial for test usage to be relevant for the testing objective. Numerous professional principles and guidelines address the importance of appropriate and fair psychological test use. For example, the APA (2002) Ethical Principles of Psychologists and Code of Conduct encourage test use that is valid and reliable for the purpose of the assessment and the test taker. The Standards for Educational and Psychological Testing (American Educational Research Association (AERA), APA, & National Council on Measurement in Education, 1999) address numerous areas, including interpretation informed by appropriate reference groups. The Specialty Guidelines for Forensic Psychology (APA, 2013) state that test use needs to consider applicable research. Similarly, the Guidelines for Child Custody Evaluations in Family Law Proceedings (APA, 2010) indicate that interpretation of assessment data needs to consider the context of the child custody evaluation. In addition, all these documents emphasize the importance of fairness and avoiding unwarranted bias.

The PAI (Morey, 2007) is an omnibus objective measure of psychological disorders, personality functioning, and related features. It is the third most frequently used measure of that type in custody evaluation (Ackerman & Pritzl, 2011), but prior to a very recent article (Hynan, 2013b), there were no published data specific for such use. Regarding tests commonly used in custody evaluation, prior to the research described in this book, there were published custody evaluation data that included gender comparisons only for the Minnesota Multiphasic Personality Inventory-2 (MMPI-2) (Bagby, Nicholson, Buis, Radovanovic, & Fidler, 1999; Bathurst, Gottfried, & Gottfried, 1997; Siegel, Bow & Gottlieb, 2012; Strong, Greene, Hoppe, Johnston, & Olesen, 1999) and the Millon Clinical Multiaxial Inventory-III (MCMI–III) (McCann et al., 2001), though the latter measure has been questioned in terms of its validity (Rogers, Salekin, & Sewell, 1999) and gender fairness (Hynan, 2004). Other custody evaluation data from the MMPI-2 (Ezzo, Pinsoneault, & Evans, 2007; Posthuma & Harper, 1998; Siegel, 1996; Siegel & Langford, 1998) and NEO Personality Inventory (Langer, 2011) did not include useful gender comparisons for all main scales.

The PAI has 11 scales of clinical functioning: Somatic Complaints (SOC), Anxiety (ANX), Anxiety-Related Disorders (ARD), Depression (DEP), Mania (MAN), Paranoia (PAR), Schizophrenia (SCZ), Borderline Features (BOR), Antisocial Features (ANT), Alcohol Problems (ALC), and Drug Problems (DRG). There are four validity scales: Inconsistency (INC), Infrequency (INC), Negative Impression Management (NIM), and Positive Impression

Management (PIM). Five scales pertain to treatment considerations: Aggression (AGG), Suicidal Ideation (SUI), Stress (STR), Nonsupport (NON), and Treatment Rejection (RXR). Also, there are two interpersonal scales: Dominance (DOM) and Warmth (WRM).

The Positive Impression Management (PIM) validity scale, the main measure of defensiveness, is especially important because evaluators need to strongly consider the extent to which parents are trying to present themselves in the best possible light, and such clients have been found to manifest moderately elevated levels on the MMPI-2, as described in later in this book and elsewhere (Bagby et al., 1999; Bathurst et al., 1997; Posthuma & Harper, 1998; Siegel, 1996; Siegel et al., 2012; Strong et al., 1999).

There is good evidence for the reliability and validity of the PAI. For example, except for two validity scales (ICN and INF), the internal consistency and test-retest reliability are adequate to good, and there is considerable evidence of concurrent validity (Morey, 2007). Additional evidence of validity can be seen in a number of clinical and offender samples (e.g., Edens, Hart, Johnson, Johnson, & Olver, 2000; Jacobo, Blais, Baity, & Harley, 2007).

THE RESEARCH PROJECT

A main objective of this research was to provide relevant data for child custody evaluators. Because of patterns of MMPI-2 findings in custody litigant samples (Bagby et al., 1999; Bathurst et al., 1997; Siegel et al., 2012; Strong et al., 1999), it was reasonable to expect that there would be important differences between the PAI responses of custody evaluation parents and the results of the standardization sample (Morey, 2007). More specifically, those previous MMPI-2 studies reported that custody litigants manifested increases in elevations on traditional scales of defensiveness in the magnitude of approximately one-half to one standard deviation, and clinical scale elevations were within the normal range. Practicing evaluators have had the opportunity to use such empirical information regarding the MMPI-2, and now have a similar opportunity with the PAI.

Archival data from the author's practice in suburban Chicago served as the database. Reliance on PAI data from one practice follows the position of leading psychologists (Stricker & Trierweiler, 1995) that practitioners can make valuable contributions to research by functioning as local clinical scientists, and is extremely relevant for the custody evaluation field which has had too little empirical data available to provide a good scientific foundation.

All 250 participants were legal parents. That number was far above the requirement for a conventional power level of .80 (meaning an 80% probability of rejecting a false null hypothesis) given a statistical significance level of

.05 and a goal of identifying at least a medium effect size (Cohen, 1992). Parental demographic data were based on information completed on the PAI answer sheet. Mothers averaged 37 years of age ($SD = 6.09$) and fathers 40 ($SD = 7.51$). Mothers and fathers both had an average of 15 years of education ($SD = 2.57$). There was a mean of 1.72 children per family ($SD = .75$). The vast majority of participants were Caucasian.

All tests were completed as a part of evaluations ordered by court. Twenty-seven tests were completed in accordance with a local court rule for a condensed evaluation, and the rest were completed according to standard orders without any such limitation. All tests from 1998 through 2009 were used in this analysis. Almost all tests had no unanswered items, and none had more than 17 unanswered, the maximum allowed for interpretation (Morey, 2007). The author administered all tests in booklet form in the office setting. All were computer scored by Psychological Assessment Resources.

Initial findings (Hynan, 2013b) showed that custody evaluation parents manifested moderate defensiveness, associated with below-average mean scores on clinical scales and modestly elevated means on interpersonal scales. Perhaps obviously, it is extremely important for tests used in custody evaluations to be fair in gender comparisons, and such fairness has not always been found in relevant research (Hynan, 2004). There were statistically significant gender differences on seven PAI scales. The mean for fathers on MAN was higher than for mothers, and that difference was clinically significant. Although that pattern of results is inconsistent with epidemiological findings, a significant elevation on MAN is likely to occur only infrequently for both genders. Otherwise, findings suggest that the PAI has adequate gender fairness, as the statistically significant differences tended to reflect findings from research on the prevalence of relevant mental health disorders.

The current research extends the analyses described above in a number of ways. First, statistical analyses were carried out to more closely examine the extent to which defensiveness on the PAI influenced scores on clinical, treatment consideration, and interpersonal scales. Next, an investigation of predecree versus postdecree cases took place. Also, there was an initial exploration about how especially challenging features of evaluations such as allegations of substance abuse, domestic violence, and/or child abuse might influence PAI scores.

DEFENSIVENESS

As described earlier, research has found that a moderate degree of defensiveness has been consistently manifested by custody litigants on the MMPI-2 and PAI. Such defensiveness is to be expected given the nature of the assessment, though it also needs to be carefully considered in test interpretation and over-all conceptualization of the evaluative information. Therefore, I carried out more detailed data analyses focused on defensiveness, similar to approaches used earlier by Bathurst et al. (1997) and Bagby et al. (1999).

It was hypothesized that parents who had elevated PIM scores (under-reporters) would manifest generally lower clinical scale scores than others who did not have elevations on PIM (non-underreporters). Somewhat simi-larly, it was anticipated that underreporters would generally show higher scores than non-underreporters on both interpersonal scales.

The PAI has two general cutoff points for PIM. As described in the test manual (Morey, 2007), if an individual obtains a PIM score of 68 T or above, the overall profile is considered invalid, and no substantive interpretation should take place. If a respondent has a PIM score at or above 57 T, the profile needs to be considered with caution.

Therefore, two separate sets of analyses were carried out regarding defen-siveness. One set of analyses looked at individuals who had a PIM score of 68 T and above versus those who scored below 68 T. The other analyses in-vestigated respondents who had PIM scores at or above 57 T, versus those who scored below 57 T.

Pim Scores at or Above 68 T

There were 55 parents who had PIM scores at or above 68 T (underreport-ers) and 195 had scores below 68 T (non-underreporters). A multivariate analysis of variance was carried out using this bifurcation of PIM scores as the independent variable. The dependent variables were the clinical, treatment consideration, and interpersonal scales. There was a significant interaction of PIM category and scale, $F(17, 232) = 8.70$, $p. < .001$.

To more closely examine this finding, ANOVAs were carried out for each of the relevant PAI scales. Non-underreporters had significantly higher mean scores (all $ps < .02$) on all clinical scales except DRG, which was nonsignifi-cant. On treatment consideration scales, non-underreporters had significantly higher mean scores on AGG, SUI, and NON ($ps < .03$), and STR was mar-ginally significant ($p = .084$). Underreporters had significantly higher mean scores on the treatment consideration scale RXR and the interpersonal scales DOM and WRM ($ps < .02$).

In some circumstances, there can be statistically significant differences on psychological tests that are small in magnitude and not clinically meaningful, especially when sample sizes are quite large (e.g., Butcher, Graham, & Ben-Porath, 1995). Consequently, statistically significant differences all throughout this book were examined for effect sizes using the Cohen (1992) d statistic. Effect sizes below .2 are considered trivial, those between .2 and .49 small, those between .5 and .79 medium, and those above .8 are categorized as large by Cohen. Most of the statistically significant differences described in this section had a medium or large effect size.

For both underreporters and non-underreporters, the mean scores on all clinical scales were all below 50 T, well below the range of concern about any clinical condition. On treatment consideration scales, the means for both groups were primarily near or below 50 T, also. The exception was for RXR: underreporters had a mean of 64 T and non-underreporters a mean of 56 T. Therefore, on RXR, parents who showed excessive defensiveness not surprisingly manifested a belief that treatment was unnecessary, and as might be expected, RXR was significantly correlated with PIM (Hynan, 2013b). However, the RXR scale has minimal relevance within the context of custody evaluation.

On interpersonal scales, the mean scores for DOM were a bit above average for both groups, though WRM underreporters had a mean of 62 T versus 57 T for non-underreporters. Therefore, excessively defensive parents showed a tendency to portray themselves as particularly warm and supportive, which are clearly positive features in parenting.

Pim Scores at or Above 57 T

There were 184 parents who had a PIM score of 57 T or above, and 66 with a PIM score of below 57 T. Therefore, only 26 percent of the sample scored in the defensiveness range that suggests neither invalidity nor a need for caution in interpretation. A second multivariate analysis was carried out using this 57 T division of PIM scores as the independent variable. The same scales as described above were the dependent variables. Once again, there was a significant multivariate interaction of PIM category and scale, multivariate $F(17, 232) = 6.70, p. < .001$.

In order to gain more detailed information about this finding, ANOVAs were carried out. Not surprisingly, the pattern of these results was very similar to the findings above when the cutoff score of 68 T was used. Specifically, parents who had PIM scores below 57 T had significantly higher mean scores on all clinical scales (all $ps < .03$) except DRG, which was not significant. On treatment consideration scales, the group with PIM scores below 57 T had higher mean scores on AGG, STR, and NON (all $ps < .001$), and on SUI, the difference approached the conventional level of statistical significance ($p = .085$). On RXR and WRM, parents with PIM scores of 57 T and above had significantly higher mean scores ($ps < .001$), and on DOM, they had marginally significant higher scores ($p. = .056$). Most of the statistically significant differences had effect sizes in the medium to large range.

For this comparison using a PIM score of 57 T as the cutoff, both groups again had mean scores of under 50 T on all clinical scales. The group that had a PIM score at or above 57 T had mean scores on RXR and WRM of 59 T, which were the highest mean elevations for this analysis.

The hypothesis that individuals who manifested higher levels of defensiveness would show lower elevations on clinical scales was supported. Also, there was support for the hypothesis that relatively defensive parents would have somewhat higher scores on interpersonal scales.

It is important to note that PAI clinical scale elevations were below the average of 50 T regardless of whether or not parents were categorized as having responded defensively. This pattern reflects the overall finding that this group of custody litigants manifested lower than usual clinical scale elevations and somewhat increased elevations on interpersonal scales (Hynan, 2013b). The PAI was designed to identify the presence of clinical problems and related features, and the manual (Morey, 2007) does not offer clinical interpretations for low clinical scale scores, other than to imply that they represent normal range functioning.

PREDECREE VERSUS POSTDECREE LITIGANTS

Professionals in the divorce field have noted that individuals who have never gone through separation or divorce sometimes present differently from those who have already gone through a process to arrive at a decision about child custody and time sharing. For parents who have never gone through the process before, one or both often experience considerable distress. Some of the distress is associated with the adult relationship falling apart, the interface of that process with the impact on the children, and the children's visible responses. For parents who have gone through it before and are dealing with a possible modification, some appear to have their lives more settled as compared to individuals meeting such life stresses for the first time. However, there are also postdecree individuals who present as repeatedly frustrated and distressed in other ways, and who continue repeated litigation over the children. Numerous judges and attorneys have commented that there is a very small proportion of parents who take up an enormously disproportionate amount of courts' time and attention.

Consequently, it was important to ascertain whether there were differences in PAI responses between parents who were going through the separation and/or divorce process for the first time, and those who were involved in efforts at postdecree modification. There were competing hypotheses about the possible impact of predecree versus postdecree timing of the litigation on PAI scores. One hypothesis was that predecree parents would show generally higher scores, especially on clinical scales, based on the expectation that they experienced higher levels of psychological distress than postdecree individuals. The alternate hypothesis was that postdecree respondents experienced significant psychological dysfunction that contributed to their return to court, and therefore their PAI scores, especially on clinical scales, would be generally higher than predecree parents.

For parents who had been married to one another, the identification of predecree versus postdecree cases was based on whether or not they had been through a prior legal process that led to the establishment of custody and time-sharing routines. For parents who had never been married to one another, the identification of predecree versus postdecree cases depended on whether or not they had already gone through any type of process, even by means of informal agreement, that had led to time-sharing routines.

For the statistical analysis, the categorization of whether it was a predecree case or a postdecree modification is labeled as timing. That categorization was missing for four individuals, and therefore there were 246 parents included in this analysis. There were 168 parents categorized as predecree and 78 as postdecree.

An initial step in the statistical analysis was to conduct a multivariate analysis of variance that included both timing and parent gender, in order to determine whether there might be a pattern such as higher scores for predecree mothers but not fathers. The significant results for gender alone are briefly summarized earlier in this chapter and described in more detail elsewhere (Hynan, 2013b). There was a significant multivariate effect for the interaction of timing and scale, $F(21, 222) = 5.44$, $p. < .001$, but the interaction of timing, gender, and scale was not significant.

In order to examine the statistically significant effect for timing, ANOVAs were carried out for each of the PAI scales. Predecree parents had a significantly higher mean score (55.91) on STR than did postdecree individuals (45.97), $F(1, 244) = 63.04$, $p. < .001$. Postdecree individuals had a significantly higher mean (45.86) on SUI than did predecree parents (44.57), $F(1, 244) = 5.71$, $p. = .018$. No other scales showed statistically significant differences. The effect size for STR was 1.15, and for SUI was .29.

Therefore, there is evidence that parents who go through custody evaluations prior to a decree generally experience a great deal more stress than do those in postdecree litigation. These results support the impression that the separation and divorce process is highly challenging emotionally. At the same time, the absence of higher scores for the predecree group on the clinical scales provides support for the impression that custody litigants generally are psychologically healthy. The clinically small but statistically significant difference on SUI is more difficult to interpret. It is important to note that both groups had scores on SUI of approximately one-half standard deviation below the standardization sample mean. Therefore, a reasonable interpretation would be that both groups reported a lower than average level of thoughts and emotions related to suicide, and that predecree parents reported slightly fewer such feelings and thoughts than did postdecree cases. At the same time, given the small size of the difference and the absence of similar empirical evidence, it is possible that the result for SUI largely represents error variance.

CONTENTIOUS PARENTAL ALLEGATIONS

A considerable proportion of custody evaluations include allegations of substance abuse, domestic violence, and/or child abuse. Such allegations typically contribute toward heated parental accusations and denials of misconduct. The presence of any of these allegations generally leads to a relatively complicated and challenging evaluation. Of course, in a significant number of these cases, more than one type of allegation is present. In practice, there is often an association between claims of substance abuse by a parent and allegations that individual is particularly inclined toward physical aggression toward the spouse when intoxicated. Somewhat similarly, at times a parent is accused of having been abusive both toward their spouse and one or more children.

The current research project included an examination of PAI scores in terms of whether or not substance misuse, domestic violence, and/or child abuse were identified as areas of concern within the family. In the vast majority of these cases, classification as to the presence or absence of one or more of these behavioral patterns was based on the report of one or both parents. In a few instances, neither parent made such a claim, but it became clear during the evaluation that there was considerable reason for concern. For example, in a few cases, both parents reported there had been child physical discipline that would generally have been considered excessive, but neither one believed there was anything wrong with it. In other infrequent instances, neither parent expressed any concern about domestic violence, but during interviews it became evident that one or more physical altercations between the parents had taken place.

It is extremely important to keep in mind that the PAI was not designed to try to identify the presence of domestic violence or child abuse. Obviously, two of the scales, ALC and DRG, are aimed to try to identify relevant substance misuse. This portion of the research is exploratory in nature.

The categorization of the presence or absence of substance misuse, domestic violence, and/or child abuse was carried out in terms of the case, and not the individual parent. In other words, if any family member described that any of these three problem areas were present, or it became otherwise evident during the course of the evaluation that any of them were present, then the case fell into the relevant categorization. Accordingly, the PAI profiles of both parents were categorized as the relevant problem area having been present.

For the sake of clarity in presenting statistical analyses, if a parent was categorized as belonging to a case in which a relevant allegation or evidence was present, the independent variable is labeled as yes, and no is used as the group label if no such allegation or evidence was present.

For a few cases, there was only one relevant PAI because only one parent completed the evaluation. Because there continued to be a great deal of disagreement between many parents as to which, if either, parent carried out substance misuse, domestic violence and/or child abuse, and there was seldom clear, objective evidence, it was not possible to reliably identify individual parents as to whether or not they had manifested such problem behaviors.

Substance Misuse

Concerns about parental substance misuse occurred quite frequently. There were 97 of 250 parents, or 39%, who were involved in cases that included allegations of parental substance misuse.

On three scales, yes parents had higher mean scores: ANT, $t(248) = 2.98$, $p = .003$; ALC, $t(248) = 4.56$, $p < .001$; and AGG, $t(248) = 2.08$, $p = .038$. It is understandable that the presence of substance misuse allegations or evidence yielded a higher score on ALC, as well as scales focused on behaviors that are often associated with alcohol problems. However, it is important to note that the mean scores for both the yes and no groups on all three scales were below 50 T. Effect sizes were small for ANT and AGG, and medium for ALC.

In general, interpretation of results regarding the possible substance misuse needs to rely substantially on other information to confirm or disconfirm that such a problem might be present. Future research in this area could be very productive if it focused on the independent identification of custody litigants who manifested substance abuse and comparing their response patterns with similar parents who clearly did not misuse substances.

Domestic Violence

Of the three types of problem behavior, for parents who completed the PAI, domestic violence occurred most frequently. There were 117 of 250 parents, or 47%, categorized as yes for domestic violence.

On three scales, parents in the yes group had higher mean scores than those in the no group: on INC, $t(248) = 2.07$, $p. = .04$; PAR, $t(248) = 2.09$, $p = .037$; and STR, $t(248) = 2.36$, $p = .019$. On ALC, the no group had a higher mean than the yes group, $t(248) = 2.15$, $p = .033$. In retrospect, it seems understandable that the involvement of domestic violence would lead to heightened experiences of stress and suspiciousness. It is much less clear why the statistically significant effects for INC and ALC took place. On all statistically significant scales except for STR, both the yes and no groups had mean scores less than 50 T. On STR, the yes group mean was 55 and the no group mean was 52. Effect sizes were small for all four scales.

These exploratory findings appear to be the only published ones for the PAI relevant for domestic violence concerns within custody litigation. Selected MMPI-2 research regarding domestic violence perpetrators is briefly summarized in the chapter on that instrument. Potentially useful future PAI research might involve comparison of scores between parents who were accurately identified either as perpetrators of domestic violence or not having carried it out.

Child Abuse

In the sample of parents who completed the PAI, 82 of 250, or 33%, were involved in cases with allegations or evidence of child abuse. There were statistically significant higher mean scores for the yes group on four scales: INC, $t(248) = 2.11$, $p = .036$; NIM, $t(248) = 3.53$, $p < .001$; PAR, $t(248) = 3.20$, $p = .002$; and ANT, $t(248) = 2.38$, $p = .018$. Again, mean scores for both the yes and no groups were less than 50 T across all four scales. It appears understandable that the presence of child abuse would be associated with higher levels of antisocial behavior, and it might be expected that concern about the presence of child abuse would be associated with suspiciousness. It is much less clear for what reasons the other two scales had shown elevations. Effect sizes were small for all four scales.

The current finding appears to be the only published one of its type regarding the PAI and child abuse. See the chapter on the MMPI-2 for a brief summary of a previous child abuse study using that measure.

IMPLICATIONS

These test results expand on the initial PAI findings for custody litigants reported earlier (Hynan, 2013b). These findings also provide a potential springboard for future PAI research with child custody evaluation parents.

The most clear cut difference between the current results and the data reported in the standardization sample (Morey, 2007) is the elevation on the PIM scale. Overall, that elevation is about one standard deviation higher than the standardization sample mean. When the 68 T cutoff for profile invalidity is used, 22% of the current sample is at or above that level. There is no known summary analysis for the PAI of other custody evaluation samples, though in a small sample of parenting capacity evaluations, 18% of respondents had a

PIM score of 68 T score higher (Carr, Moretti, & Cue, 2005). Morey (2007) presented a brief summary of other published research on the PIM scale. For the MMPI-2, a somewhat higher base rate for excessive defensiveness of .30 was identified in a meta-analysis (Baer & Miller, 2002). As described above, there is a second, lower PIM scale cutoff of 57 T. At or above that score, caution is needed in the interpretation of clinical and other scales. That is, PIM scores at or above 57 T but below 68 T are best viewed as being in a gray area, in which caution is needed but useful clinical and related data may still be drawn from the PAI. As noted above, the PAI manuals (Morey, 2007) did not describe interpretive considerations for low PIM scale scores, other than to indicate that they are representative of apparently honest responding.

Custody evaluators may wish to be aware of other more complex measures of defensiveness on the PAI. The Defensiveness Index (DEF; Morey, 1996) and the Cashel Discriminant Function (CDF; Cashel, Rogers, Sewell, & Martin-Cannici, 1995) both involve calculations based on a number of PAI indices, including PIM, and are described by Morey (2007). However, it is not clear that either adds incremental validity over the PIM scale alone, and the current research did not include them.

The analyses regarding the PIM defensiveness scale and its impact on other scale elevations show that this sample of custody litigant parents manifested clinical scale scores with very few significant elevations, regardless of what defensiveness category they fell into. It is important that this pattern of results suggests that defensive responding did not consistently hide test scores representative of psychological dysfunction and thus did not diminish the utility of the PAI. However, it remains an open question regarding whether high PIM scores are representative of comparatively healthy individuals answering questions in a defensive manner, and/or to what extent the defensiveness may in fact cover up psychopathology in certain parents.

The generally lowered mean scores on all clinical scales and the modestly higher means on the interpersonal scales are likely influenced to some extent by the moderate defensiveness found in these PAI respondents. It is important to note that the PAI does not have any clinical score adjustments similar to the *K* scale correction in the MMPI-2.

Because the PAI and MMPI-2 both use T scores, results of the two tests can be directly compared. Overall, when used in custody evaluation, the PAI may appear less sensitive to the presence of psychological disorders as compared to the MMPI-2. For example, as shown later in this book, the mean scores for MMPI-2 clinical scales when used with custody litigants are generally somewhat higher than the corresponding means for PAI clinical scales.

More specifically, for the PAI, elevations at or above 60 T on clinical scales are described generally as indicative of a modest or moderate degree of dysfunction, and at or above 70 T as more prominent disturbance (Morey, 2007).

In the current sample, the PAI clinical scales with the highest frequencies of elevations at or above 60 T were MAN (9%), PAR (4%), and DRG (4%). They were less often elevated in the current test archive than the most frequently elevated MMPI-2 clinical scales (*Pd* 11%, *Hy* 8%, and *Pa* 6%), even though these MMPI-2 elevations are based on that measure's higher standard cutoff of 65 T.

The PAI manual (Morey, 2007) listed raw to T score conversions separately for the census-matched standardization sample and a clinical sample. PAI scoring and interpretation should rely on the census-matched data, in part because the preponderance of evidence is that custody evaluation parents generally do not present with major clinical problems. As a general procedure, an evaluator should give a great deal of consideration to relying largely on interpretive considerations described in the manual.

At the same time, it is crucial for practitioners to make conclusions about custody evaluation participants only after examining the totality of information from additional sources of data such as interviews, observations, and information from collateral sources. In this manner, convergent information from numerous sources would reasonably have more weight than relatively small details from any one source, such as testing.

For example, in a hypothetical case, interview data and collateral information indicated that a father experienced aspects of depression that had an impact on his parenting, but his score on the relevant DEP scale was 59 T. Because such an elevation is close to, but just below a classification of an individual likely manifesting unhappiness, pessimism, and self-doubts (Morey, 2007, p. 37), and such an elevation is above more than 80% of respondents in a normal distribution, that score would appear to provide support for the inference that he is depressed. However, such a score in isolation should not lead to such a conclusion, and may be attributable to error variance.

Because custody evaluations involve comparisons between parents, it is crucial to keep in mind that a small difference in test scores between parents may not be clinically significant. A number of authorities have described that score differences that are within the standard error of measurement tend not to be clinically significant (e.g., Butcher et al., 1995, Morey, 2007). The standard error of measurement for most PAI clinical scales is approximately 4, and is about 3 for ANT and ALC. The standard error of measurement for the PAI is somewhat smaller, due to generally higher reliability coefficients, as compared to the MMPI-2, which generally has a standard error of measurement of 5 for clinical scales.

Such statistical information that pertains to clinical significance can be very important in practice in certain cases in which comparisons are made between the scale elevations of competing parents. These comparisons can become especially tricky when one parent has scored just above an identified cutoff point and the other has scored just below it. For example, on BOR, the test manual stated that at elevations of 70 T or above, individuals are likely to be impulsive, labile, angry, suspicious, and saddled with relationship problems (Morey, 2007). Individuals with elevations just below 70 T tend to have mood, impulse control, and interpersonal problems, though at a somewhat less intense level. In a hypothetical case in which Parent A had a score of 71 T and Parent B scored 68 T, their score difference is within the standard error of measurement and therefore that difference is not clinically significant even though one is above and the other below the 70 T cutoff.

There are numerous statistical analyses described in this chapter, and a significant proportion of them did not yield significant results. When such repeated analyses occur, it is important to question whether some of the statistically significant ones, especially those that are small in magnitude, are simply due to error variance. For instance, with a significance level set at .05, if 20 statistical analyses are carried out, one of them is likely to be significant just by chance. Two potentially useful ways of ascertaining whether such statistically significant differences are representative of the actual population differences involve empirical or conceptual approaches. The empirical approach would be to compare the significant results with other research findings, and if there is convergence, it is more likely to reflect an actual difference. However, there unfortunately are no published comparison data for the PAI with custody evaluation parents other than what has been drawn from the current sample (Hynan, 2013b). A conceptual approach would look at whether the results seem to make sense in light of other related knowledge. However, a relative weakness of relying only on this conceptual approach is that, as described in Chapter 3 in a different context, any individual might be overly inclined to intuitively conclude that findings which appear to confirm one's previously held beliefs are accurate, whereas others are spurious.

Limitations of the current research include the fact that the current sample was all from one practice in a limited geographical area, and there were very few non-Caucasian parents. However, these characteristics have been found in past MMPI-2 research with custody evaluation parents, and the largest prior custody evaluation test sample (Bathurst et al., 1997) was all drawn from one practice. In addition, prior research studies (Bagby et al., 1999; Bathurst et al., 1997) that listed demographic characteristics such as parental age and level of education, and numbers of children had data that were quite similar to that of the current study.

The reality, which seems unlikely to change, is that there has been little quantitative research on individuals undergoing custody evaluations, as academia has shown very little interest in the area (Grisso, 2005). If there is to be an expansion of solid research-based evidence with custody evaluation participants, practitioners are likely to be the individuals to carry it out. Therefore, the current research both can be of direct benefit to custody evaluation practitioners and can provide a potential platform for others to further such empirical knowledge.

A number of practical considerations are extremely important for custody evaluators because of the court-related nature of the process. It is crucial that there be adequate monitoring and supervision, as well as reasonable comfort and quiet, when individuals complete tests. There are a number of good ways to provide such a testing environment. What is most necessary is that parents have sufficient opportunities to comfortably focus and complete their tests, and do not have opportunities for access to any type of electronic, paper or other communication that could provide coaching regarding the ostensibly correct answers.

Some evaluators rely on computerized test interpretation. For the PAI, it appears that if an evaluator purchases computerized scoring, interpretation is automatically sent with the scoring. There are a number of drawbacks in relying on computerized test interpretation. Such interpretations rely on proprietary information that is not generally available, and therefore it is not possible to know the scientific validity of the interpretive statements. Garb (1998) summarized the results of research on computerized psychological test interpretation. He reported frequent problems in terms of consistent external validity of interpretive statements and noted weaknesses in automated assessment programs in fields such as medicine and business.

More recently, Flens (2005) maintained that there were additional reasons for caution about the use of computerized test interpretations, especially from an ethical standpoint. He described that a letter of inquiry had been sent to the APA Ethics Committee about possible reliance on such computerized interpretations. The Ethics Committee response, in brief, was that practitioners should be very cautious about their use, especially because of the routine absence of specific information about how such test interpretations were generated.

In closing this chapter, it should also be noted that the use of the PAI in child custody evaluation would be significantly aided if there were external validity data specifically regarding custody litigation parents. In fact, such external validity data would be helpful for all psychological tests regularly used in custody evaluations.

Chapter 9

THE PARENT-CHILD RELATIONSHIP INVENTORY (PCRI): EXPANDED RESEARCH

PRACTICE CHECKLIST

_____In the custody evaluation sample, parents generally had scores that were better than the standardization sample.

_____The PCRI identified only 3% of parents as having responded defensively, a small fraction of what had been found on the MMPI-2 and PAI.

_____The PCRI defensiveness scale (SOC) appears ineffective with custody evaluation parents.

_____The PCRI shows good gender fairness.

_____The MMPI-2 scales L and K and the PAI scale PIM may be useful in shedding light on the level of PCRI defensiveness, especially if administered during the same session.

_____There is more consistent evidence of PCRI external validity regarding mothers than fathers.

_____The AUT scale may need to be disregarded because of weak psychometric data.

_____Always compare and integrate psychological test results with other evaluative information.

Note: This form is a guide to promote productive reasoning and good practice. It is not comprehensive or all-inclusive and does not replace adequate training and experience.

Because child custody evaluation has a primary goal of clarifying what is in children's best interests, there is a great deal of focus on interactions between children and parents. Psychological testing is frequently used to try to shed light on parent-child interactions from an objective standpoint.

It is highly relevant for custody evaluators that many state statutes make reference to the relationships between children and parents in child custody determinations. For example, the UMDA (NCCUSL, 1979) indicates that the relationship between the child and each parent is a factor to be considered in custody determination, and the Specialty Guidelines for Forensic Psychology (APA, 2013), state that forensic examiners need to include a focus on legally relevant factors in their assessments. Also, gender fairness is especially important in custody evaluations because they characteristically compare the parenting of mothers and fathers. See the prior chapter for more detailed descriptions of relevant standards and guidelines, as well as information about gender fairness in psychological testing.

The Parent-Child Relationship Inventory (PCRI) is a parental self-report measure that covers a number of important aspects of parenting. Heinze and Grisso (1996) recommended the PCRI as a useful instrument in child custody evaluation. Recent survey research (Ackerman & Pritzl, 2011) that asked evaluators about test usage reported that the PCRI is the third most used parenting measure in custody evaluation.

It is noteworthy that the two measures rated as used more in that survey have had limitations for custody evaluation use. The Parenting Stress Index (PSI), prior to its recent revision (Abidin, 2012) relied on a standardization sample that included 13 times as many women than men. Although the new, fourth edition of the PSI was greatly improved by having approximately equal numbers of women and men in its normative sample, it remains the case that the vast majority of published research using the measure relied on former norms and administered it primarily to females. A table in a recent book chapter (Abidin, Austin, & Flens, 2013) described preliminary norms for child custody cases, but it did not include gender comparisons and relied on scores from the older edition of the PSI. All these factors led to interpretation difficulties when comparing scores of mothers and fathers. The Child Abuse Potential Inventory (Milner, 1986) was designed only to measure moderate or greater levels of child physical abuse and its best general use is in settings in which the base rate for such abuse is approximately 50%, which is quite different from what is found in custody evaluation cases.

There are six PCRI content scales and one validity scale included in this investigation. Higher scores on the content scales represent more positive functioning. The Parental Support scale (SUP) pertains to the degree of emotional and social support received by a parent. The Satisfaction With Parenting scale (SAT) assesses the degree of enjoyment and fulfillment associated with being a parent. The Involvement scale (INV) represents the level of a parent's interaction with and knowledge of the child. The Communication scale (COM) assesses parental perceptions of communication quality with the child. The Limit Setting scale (LIM) focuses on the parent's experience in carrying out limit setting. The Autonomy scale (AUT) represents parental ability to promote child independence. On the validity scale, Social Desirability (SOC), lower scores indicate greater defensiveness by portraying the parent-child relationship in a socially desirable light. SOC is particularly important because custody evaluation parents are often expected to present themselves in an unrealistically positive light. As noted elsewhere in this book, custody evaluation parents have been found to manifest moderately elevated defensiveness on the PAI and MMPI-2.

It is important to emphasize that the PCRI and other parenting inventories do not claim to assess parenting in its entirety, as can be seen in each of the manuals of the measures described here. In fact, a good argument has been made that a complete model of parenting competency does not even exist (Azar et al., 1998).

The PCRI manual (Gerard, 1994) showed evidence of adequate test reliability and validity with three different samples. A number of authorities (Marchant & Paulson, 1998; Otto & Edens, 2003) described that the PCRI would benefit from more extensive reliability and validity data beyond what was contained in the manual. More recently, Coffman et al. (2006) described evidence of generally very good PCRI reliability; also, there was good validity with parents of adolescents, though validity was more consistently positive in mother-adolescent than father-adolescent relationships. In other research, the PCRI has been used in areas such as adolescent behavior problems (Oliver, Guerin, & Coffman, 2009) and autism (Osborne & Reed, 2010).

A recent study used the PCRI in a simulated child custody experiment (Tobin, Seals, & Vincent, 2011). Parents were instructed to respond either as if they were participating anonymously in a research project, or as though they were involved in a child custody evaluation. Results showed better content scale scores and more defensiveness under the custody evaluation instructions.

THE RESEARCH PROJECT

A main objective of this study was to provide expanded PCRI data for evaluators, as only one published study (Hynan, 2013a) has used it with actual custody litigants. The availability of relevant reference data is especially useful when there are characteristics of individuals being tested that include a reasonable expectation of response patterns different from the standardization sample.

Archival data from the author's practice in suburban Chicago served as the database. As described in a seminal article by Stricker and Trierweiler (1995), practitioners potentially make substantial contributions to a field of knowledge when they act as local clinical scientists and collect valuable research information, which potentially can be replicated by others, just as academic scholars in one location collect data potentially to be supported or refuted by researchers in different laboratories. As repeatedly emphasized in this book, the custody evaluation field will have a more sound scientific foundation as more relevant empirical data are collected and disseminated.

All 214 participants were legal parents. The number of participants was far above the requirement for a conventional power level of .80 (Cohen, 1992), as described in more detail in the prior chapter.

Parental demographic data were based on information completed on the PCRI answer sheet. Mothers averaged 37 years of age $(SD = 6.16)$ and fathers 40 $(SD = 7.66)$. Mothers had a mean of 14 years of education $(SD = 2.60)$ and fathers 15 $(SD = 2.52)$. There was a mean of 1.72 children per family $(SD = .74)$. The vast majority of participants were Caucasian.

All tests were completed as aspects of evaluations ordered by court. Twelve tests were completed in accordance with a local court rule for a condensed evaluation, and the rest were completed according to standard orders without any such limitation. All tests from 2000 through 2009 were used. Almost all tests had no unanswered items. None of the tests had more than seven items unanswered or that included more than one response. Gerard (1994) indicated that tests with eight or more unanswered or multiple-response items should not be interpreted. Also, all tests had adequate response consistency, as evidenced by all having a maximum Inconsistency score of 1. The author administered all tests in paper form in the office setting. All were computer scored by Western Psychological Services.

Prior research (Hynan, 2013a) drew on the same custody evaluation archive as employed here and found that most content scales had scores one-half to one standard deviation better than the standardization sample means. However, SOC, the validity scale, identified only 3% of parents as responding defensively. That study reported that overall scores on the PCRI manifested no differences between mothers and fathers and thus appeared to show good gender fairness.

The current research expanded upon the prior custody evaluation PCRI study. First, it more closely examined findings on defensiveness. Second, it investigated PCRI score differences between predecree and postdecree parents, including how that categorization interacted with gender. Third, the current study carried out exploratory analyses regarding how the presence or absence of substance abuse, domestic violence, or child abuse influenced PCRI scores.

DEFENSIVENESS

The PCRI SOC scale that measures defensiveness through presenting oneself in a socially desirable manner can range from a score of 5 through 20. A SOC score of 9 or less is defined as representing excessive defensiveness, and such scores mean that the results of content scales should generally be regarded as invalid (Gerard, 1994). As noted above, only 3% of this custody evaluation sample responded in such a manner. More than 88% of respondents had SOC scores of 10 through 16. Therefore, there was a very limited range of scores, and when compared to defensiveness scales on other psychological tests, SOC manifested significant limits in performance (Hynan, 2013a).

When correlations between SOC and other defensiveness scales are examined, two are small but statistically significant and one is not significant. The correlations are negative because lower SOC scores are representative of greater defensiveness, whereas higher scores on the other relevant scales show heightened defensiveness. Specifically, in the test archive that provided the data analyzed in this book, there were statistically significant correlations between SOC and the PAI PIM scale (n=202) (r = -.28, p <.001), and between SOC and the MMPI-2 L scale (n=133) (r = -.29, p = .001), but the correlation between SOC and the MMPI-2 K scale was not significant (r = -.11).

For evaluators, these correlations are less likely to be practically meaningful than comparisons between the proportions of respondents who were categorized as answering questions in an excessively defensive manner. That is, in the current custody evaluation psychological testing archive, the main MMPI-2 and PAI scales of defensiveness showed elevations at rates that were 7 to 14 times higher than the SOC scale.

The proportion of parents identified as defensive on the PCRI in the current study is essentially identical to that found in the custody evaluation simulation by Tobin et al., (2011). Apparently from a research standpoint, those authors concluded that SOC was effective in detecting effort to present in a socially desirable manner. However, from the perspective of a practicing evaluator, the differences in mean SOC scores were practically nonexistent between subjects instructed to answer questions like research participants as compared to those instructed to respond as if they were custody evaluations, as can be seen in Table 2 of that study (p. 292).

Therefore, the most reasonable conclusion is that the SOC scale is ineffective in identifying custody evaluation parents who have answered questions in a defensive or socially desirable manner. Because it is likely that, in custody evaluations, the PCRI would be administered together with the MMPI-2 and/or PAI, it would be more reasonable to rely on the appropriate scale or scales of one of those other measures to give an indication of defensiveness on PCRI content scales, especially if they were administered during the same appointment (Hynan, 2013a). An alternate hypothesis is that custody evaluation litigants are likely to respond defensively much more frequently on measures of personality and psychological dysfunction as opposed to one that focuses on parenting. However, given that, on the whole, child custody evaluations are primarily focused on what is best for children, such an alternate hypothesis appears implausible.

PREDECREE VERSUS POSTDECREE LITIGANTS

Parental experiences prior to a legal decree having been entered appear quite different in many ways from experiences after a decree has been in effect. It might be expected that such different experiences would lead to different response patterns on parenting measures such as the PCRI. Because these statistical analyses investigated group differences, predictions need to rely on anecdotal generalities about family composition and interaction before and after the decree, and need to overlook numerous diverse experiences within the predecree and postdecree groups.

For example, in the postdecree group, almost all families would be living in separate households, with each parent having a somewhat lesser amount of contact with the children. Consequently, it was predicted that postdecree parents would have lower scores on INV and COM than predecree parents. However, because in most intact families mothers have had more direct contact with the children than fathers, it was also predicted that there would be an interaction effect such that the lower postdecree scores on the INV and COM scales would be more pronounced for mothers than for fathers.

In predecree households, especially when parents might still be residing together, parents frequently convey an impression that the other parent does little to nothing to actively support their parenting (and some complain that the other parent interferes with it). Because such frustrating circumstances tend not to be present in postdecree households, it was predicted that the postdecree group would show higher scores on SUP.

Also, in a number of families, fathers act as the more vigorous limit setters, especially about relatively major behavioral concerns (even though the frequency of limit setting overall is sometimes higher by mothers). Because many mothers experience an increased requirement to carry out limit setting directly after the parents have split up, it was predicted that mothers in the postdecree group would manifest higher scores on LIM than predecree mothers.

In the statistical analyses, timing was used to describe the predecree versus postdecree categorization. Timing category data were missing for four parents.

A multivariate analysis of variance was carried out with timing and gender as between-subjects factors, and the six PCRI content scales as the multiple dependent measures. Results showed significant interaction effects of timing by scale, multivariate $F(5, 202) = 4.02$, $p = .002$; and timing by gender by scale, multivariate F $(5, 202) = 2.66$, p $= .025$. Descriptive statistics (T-score means) are displayed in Table 2.

Table 2
MEAN PCRI CONTENT SCALE SCORES BY TIMING AND GENDER

| | Predecree | | Postdecree | |
Scale	Mothers	Fathers	Mothers	Fathers
SUP	55.08	55.14	57.00	60.31
SAT	60.64	61.65	59.03	60.72
INV	57.34	58.42	57.87	57.25
COM	53.45	55.42	52.90	52.63
LIM	59.04	60.55	63.17	60.17
AUT	52.07	53.49	51.37	49.59

Note: SUP = Support; SAT= Satisfaction; INV = Involvement; COM = Communication; LIM = Limit Setting; AUT = Autonomy.

The significant multivariate effect for timing was examined by means of an ANOVA carried out for each of the scales. The postdecree group had higher scores ($M = 58.71$) than the predecree group ($M = 55.11$) on SUP, $F(1, 208) = 6.71$, $p = .01$, and this difference had a small effect size of .38 (Cohen, 1992). No other scale showed a statistically significant difference. However, on AUT, there was a marginally significant difference such that the predecree group ($M = 52.78$) manifested higher scores than the postdecree parents ($M = 50.45$), $F(1, 208) = 3.03$, $p = .083$, with a small effect size of .26.

In examining the timing by gender interaction (see *Ms* in Table 2), it is useful to first look at the differences between mothers and fathers at the predecree stage, and then compare those differences to postdecree scores. A pattern emerges that fathers had higher predecree means than mothers on each of the six content scales, though effect sizes reached a small level only for INV ($d = .22$) and COM ($d = .27$). At the postdecree stage, fathers showed higher scores than mothers only on SUP ($d = .38$) and SAT ($d = .23$), and they manifested lower scores than mothers on LIM ($d = .40$).

In addition, it is useful to examine the timing by gender interaction by comparing the predecree and postdecree scores of mothers, and to also do so for fathers. On the SUP scale, there was a higher postdecree than predecree mean for mothers with a small effect size (.21) and a higher postdecree than predecree mean for fathers with a medium effect size (.53). On SAT, mothers showed a lower postdecree than predecree mean ($d = .24$), and there was no difference for fathers predecree versus postdecree. There was no predecree versus postdecree difference for either mothers or fathers on INV, and fathers only manifested a lower postdecree mean on COM ($d = .29$). On LIM, only mothers manifested a difference, which involved a higher postdecree mean, with an effect size that was at the upper end of the small range ($d = .49$). On AUT, only fathers manifested a difference, which involved a lower postdecree score ($d = .42$).

It is noteworthy that test score differences are generally considered clinically significant if they meet or exceed the standard error of measurement (SEM), which ranges from 3 to 5 for the PCRI content scales (Gerard, 1994, p. 23). The higher postdecree versus predecree SUP mean for fathers and the higher postdecree versus predecree LIM score for mothers met this criterion.

Overall, the predictions were partially supported by the results. As predicted, there was a significant effect for SUP such that parents experienced more support postdecree than predecree. It was interesting that this effect was more pronounced for fathers than mothers. Also consistent with predictions, mothers reported stronger limit setting postdecree as compared to predecree. However, contrary to expectations, parents generally did not have lower INV and COM scores postdecree as compared to predecree.

Aside from the predictions, the medium effect size difference for fathers having experienced more support as a parent in the postdecree versus predecree phase is quite noteworthy, and suggested that fathers may generally feel better in the parental role after the separation or divorce has been finalized. The medium effect size difference for mothers having reported higher levels of limit setting postdecree than predecree indicates that women may generally increase their limit setting activity in the postdecree phase. It is interesting that parental ratings of promoting autonomy decreased in the postdecree phase, which may represent increased concern that the children may have more than optimal autonomy associated with spending time with the other parent.

CONTENTIOUS PARENTAL ALLEGATIONS

As indicated previously, a significant proportion of child custody evaluations include allegations of substance abuse, domestic violence, and/or child abuse. The current statistical analyses look at whether the possible presence of such features has an influence on PCRI scores. The categorization of each participant in terms of whether or not substance misuse, domestic violence, and/or child abuse was an area of concern took place in exactly the same manner as was described in Chapter 8. Also, it is similarly important to keep in mind that the PCRI was not designed to try to identify the presence of any of these behavioral features. These analyses were exploratory in nature, and therefore no specific predictions were made.

In this sample of custody evaluation parents, there were 83 (39%) with and 131 without allegations or evidence about substance abuse. Using the statistical contrasts described below regarding the other allegation categories, no significant differences were found between parents with and without substance abuse concerns. The current study is the only known one that pertains to substance abuse and the PCRI. For general coverage about substance misuse in the child custody evaluation context, see Chapter 12 in this book and the article by Schleuderer and Campagna (2004).

Domestic Violence

Of the parents who completed the PCRI, there were allegations or evidence of domestic violence for about half. Specifically, allegations/evidence of domestic violence were present for 108 (labeled as yes) and not present for 106 (labeled as no).

There were consistent findings that parents in the no group had higher PCRI scores than those in the yes group. Specifically, the no group had higher mean scores on SUP, $t(212) = 2.43$, $p = .016$; SAT, $t(212) = 2.18$, $p = .030$; INV, $t(212) = 2.13$, $p = .035$; COM, $t(212) = 2.27$, $p = .028$; and AUT, $t(212) = 3.40$, $p = .001$. There was no significant difference on LIM. On all six scales, the means for both the yes and no groups were at or above the 50 T average. For the statistically significant scales, effect sizes were all small.

Such a consistent pattern of findings indicates that the absence of allegations or evidence about domestic violence is associated with responses indicative of better parenting. However, given that the yes group had at least average mean scores, it is noteworthy that the presence of domestic violence concerns did not lead to below-average scores, but simply less high ones.

There are no known studies other than the present one regarding domestic violence and PCRI scores. For further coverage about domestic violence and child custody matters generally, see Chapter 12 in this book.

Child Abuse

There were 70 (33%) of 214 individuals who completed the PCRI who were classified as being involved in cases in which there were allegations or evidence of child abuse. For purposes of describing the statistical findings, the yes and no labels were employed again.

Interestingly, the same pattern of results occurred as described above regarding parents in cases in which there was concern about domestic violence. Specifically, the no group obtained higher PCRI than the yes group scores on SUP, $t(212) = 2.27$, $p = .024$; SAT, $t(212) = 3.32$, $p = .001$; INV, $t(212) = 3.48$, $p = .001$; COM, $t(212) = 3.73$, $p < .001$; and AUT, $t(212) = 2.47$, $p = .014$. There was no significant difference on LIM. Again, the main scale scores for both groups were at or above 50 T. On the statistically significant scales, effect sizes were small, except for COM, which had a medium effect size. Based on the SEMs reported in the PCRI manual (Gerard, 1994), the mean differences for INV and COM were clinically significant.

This consistent pattern of scores indicates that parents, in cases in which there was no concern about child abuse, reported higher levels of parenting than those parents for whom there were allegations or evidence of child abuse. Again, however, because mean scores even for the yes group were at or above average, the presence of child abuse concerns did not lead to below-average scores, but simply less high ones.

Gerard (1994, pp. 34–36) reported correlations in the expected directions between a number of PCRI content scales and reports of disciplinary measures consistent with abusiveness, such as hitting, spanking, and threats; also, there were expected correlations with nonabusive parenting behaviors such as praise and reasoning. In a separate high-risk sample of adolescent mothers, PCRI mean scores were consistently below average on content scales. For further information about child abuse within the custody evaluation context, see Chapter 12.

IMPLICATIONS

As explained elsewhere, (Hynan, 2013a), findings on the SOC scale lead to a conclusion that, within the context of child custody evaluation, it should not be relied upon as a measure of social desirability or other defensiveness. If possible, evaluators could administer another measure such as the PAI or MMPI-2, preferably during the same appointment as the PCRI, and use the relevant scale(s) to gauge PCRI defensiveness.

It is noteworthy that SOC had a statistically significant correlation with the MMPI-2 L scale but not the K scale. Because L is believed to more represent a tendency to purposefully present oneself in an unrealistically positive manner, and K is perceived as representing a relatively greater degree of limited insight about oneself, such a pattern of correlations suggests that SOC may reflect relatively intentional efforts at impression management.

The lower predecree than postdecree scores on SUP suggest that an important part of predecree life problems is the limited support parents feel they experience. It is likely that at least a good portion of this experience is due to parents feeling that the other parent gives them too little support in their interactions with the children. Predecree parents experience significantly higher stress (as seen in the STR scale of the PAI, see Chapter 8), and it is likely that these phenomena are associated with one another. That is, it is likely that at least an important aspect of the stress experienced by parents in the predecree phase is associated with the relatively low level of support they experience in parenting.

The interaction effect of parent gender and timing on PCRI scores is particularly interesting in terms of understanding parental experiences at different phases of the family dissolution process. It is also interesting in light of the fact that PCRI final T scores were created to be predominantly gender neutral.

It is clear that neither gender has superiority in parenting competency (Downey, Ainsworth-Darnell, & Dufur, 1998). However, it is important, especially for evaluators, that research has found a number of different patterns in mother-child versus father-child interactions. Attachment that occurs with mothers of young children tends to involve comfort and soothing, whereas the type that takes place with fathers tends to be more adventurous and engaging of the external world. For children from elementary school years through adolescence, interactions with mothers tend to be both more positively and negatively emotionally charged than with fathers. Adolescents tend to be more comfortable discussing emotional material with mothers and more tend to look to fathers to obtain factual or practical information (Bornstein, 2002; Laursen, 1995; Pruett & Pruett, 2009; Steinberg & Silk, 2002).

The PCRI manual (Gerard, 1994) described a study that showed a pattern of gender score differences consistent to some extent with these differences described here. That research used a linear T-score transformation that was *not* the same as the T-score transformation used in constructing the final PCRI norms. The results showed a number of statistically significant gender differences, but the sizes of the differences were small and considered not clinically significant. Specifically, mothers had higher scores than fathers on INV and COM, and fathers had higher scores than mothers on SUP and LIM.

Returning to the findings of the custody evaluation sample, in retrospect, the pattern of higher PCRI scores for parents not involved in cases with concern about domestic violence or child abuse is understandable and it is important that this measure reflects such differences. At the same time, it is crucial that evaluators not rely primarily on the PCRI or the other tests described in this book to try to identify behaviors such as domestic violence and/or child abuse. As noted above, this research is exploratory only.

In general, it is crucial for evaluators to be cognizant about both the strengths and other limitations of the PCRI. Although it covers important and relevant content areas and now has comparison data specific to custody evaluation, it does not cover all relevant aspects of parenting and would benefit from more extensive reliability and validity data. External validity indicators are more consistently present for mothers than fathers, and the AUT scale shows such notable limitations in this regard that it perhaps should not be relied upon (Coffman et al., 2006). There are inevitable limits in the type and extent of information that can be extracted especially from brief parental self-report instruments (Grisso, 2003).

Of course, it is absolutely necessary to combine the results of any psychological test with other sources of relevant information. For example, it is crucial to carry out direct parent-child observations, obtain information from knowledgeable collaterals, and interview children about their perspectives regarding interactions with parents (e.g., Austin, 2002; Hynan, 1998, 2003).

The primary limitations of the current study, and the factors mitigating those limitations, are described in the prior chapter on the PAI. Despite the limitations of the current study, the custody evaluation field is likely to benefit from having a good-size reference sample for this test. Custody evaluations obviously focus on parent-child interactions and benefit from the appropriate use of empirical foundations.

Especially if custody evaluators keep firmly in mind both the strengths and limitations of the PCRI, these data can assist the field by potentially reducing reliance on questionable methods. In the past, the custody evaluation field has been criticized for excessive reliance on unscientific methods and evaluator personal values and biases (e.g., Emery et al., 2005; Erickson et al., 2007).

The practicing custody evaluator needs to keep a number of crucial matters in mind when carrying out testing with the PCRI or any other instrument. As described in more detail in the previous chapter on the PAI, such considerations include sufficient monitoring of individuals who are completing tests, the provision of reasonable comfort for test takers, and the exercise of considerable caution about the use of computerized test interpretation. It is also relevant that no psychological test has reliability and/or validity data specifically drawn from child custody litigants.

The following reality is crucially important for custody evaluators, and it bears repeating. No aspect of evaluative information should be relied upon in isolation. It is necessary to look for convergent information about the best interest of children when reviewing all sources of data.

Chapter 10

THE MMPI-2: NEW RESEARCH

PRACTICE CHECKLIST

There are a number of consistent findings from MMPI-2 empirical studies of child custody litigants, including:

____Moderate mean elevations on scales *L* and *K*.

____Proportions of elevations on *L* range from 20 to 36%.

____Proportions of elevations on *K* range from 21 to 42%.

____Mean scores on main clinical scales are in the normal range.

____Mean clinical scale elevations are in the normal range even when only those parents who have not responded defensively are considered.

____Highest mean clinical scale scores and proportions of elevations are on *Hy*, *Pd*, and *Pa*.

____There are no clinically significant gender differences on main scales.

____A high score on *L* or *K* does not necessarily mean that the respondent is hiding psychopathology.

____Always look for the presence or absence of convergence between test results andother evaluative information.

Note: This form is a guide to promote productive reasoning and good practice. It is not comprehensive or all-inclusive and does not replace adequate training and experience.

As described in prior chapters, because research indicates that parental psychological dysfunction can have a negative impact on children of divorce (e.g., Langford, 2009) it is important to assess parental functioning in part through psychological testing. The MMPI-2 is by far the most frequently used test in custody evaluation (e.g., Ackerman & Pritzl, 2011; Quinnell & Bow, 2001), and there is evidence that it is the only one that is used in the majority of evaluations (Hagen & Castagna, 2001). Experienced and aspiring custody evaluation practitioners are likely to be familiar with the MMPI-2, though individuals who would like much more detailed information may wish to refer to the manual (Butcher et al., 2001) and/or interpretive guides (e.g., Butcher et al., 2006; Graham, 2011; Greene, 2010; Pope et al., 2006).

The MMPI-2 is the only psychological test that previously had been used in multiple independent research studies with custody evaluation samples. There was even a relatively small study that used the original MMPI, which generally is no longer used in practice, with custody evaluation parents (Ollendick & Otto, 1984).

A primary reason that the current MMPI-2 analysis is important to the field is that the greater the comprehensiveness of available MMPI-2 data specific to the custody evaluation context, the greater confidence evaluators (and other consumers of such information) can have that such reference data are applicable for their cases. In other words, there is more reason for confidence in the applicability of such scores with greater numbers of samples and total subjects (AERA, 1999). Such confidence is especially warranted when there are commonalities in the data from entirely different sources, such as different researchers using information from different geographic localities, and across distinct time periods. An additional reason that the current MMPI-2 data and analyses are important is that they more closely examine vital gender comparisons that are highly relevant to concerns about fairness between women and men. Furthermore, this research extends analyses to examine important differences between types of custody evaluation (especially contrasts that involve a hybrid mediation-evaluation model) and predecree versus postdecree cases.

Experienced evaluators and those in the legal profession are highly aware that, in disputed custody cases, allegations regularly arise about highly challenging matters such as substance abuse, domestic violence, and/or child abuse. The current MMPI-2 research includes initial investigations about how those challenging factors may influence parental MMPI-2 scores.

A brief review of prior MMPI-2 research in child custody evaluation is warranted. The first published study to report on MMPI-2 scores of custody evaluation parents was carried out by Siegel (1996). It included a relatively small sample of 80 parents, and focused only on the traditional validity scales L, F, and K. Siegel contrasted scores from his sample with a Caucasian normative group from the MMPI-2 standardization sample (Butcher et al., 1989). He reported that his custody evaluation sample had higher mean scores than the standardization sample on L and K, and men only had lower scores on F. Focusing on the same three validity scales, Siegel and Langford (1998), in a small study, found that mothers who appeared to have manifested parental alienation syndrome showed slightly higher defensiveness than mothers who had not done so; the difference was statistically but not clinically significant.

In what previously had been the largest single MMPI-2 custody evaluation study, Bathurst et al. (1997) reported on the results of 508 parents, included all main scales, and examined both gender differences and whether or not subjects were classified as having responded defensively. Bagby et al. (1999) had a primary focus on defensive responding, and included data on all main scales (plus some nontraditional validity scales) as well as gender comparisons.

A number of other researchers have looked primarily at defensive responding by custody evaluation parents. For example, a group of academics and practitioners collaborated to investigate whether MMPI-2 validity scale items could be accurately classified as primarily measuring either a conscious effort to present oneself in an unrealistically positive light versus a more unintentional self-deception that was defensive in nature (Strong, Greene, Hoppe, Johnston, & Olesen, 1999). Posthuma and Harper (1998) compared MMPI-2 validity scale scores of custody litigation parents with personal injury litigants.

Ezzo, Pinsoneault, and Evans (2007) compared MMPI-2 scores of parents litigating possible termination of parental rights with child custody litigants. The child custody evaluation participants were divided into groups of either married or unmarried parents.

Pope, Butcher and Seelen (2000) briefly referred to MMPI-2 data previously collected by Butcher from numerous custody evaluators (including Bathurst et al. (1997)) in disparate geographical locations. The Pope et al. summary focused on mean scores for scales L and K, and clinical scales with the most frequent elevations. However, a conventionally detailed data description and analysis appears not to have been published in any generally available journal or book.

Recently, MMPI-2 research on high-conflict custody litigation cases was carried out by Siegel, Bow, and Gottlieb (2012). They operationally defined high-conflict cases as those that included protective orders; protracted litigation; and/or specific allegations of domestic violence, mental illness, child abuse, or substance abuse. In general, they reported higher scores on a number of validity and clinical scales in their sample as compared to a number of the prior custody evaluation studies and the standardization sample.

THE RESEARCH PROJECT

Archival information from my practice in suburban Chicago served as the database. There was a total of 557 parents, with near equal numbers of mothers (n = 277) and fathers ($n = 280$).Therefore, it is the largest single MMPI-2 study to date with child custody litigants. All participants were legal parents. The parental demographic data that were available were based mainly on information completed on the MMPI-2 answer sheet. Mothers averaged 37 years of age ($SD = 6.48$) and fathers 39 ($SD = 6.83$). Mothers had a mean of

14 years of education ($n = 170$, $SD = 2.41$) and fathers 15 ($n = 173$, $SD = 3.02$). There was a mean of 1.75 children per family ($SD = .79$). The vast majority of participants were Caucasian.

All usable MMPI-2 protocols from court-ordered evaluations in 1993 through 2009 were included in the study. There were 11 tests with *Cannot Say* scores over 10, or *TRIN* or *VRIN* T-scores of 80 or greater (Graham, 2006) that are not included here. The author administered all tests in booklet form in the office setting. All were computer scored by Pearson, except for 63 that were hand scored. All hand scoring went through multiple accuracy checks by two individuals.

There were three types of custody evaluations. Conciliation was a hybrid of mediation and evaluation that was used until 1998. Condensed evaluations had a general limit of 15 hours of office time. Standard evaluations did not have hybrid or condensed formats. They are described in more detail in the relevant section below.

There were a number of goals of this MMPI-2 research project. The most general objective was to obtain descriptive data relevant for custody evaluation practitioners, in order to augment results of prior research and thereby provide a more comprehensive and updated knowledge base. The only previous MMPI-2 custody evaluation research that included useful gender comparisons for practitioners on all main scales was carried out by Bathurst et al. (1997), Bagby et al. (1999), and Siegel et al. (2012). The first study involved clients from a practice in Southern California, the second used clients from the Toronto area, and in the third, clients were from Texas and Michigan. Obviously, two of those prior excellent studies were published quite a number of years before the research program being described here, though it needs to be acknowledged that the earliest test protocols completed in the current study were done before the Bathurst and Bagby project were published. The Ezzo et al. (2007) gender comparisons combined cases undergoing custody evaluations with others going through termination of parental rights litigation, so those contrasts are not directly useful for custody evaluation practitioners.

Relevant descriptive data can be seen in Table 3. The validity scales that measure defensiveness, *L* and *K*, are elevated slightly more than one standard deviation above the MMPI-2 standardization sample (Butcher et al., 2001) mean. The clinical scales all have mean scores within the normal range.

In general, MMPI-2 scores are considered elevated if they have T-scores of 65 or higher. For the clinical scales (not including *Mf* and *Si*), elevations at that level are sometimes referred to as being in the clinical range. On *L*, 36% of respondents had elevated scores, and on *K*, 42% had elevations. These percentages are somewhat higher than what had been reported in prior research. In the Bathurst et al. (1997) sample, 20% and 21% of respondents had elevations on *L* and *K*, respectively.

Table 3
DESCRIPTIVE STATISTICS (T-SCORES) BY GENDER

Scale	Total		Mothers		Fathers	
	M	SD	M	SD	M	SD
L	60.88	11.78	62.06	12.25	59.71	11.21
F	45.63	6.52	46.16	6.46	45.12	6.54
K	62.14	8.63	62.86	9.14	61.43	8.03
Hs	50.49	7.00	49.81	7.19	51.16	6.75
D	47.31	7.11	46.94	6.90	47.68	7.31
Hy	54.03	7.61	53.37	7.86	54.67	7.31
Pd	55.14	7.97	55.45	8.05	54.82	7.88
Mf	49.86	8.49	53.46	7.56	46.29	7.84
Pa	52.07	8.76	51.53	8.53	52.60	8.99
Pt	48.49	6.59	48.01	6.53	48.95	6.63
Sc	48.91	6.64	49.73	6.63	48.10	6.56
Ma	48.39	7.71	48.46	7.90	48.33	7.54
Si	42.29	7.08	42.15	6.85	42.43	7.31

Note: L = Lie; F = Infrequency; K = Correction; Hs = Hypochondriasis; D = Depression; Hy = Hysteria; Pd = Psychopathic Deviate; Mf = Masculinity-Femininity; Pa = Paranoia; Pt = Psychasthenia; Sc = Schizophrenia; Ma = Hypomania; Si = Social Introversion.

In the current sample, there were 127 parents (23%) who had clinical scale elevations. Consistent with the pattern of mean scores, respondents had the highest proportions of scores in the clinical range on scales Pd (11%), Hy (8%), and Pa (6%). On all the other clinical scales, the proportions of significant elevations were 5% or less. In general, past research has also found those three clinical scales to have had the highest mean scores and proportions of elevated scores (Bagby et al., 1999; Bathurst et al., 1997; Siegel et al., 2012).

Code types are frequently used in interpretation. Because inferences about symptoms should be avoided unless the T scores within the code types use a cutoff of 65 (Graham, 2011), such a categorization is used here, and only 43 profiles met this criterion. The most frequent code type was 34/43 (11 profiles), and there were a total of 22 with one of the following: 36/63, 46/64, 49/94, or 13/31.

GENDER

As previously emphasized, it is extremely important for there to be gender fairness in all custody evaluation procedures and conceptualizations. Psychological testing with custody litigants has found different patterns of results depending upon the test. Although research (Hynan, 2004) had found inadvertent bias against women in the prior scoring system of the MCMI-III, and a number of modest gender differences on the PAI (Hynan, 2013b), previous MMPI-2 research (Bagby et al., 2009; Bathurst et al., 1997; Siegel et al., 2012) found very little difference between the scores of mothers and fathers. At the same time, in those studies, a number of small gender differences could be seen in an inspection of mean scores. In addition, Bathurst et al. (1997) reported a statistically significant difference for gender when a multivariate analysis of variance was conducted.

In that study, follow-up univariate analyses identified statistically significant gender differences on scales F and D. Although the article's narrative described that men scored slightly lower than women on those two scales (p. 208), the relevant table of descriptive statistics (p. 207) showed that men actually had a slightly higher mean score than women on scale D. The small sizes of the differences led the authors to conclude that they were not clinically significant.

An additional and relevant complication is that a lack of mean score differences between genders or ethnic groups does not necessarily mean a lack of test bias. For example, Butcher et al. (1995) stated that an absence of test bias between groups would be demonstrated by the test having equal predictive validity for both groups with respect to appropriate criterion measures.

The gender comparisons included all 557 legal parents. Consistent with the findings of prior research, it was predicted that gender differences in the current study would be nonexistent or small, and not forensically meaningful.

The initial statistical analysis was a multivariate analysis of variance. In order to test for the possibility of an interaction effect (e.g., whether mothers only might manifest lower scores on conciliation), the multivariate analysis included both gender and type of evaluation as between-subjects factors. The 13 MMPI-2 scales were the multiple dependent measures. Results showed significant interactions of gender by scale, Wilks' Lambda = 12.68, $F(12, 531)$, $p < .001$; and type by scale, Wilks' Lambda = 1.59, $F(24, 1062)$, $p = .035$; but the interaction of gender by type by scale was not significant, Wilks' Lambda = .72, $F(24, 1062)$.

Gender differences were examined through a univariate analysis of variance carried out for each scale. See Table 3 for means and standard deviations. Women had higher scores on L $(F(1, 555) = 5.58$, $p = 0.19)$; Mf $(F(1, 555) = 120.87$, $p < .001)$; and Sc $(F(1, 555) = 8.54$, $p = .004)$. Men had higher scores on Hy (F(1, 555) = 5.21, p = .023); and Hs (F(1, 555) = 4.09, p = .044). All other gender comparisons were not significant.

As described earlier, there can be statistically significant differences that are small in magnitude and not clinically meaningful, especially when the sample sizes are quite large (Butcher et al., 1995). Consequently, the statistically significant gender differences here were examined for effect sizes using the Cohen (1992) d statistic. Effect sizes below .2 are considered trivial, those between .2 and .49 small, those between .5 and .79 medium, and those above .8 are categorized as large.

On the clinical scale that had a statistically significant higher mean for women, Sc, the effect size was small at .25. On the clinical scales that had statistically significant higher scores for men, Hs and Hy, the effect sizes of .19 and .17, respectively, were at a trivial level.

Scale Mf represents gender-relevant attitudes of the test taker and not psychological symptoms. The gender means in Table 3 show a slightly above-average score for women, which represents a very mild tendency toward relatively masculine attitudes, and a slightly below-average score for men, which also represents a very mild tendency toward comparatively masculine attitudes. Therefore, the large effect size of .93 manifests a modest tendency by both mothers and fathers to endorse relatively masculine attitudes.

The gender differences found in the current study mostly occurred on scales different from the Bathurst et al. (1997) statistical analysis. Bagby et al. (1999) and Siegel et al. (2012) did not include statistical analyses of gender differences. However, an examination of relevant descriptive statistics of those two studies found a number of interesting similarities with the current research. In all four studies, mean F scores were higher for women (in the current study the difference was marginally significant, p = .06, and the effect size was .20), with effect sizes of .43 for Bagby et al., .37 for Bathurst et al, and .51 for Siegel et al. Also, the means for Sc were higher for women in all studies, with effect sizes of .21 for Bagby et al., .17 for Bathurst et al., and .20 for Siegel et al.

Overall, the results of the current study support the hypothesis that gender differences would be small or nonexistent. At the same time, it is noteworthy that the current study and the prior ones that included relevant gender comparisons all found women to have higher scores than men on F and Sc. Although the effect sizes were all small, such consistency in results is strongly suggestive of actual population differences and not just random variance or statistical noise.

In order to understand this phenomenon, it is important to note that mean scores for both F and Sc for men and women across all four studies were almost all below average. Also, it is noteworthy that there is conceptual overlap between the scales F and Sc in that both, to some extent, represent the admission of highly unusual experiences; correlations in separate large samples between the two scales are reported as .71 (Butcher et al., 2001) and .87 (Greene, 2000). Therefore, it appears that the custody evaluation context leads parents to generally decrease the extent to which they disclose highly unusual experiences, which is understandable given the generally moderately elevated defensiveness seen in numerous studies with custody litigants on the MMPI-2 and the PAI (Hynan, 2013b).

As noted repeatedly earlier in this book, gender comparisons are crucial in child custody evaluations because of the central importance of fairness. On the surface, the fact that all gender differences (other than the unusual scale *Mf*) had small effect sizes suggests that there is no gender bias on the MMPI-2 when used in child custody evaluation. However, as noted by Butcher et al. (1995), an absence of score differences does not necessarily mean an absence of bias. Although the MMPI-2 continues to be an extremely useful measure for custody evaluation practitioners and many others, it is important to raise questions about whether patterns of MMPI-2 scores for women and men should generally manifest meaningful differences.

More specifically, epidemiological research has consistently found a number of differences between genders in terms of the prevalence of certain disorders. For example, women have been found to have significantly higher prevalence rates of depressive and anxiety disorders than men, and men have been found to have higher prevalence rates of antisocial personality and substance dependence (Eaton, Keyes, Krueger, Balsis, Skodol, et al., 2012; Grant, Hasin, Stinson, Dawson, Chou, et al., 2004; Vesga-Lopez, Schneier, Wang, Heimberg, Liu, et al., 2008; World Health Organization, 2007). Given these gender differences in prevalence base rates, it might be expected that, at least in large samples, the MMPI-2 would show higher mean scores for women on scales such as *D* and *Pt*, and higher ones for men on *Pd*. However, such differences characteristically do not occur when T-scores, the common forensic and clinical scoring application, are used, including in the standardization sample (Butcher et al., 2001).

In contrast, when MMPI-2 raw scores were used, a number of expected gender differences occurred in a sample reported by Greene (2000), such as higher mean scores for women on *D* and *Pt*. However, the T-score conversion purposefully removes such differences. Thus, while that conversion appears to lead to gender equality, it is reasonable to question whether the test would be more accurate if the actual gender differences found in prevalence research were reflected in T-score gender differences on relevant MMPI-2 scales.

Because MMPI-2 clinical scale mean scores are generally below average for custody litigants, gender differences are likely to be important only for the small proportions of parents who have relevant elevated scores. For practitioners, such concerns about gender differences may be most likely to occur on scale *Pd*, because it is elevated in 11% of the current sample, and, as noted above, is one of the three clinical scales with the highest percentages of elevations in prior custody evaluation research.

TYPE OF EVALUATION

As described earlier, the current research project includes comparisons between MMPI-2 scores of three different types of custody evaluations. No known prior research has included such an analysis.

One type of evaluation, called conciliation, was a hybrid of mediation and evaluation. It was in effect in the DuPage County, Illinois domestic relations court through 1998. Families with disputed child custody were routinely referred. Conciliation started with a mediation process. If the mediation was not successful at arriving at an agreement, the psychologist would conduct an abbreviated evaluation. Afterward, there was a return to mediation, which involved the psychologist using feedback and recommendations from the evaluation process in a final attempt to reach a mediated agreement with the parents.

Condensed evaluations had a structure that did not involve any mediation, but set a general limit of 15 hours of office time to complete the evaluation procedures, not inclusive of the report. It was used for many cases in DuPage County after the conciliation program was discontinued. If parents were in agreement to extend beyond 15 hours, and there was no objection from the judge or attorneys, the psychologist could do so. The time limit was designed to contain expenses for families.

The standard type of evaluation did not include any mediation or established time limits. Standard evaluations were carried out pursuant to court orders from various jurisdictions in the greater Chicago metropolitan area.

Over the decades that mediation regarding child custody has been in place, a number of hybrid mediation models have been reported (Lowry, 2004; Pickar & Kahn, 2011; Shienvold, 2004). Although considerable custody mediation research has been carried out (e.g., Beck, Sales, & Emery, 2004; Emery, 2012), there appears to be no research that compared different types of mediation and reported on parental experiences such as emotional distress. The only known published research that has compared different types of mediation found a more positive outcome when children were directly involved in the process (McIntosh, Wells, Smyth, & Long, 2008).

When the conciliation program was in effect, a number of the providers and others within the court system hypothesized that it was less stressful for participating parents than going through a traditional evaluation. Those individuals believed that the mediation focus on arriving at a cooperative agreement might lead participants to be more relaxed, less suspicious, and thereby more likely to reach an agreement, as compared to the experience of a more typical evaluation. More specifically, some psychologists believed that conciliation participants might have lower scores on *Pa* than parents going through other types of evaluation. Other practitioners believed there was unlikely to be any difference in MMPI-2 responses between different types of evaluation.

Therefore, these statistical analyses were exploratory and not predictive. There were 163 parents who went through conciliation, 210 had condensed evaluations, and 177 had standard evaluations. Type of evaluation information was missing for seven parents. As described above, a multivariate analysis found a statistically significant result for type of evaluation. In order to more closely examine that result, univariate analyses of variance were carried out.

There were significant differences only on scales K ($F(2, 547) = 3.66$, $p = 0.27$); Pd ($F(2, 547) = 4.93$, $p = .008$); Mf($F(2, 547) = 4.93$, $p = .04$); and Sc ($F (2, 547) = 3.11$, $p = .045$). See Table 4 for means and standard deviations. An examination of the means indicates that conciliation was lower than the other two types of evaluation on K, Pd, and Sc. The condensed evaluation manifested a higher score on Mf than did the other two types of evaluation.

To more closely examine these differences, effect sizes were inspected. On scale K, there was an effect size of .29 regarding the difference between standard and conciliation. On Pd, there was an effect size of .36 regarding the difference between standard and conciliation. There was an effect size of .28 regarding the difference between standard and conciliation on Sc. The difference between condensed and standard on Mf had an effect size of .25. No other comparisons on any of the four scales had effect sizes of .20 or greater.

Therefore, conciliation appears to have led to modestly lower scores on measures of defensiveness and maladaptive behavior, as compared to the standard evaluation. However, there did not appear to be any effect in terms

Table 4
STATISTICALLY SIGNIFICANT MMPI-2 SCALES BY EVALUATION TYPE

Scale	Conciliation		Condensed		Standard	
	M	*SD*	*M*	*SD*	*M*	*SD*
K	60.83	8.91	62.26	8.39	63.34	8.40
Pd	53.67	7.50	55.15	8.67	56.37	7.34
Mf	49.83	8.14	50.84	8.67	48.64	8.54
Sc	47.87	5.99	49.10	7.19	49.62	6.53

Note: K = Correction; *Pd =* Psychopathic Deviate; *Mf =* Masculinity-Femininity; *Sc =* Schizophrenia.

of suspiciousness by parents, as indicated by the lack of a significant difference on *Pa*, the most directly relevant MMPI-2 scale.

These findings suggest that conciliation may have led participants to feel somewhat more open and honest, and to endorse fewer items representative of impulsiveness and highly unusual experiences as compared to those who went through the standard form of evaluation. In that regard, the conciliation format may have provided a buffer against aspects of psychological distress that can accompany the divorce and custody dispute experience. If that format does actually lead to greater openness and less distress, it could potentially foster the type of cooperation that increases the likelihood of an agreement about custody.

The higher score on *Mf* for condensed as compared to standard evaluations suggests that those who took part in the condensed type were somewhat less likely to endorse relatively traditional gender attitudes. However, it is difficult to identify what aspects of the condensed format might have led to such an effect.

There are a number of limitations regarding this research on type of evaluation. As described elsewhere, this was archival research, and there was no random assignment. Therefore, the differences for type of evaluation could have been due to other factors. For example, the lower scores on a number of scales for conciliation could have been due to the fact that those evaluations occurred a number of years ago, when there may have been a different quality to many of the evaluations that took place. For example, when the conciliation program was in effect, disputed cases were more frequently referred, and those referrals appeared to have taken place earlier in the legal process, as compared to the condensed and standard evaluations. Some evaluators have voiced a perspective that, in more recent years, the evaluation cases that are referred are fewer in number but considerably higher in terms of complexity and the level of conflict between parents. The higher levels of complexity and conflict could partially represent greater mental health difficulties on the part of parents, which in turn could be reflected in higher MMPI-2 scores.

Another limitation is that the effect sizes are small. Also, there is no other known research that reported similar findings to provide empirical support for the current results.

It is important for evaluators to be fully cognizant of the ethical issues inherent for a practitioner combining mediation and evaluation. Although there are adherents to combining those roles (e.g., Lowry, 2004), there are ethical risks to dual roles of any type (APA, 2002; Milne, Folberg, & Salem, 2004), and evaluators need to be extremely cautious about proceeding down such a path.

Despite these limitations, the current results are important because they provide empirical evidence that a hybrid mediation-evaluation process might allow for a more open and less distressing experience that would have the potential of reaching settlements about disputed child custody. In that regard, this study is best seen as a possible springboard for others to conduct research comparing different types of mediation or different forms of evaluation in terms of parental experiences and/or possible outcomes.

DEFENSIVENESS

Prior MMPI-2 research in custody evaluation (e.g., Bagby et al., 1999; Bathurst et al., 1997) has consistently found modestly higher than usual scores on scales L and K, which are the traditional validity scales that measure defensiveness. Therefore, the current study carried out similarly detailed investigation regarding defensiveness on those scales.

Following earlier research findings, it was hypothesized that individuals who had elevated scores on the traditional validity scales that measure defensiveness would manifest a number of differences in clinical scale scores when compared to others who did not show elevated validity scale scores. However, also consistent with earlier findings, it was predicted that the means of clinical scales would all be in the normal range, regardless of whether defensiveness scores were categorized as elevated or normal.

In addition, informal observation over many years of administering the MMPI-2 in custody evaluations led to an impression that scale Si tended to be unusually low (indicative of extraversion), especially when there was heightened defensiveness. Therefore, it was predicted that there would be a significant negative correlation between Si and the validity scales that defensiveness.

Somewhat similarly, both prior research (Bagby et al., 1999; Bathurst et al., 1997; Ezzo et al., 2007; Siegel et al., 2012; Strong et al., 1999) and informal observation indicated that scale Pa was among the clinical scales with the highest mean scores. At the same time, one aspect of the composition of Pa is the Harris-Lingoes subscale Naïveté, which has items that can be seen as reflecting a type of defensiveness. Therefore, it was hypothesized that there would be a modest but statistically significant positive correlation between Pa and the traditional validity scales that measure defensiveness.

Following Bathurst et al. (1997) and Bagby et al. (1999), a bifurcation of the sample was made to create two groups, in terms of whether the defensiveness scores were elevated to 65 or higher (underreporting) or whether they were below 65 (non-underreporting). Such analyses took place separately for scales L and K.

On scale L, there was a significant effect of group, multivariate $F(9, 546) = 7.26$, $p < .001$. Univariate analyses of variance were carried out to examine which scales showed statistically significant differences. Underreporting parents had higher scores on *Hs*, *D*, *Mf*, and *Sc*; though they had lower scores on *Pd* and *Pa* (all $ps < .05$).

There was also a significant effect of group on scale *K*, multivariate $F(9, 546) = 44.86$, $p < .001$. Univariate analyses showed that underreporting parents had higher scores on *Hs*, *Hy*, *Pd*, *Pt*, and *Sc*; but underreporters had lower scores on *Ma* and *Si* (all $ps < 001$).

The Pearson correlation between scales *Si* and *K* was -.35, p < .001, consistent with predictions. However, the correlation between *Si* and *L* was .06 and not significant. Contrary to expectations, there were no positive correlations between *Pa* and *K* ($r = -.08$, *ns*), and *Pa* and *L* ($r = -10$, $p < .02$).

As anticipated, consistent with prior research, even when only non-underreporting parents are considered, mean scores on all clinical scales are within the normal range. For example, the highest mean clinical elevation for non-underreporters on either defensiveness scale is 56 on *Pd*, which is almost identical to the overall mean, as can be seen in Table 3.

Therefore, even though a significant minority of respondents was in the elevated range on the relevant validity scales, such defensiveness does not appear to suppress clinical scores a great deal. When a comparison is made between the clinical scores of parents who had elevated *K* and those who were elevated on *L*, not surprisingly, the *K* scale underreporters had relatively higher clinical mean scale scores; most of those clinical scales that were higher were the *K*-corrected ones, other than *Ma*. The fact that *Ma* was not higher for underreporters might have been associated with the fact that it has a very small *K*-correction value.

It is interesting that *Hy*, which is not *K*-corrected, had a significantly higher score for parents elevated on the *K* scale (as well as a marginally higher score for those elevated on *L*, *p.* = .07). It may be due to the fact that *Hy* represents the hysterical syndrome, which in itself is typically accompanied by limitations in insight, an aspect of defensiveness often considered as represented in the *K* scale. For *Si*, the significantly lower score for *K* scale underreporters is associated with the fact that higher *Si* scores represent greater introversion, and as can be seen in the negative correlation between *Si* and *K*, the defensiveness represented by *K* is associated with parents reporting themselves to be comparatively extroverted.

Overall, when considering such a pattern of findings, there is most reason for confidence that they represent actual population differences when there is convergence with the outcomes of prior studies. The current results support the conclusions of prior research that the majority of custody evaluation parents do not manifest major psychopathology, and that the defensiveness sometimes seen in the MMPI-2 in custody evaluation litigants does not negate the overall effectiveness of this measure when used with such individuals.

PREDECREE VERSUS POSTDECREE LITIGANTS

Professionals in the divorce field at times have noted that individuals who have never gone through a separation or divorce can present differently from those who have already gone through a process to arrive at a decision about child custody and time sharing. For parents who have never gone through the process before, one or both often experience considerable distress. Some of the distress is associated with the parental relationship falling apart, the interface of that process with the impact on the children, and the children's visible responses. For others who have gone through it before, and are dealing with a possible modification, some appear to have their lives more settled as compared to individuals meeting such life stresses for the first time. However, there are also individuals who present as repeatedly frustrated after an initial agreement or judgment has taken place, and who continue to be involved with the legal system in ways that result in litigation about the children. Numerous judges and attorneys have commented that there are a very small proportion of parents who take up an enormously disproportionate amount of the courts' time and attention.

Consequently, there were competing hypotheses about the possible impact of predecree versus postdecree timing of the litigation on MMPI-2 scores. One hypothesis was that predecree parents would show generally higher scores, especially on clinical scales, based on the expectation that they experienced higher levels of psychological distress than postdecree individuals. The alternate hypothesis was that postdecree respondents experienced significant psychological dysfunction that contributed to their return to court, and therefore their MMPI-2 scores would be generally higher than predecree parents.

For parents who had been married to one another, the identification of predecree versus postdecree cases was quite easy, and was based on whether or not they had been through a prior legal process that led to the establishment of custody and time-sharing routines. For parents who never had been married to one another, the identification of predecree versus postdecree cases depended on whether or not they had already gone through any type of process, even by means of informal agreement, that had led to time-sharing routines.

For the statistical analyses, timing was used to describe the categorization of whether it was a predecree case or a postdecree modification. That categorization was missing for 10 parents, and therefore there were 547 individuals included in this analysis. There were 337 predecree and 210 postdecree parents.

A multivariate analysis of variance was carried out with both timing and gender as between-subjects factors in order to explore whether there might be any interaction effects between the two categorizations, such as whether there might be differences between women and men in one timing category, but not the other. There was a significant interaction of timing by scale, multivariate $F(12, 530) = 3.13$, $p < .001$. As described in the Gender section of this chapter, there was a significant interaction of gender by scale, but the interaction of gender, timing, and scale was not significant.

In order to more closely examine the significant multivariate effect for timing, univariate analyses were carried out. For each of the following scales, there was a statistically significant difference in the direction of predecree parents having higher scores: on L ($F(1, 545) = 8.10$, $p = .005$), D ($F(1, 545) = 5.75$, $p = .017$), Hy ($F(1, 545) = 4.40$, $p = .036$) and Pd ($F(1, 545) = 8.39$, $p = .004$). Also, on scale Pt, there was a marginally significant difference, $F(1, 545) = 3.11$, $p = .078$.

On L, the predecree mean was 62 and the postdecree mean was 59. On all relevant clinical scales, means scores were in the normal range. For all statistically significant scales, effect sizes were in the range of .22 to .25, except Hy, which was smaller. Also, on all other, nonsignificant MMPI-2 scales except Hs, means scores for predecree were higher than postdecree means.

Therefore, it appears that individuals who go through custody evaluations prior to a decree generally experience modestly more distress, and manifest somewhat greater defensiveness, as compared to parents in postdecree litigation, though the magnitude of differences did not suggest clinical significance. However, it should be noted that this study did not separate out those mainly postdecree litigants who are the "frequent flyers" in the court system. As a result, no conclusions can be made about the MMPI-2 profiles of such repeat child custody litigators.

CONTENTIOUS PARENTAL ALLEGATIONS

A considerable proportion of custody evaluations include allegations of substance abuse, domestic violence, and/or child abuse. Such allegations typically contribute toward heated parental accusations and denials of misconduct. The presence of any of these allegations generally leads to a relatively complicated and challenging evaluation. Of course, in a significant number of these cases, more than one type of allegation is present. In practice, there is often an association between claims of substance abuse by a parent and allegations that individual is particularly inclined toward physical aggression toward their spouse when intoxicated. Somewhat similarly, at times a parent is accused of having been abusive both toward the spouse and one or more children.

The current research project included an examination of MMPI-2 scores in terms of whether or not substance misuse, domestic violence, and/or child abuse were identified as areas of concern within the family. In the vast majority of cases, one or both parents specifically identified one or more than one of these behavior patterns as a problem. In a few instances, neither parent made such a claim, but it became clear during the evaluation that there was considerable reason for concern. For example, in a few cases, both parents reported there to have been child physical discipline that would generally have been viewed as excessive, but they did not believe there was anything wrong with it. In other relatively uncommon instances, neither parent expressed any concern about domestic violence, but during interviews it became evident that one or more physical altercations between the parents had taken place.

It is extremely important to keep in mind that the MMPI-2 was not designed to try to identify the presence of substance abuse, domestic violence, or child abuse. Although there are a number of MMPI-2 supplementary scales that were created to try to identify substance misuse or associated characteristics, those scale were not used in the current analyses. This section of the research is exploratory in nature.

The categorization of the presence or absence of substance misuse, domestic violence, and/or child abuse was carried out in terms of the case, and not the individual parent. See the Chapter 8 section on Contentious Parental Allegations for more detail about this matter.

Substance Misuse

Of the three types of allegations, concerns about parental substance misuse occurred most frequently. There were 225 of 557 parents, or 40%, who were involved in cases that included allegations of parental substance misuse.

Interestingly, when statistically significant differences were found on MMPI-2 scales, in each instance parents who were in the category of no allegation or evidence of substance misuse had higher mean scores than those that were classified as having such allegations present. On K, the mean for the no substance abuse group was 63 and for the group that had substance misuse allegations the mean was 61, $t(555) = 2.98$, $p = .003$. On other scales with statistically significant differences, $Mf(t(555) = 3.39, p = .001)$, $Pt(t(555) = 2.14, p = .033)$, and $Sc(t(555) = 2.39, p = .018)$, the mean scores did not show elevations. The effect sizes on all these scales were small, except Pt, which had a trivial effect size (Cohen, 1992).

This is the only known MMPI-2 research investigating substance abuse in child custody litigants. Overall, interpretation of results for specific parents may be assisted by reliance on general guides for assessing substance misuse with the MMPI-2 (e.g., Young & Weed, 2006). Future research in this area with custody litigants could be productive in terms of independently identifying persons who manifest substance misuse and comparing their response patterns with parents who clearly do not misuse substances.

Domestic Violence

There were 208 of 557 parents (37%) who were involved in cases that were categorized as having concerns about domestic violence. On two scales, those parents with allegations about domestic violence had statistically significant higher mean scores than those without domestic violence allegations. The mean on L for parents with domestic violence concerns was 63, and for those in cases without domestic violence allegations, the mean was 59, t (555) = 3.66, $p<.001$. Similarly, on Mf, parents in cases with domestic violence concerns had a higher mean (51) than those in cases without such concerns (49), t (555) = 2.09, $p = .037$. On two other scales, Hs and D, the higher means for parents in cases that included domestic violence allegations approached conventional levels of statistical significance, $ps < .09$. The effect size for L was .32 and the other effect sizes were all under .20.

Again, these preliminary findings appear to be the only MMPI-2 data relevant for domestic violence concerns within child custody evaluations. Outside the realm of custody evaluation, MMPI-2 research with male domestic violence perpetrators has shown patterns of responding that has identified three subgroups (antisocial, other psychological dysfunction, and nonpathological) previously pointed out elsewhere in the domestic violence literature (Scott, Flowers, Bulnes, Olmsted, & Carbajal-Madrid, 2009). There has been far less research with female domestic violence perpetrators, and such women did not display the same patterns of MMPI-2 scores as male aggressors (Peacock, 2009). Kahn, Welch and Zillmer (1993) reported MMPI-2 profiles for a modest sample of battered women. Future research with child custody litigants might also focus on contrasting domestic violence perpetrators with those who have not carried out that type of aggression.

Child Abuse

In the current data set, there were 151 of 557 parents, or 27%, who were involved in cases that included allegations or concerns about child abuse. The data analyses revealed that there were no significant differences on any MMPI-2 scale between the scores of parents who were involved in cases that included child abuse concerns versus those in cases without any such concerns.

Of the three crucial issues discussed here, child abuse is the only one that has been directly examined in any prior custody evaluation MMPI-2 research (Posthuma & Harper, 1998). Those researchers investigated defensiveness scales only. Their main findings compared MMPI-2 raw scores of custody evaluation litigants, some of whom were involved in cases that included allegations of child abuse, with those of litigants in personal injury cases. There do not appear to be practical applications of that comparison for custody evaluators. Posthuma and Harper (1998) did not include any statistical analyses between the different types of custody litigants; that is, there were no analyses reported between custody cases that did not include any abuse allegation, and those that included allegations of physical abuse or sexual abuse. However, an examination of scores for the traditional validity scales revealed very similar means for each of the custody subgroups.

Outside the child custody arena, MMPI-2 research on parents at risk for child abuse (Egeland, Erickson, Butcher, & Ben-Porath, 1991) identified patterns of scale elevation. However, the majority of this type of research has investigated women only, and thus by itself has very limited utility in custody evaluation.

IMPLICATIONS

Interpretive considerations for psychological tests are at an intensified level of focus and concern because of the high-stakes nature of child custody disputes. Consequently, it is extremely important for custody evaluators to look to other sources of evaluative information for confirmation or disconfirmation of testing results.

The main purpose of using the MMPI-2 in custody evaluation is to identify possible parental psychological dysfunction that would potentially have a negative impact on children. That objective is based both on consistent research findings that indicate parental psychological problems to be predictive of negative outcomes for children, and on common statutory factors that indicate the mental health of parents needs to be considered in custody determinations. Although the legal system often looks for clear lines of demarcation in terms of matter such as mental health functioning, there is no universally agreed upon MMPI-2 clinical scale elevation that always represents serious psychological problems; however, relatively higher elevations, such as those at or above a T score of 65 are more likely to accurately reflect the presence of psychological symptoms (e.g., Graham, 2011). Some authorities have recommended interpretation of scale elevations in a much less cautious manner, such as considering the highest scale, or the highest two or three scales when code types are relied upon, largely regardless of the levels of the elevations (see Bathurst et al., 1997). A primary danger of disregarding the degree of scale elevations is that then essentially all respondents potentially can be seen as a manifesting psychological dysfunction, which is contrary to the reality that most people are psychologically healthy. Also, disregard of the level of scale elevations can make MMPI-2 results essentially meaningless and can thereby degrade the integrity of the testing in custody evaluation.

As noted above, relying on code types with scale scores at or above 65 T is recommended. Also, there is greater reason for confidence about the accuracy of code types when well-defined codes are used. In well-defined codes, after the scales contained in the code type, the next highest clinical scale elevation is at least 5 T lower than the lowest scale within the code. The use of this more restrictive code definition makes for more homogenous code types, and therefore less error variance (Butcher et al., 1995), but inevitably reduces the number of applicable profiles. In the current study, there were 20 tests with well-defined two-point code types, or under four percent of the total sample.

Whether a clinical scale elevation is at 65 T or higher, or whether it is slightly below it, looking for the presence of possibly converging data in sources such as interviews, observations, other psychological testing, or collateral information is of utmost importance. If no such convergent data can be found, the evaluator must strongly consider that the test finding may simply be in error. Although some individuals outside of the field of psychology may view psychological tests as relatively infallible, evaluators need to remain fully cognizant both of their strengths and limitations. For example, an elevation into the clinical range on a relevant scale may simply be due to error variance.

The most distinct finding of this and other MMPI-2 research in custody evaluation is the moderate elevation on scales of defensiveness. The proportions of defensive profiles in the present research are slightly higher than the base rate of .30 for such applied settings reported in the meta-analysis by Baer and Miller (2002). Such data clearly refute opinions that I have heard voiced at times by certain family law attorneys that the MMPI-2 is basically useless because it almost always shows defensiveness in custody evaluation parents.

These well-documented patterns of defensiveness are obviously relevant for interpretation. For example, Butcher (cited in Bathurst et al., 1997) has indicated that, when there is a defensive response pattern, it is reasonable to consider clinical scale elevations of 60 T and above to be in the clinical range. At the same time, a number of authorities (e.g., Graham, 2011) have maintained that the amount of a clinical scale elevation on a K-corrected scale that is due to the K correction needs to be considered. For example, Pd is the most frequently elevated K-corrected clinical scale in custody evaluation, and if a significant clinical elevation is due primarily to the K correction, the respondent may not actually have the characteristics usually represented by such a scale elevation.

At times, questions are raised about whether elevated defensiveness scores are the result of situational factors, such as the custody evaluation context, versus the presence of personality characteristics such as psychological rigidity, poor insight, and/or efforts at excessive self-control (e.g., Medoff, 1999). It is certainly possible that there are sometimes elements both of situational and personality factors. For example, the Baer and Miller (2002) meta-analysis found very significant increases in *L* and *K* when experimental subjects were instructed to deny problems, present very positively, or both.

Although *L* and *K* are both measures of defensiveness, they clearly measure somewhat separate aspects of defensiveness. In the present study, the correlation between the two scales is .36, which is very close to that of the standardization sample (Butcher et al., 2001). It represents a moderate degree of overlap, but also a considerable amount of variance separate from one another. Numerous authorities (e.g., Paulhus, 1984; Strong et al., 1999) described *L* as representing more of a tendency to purposely present oneself in an unrealistically virtuous way, whereas *K* has been described as a type of defensiveness represented by self-deception or limited insight about oneself.

Interpretive guides (Graham, 2011; Greene, 2010; Pope et al., 2006) do not offer clear cutoff points, across all defensiveness scales, regarding when the overall MMPI-2 profile should be considered invalid. As a general approach, if both *L* and *K* are elevated at or above 65 T, it is reasonable to conclude that answers on clinical items and subsequent clinical scale scores are invalid. Others (e.g., Graham, 2011) have indicated that a score at or above 70 T on one of the main defensiveness scales indicates likely profile invalidity.

When one examines the main MMPI-2 custody evaluation studies, the mean T scores for *L* and *K* fall in approximately the 56 to 62 range. Such scores are most reasonably interpreted, on a group level, as representing a tendency for a significant minority of parents to respond defensively. In the interpretation of individual profiles with such elevations, it is reasonable to conclude that they represent a modest to moderate level of defensiveness, in which caution is needed in the consideration of clinical scale elevations, but the overall profile is not considered necessarily invalid.

At times, especially when testifying at deposition or trial, an attorney's questioning suggests that individual is looking for an evaluator to state that an elevated defensiveness score must mean that the parent is hiding psychopathology. However, no such conclusions can accurately be drawn just from defensiveness scale elevations. Although it is certainly possible that the parent was trying to cover up psychological problems when they completed the test, it is also possible that parent is both psychologically healthy and defensive at the same time.

Especially when interpreting clinical scale elevations, comparisons of scale elevations between the mother and father can be crucial. In such matters, it is extremely important to be cognizant of the fact that numerous MMPI-2 authorities (e.g., Butcher et al., 1995; Graham, 2011; Greene, 2010) have described differences of less than 5 T to be not clinically significant. Such a consideration can be particularly important and potentially tricky in practice when there are relevant clinical scores that straddle the traditional 65 T cutoff. For example, Parent A may have a score on *D* of 66, and Parent B a score of

62. Although Parent A's score would be categorized as being in the clinical range, and Parent B's score would be classified as below that range, the reality is that their scores would not differ from one another in a clinically important way. Such detailed considerations are especially likely to be relevant within a high-stakes matter such as disputed child custody.

The research findings described in this chapter include numerous statistically significant results, as well as a larger number of results that did not reach conventional levels of statistical significance. In these common circumstances, there is often a good question about whether some of the statistically significant findings might just be spurious and not representative of actual population differences. Two useful methods of addressing this question pertain to whether research results appear to be consistent with findings of relevant prior studies, and whether the results appear to be conceptually coherent. For example, the findings here in terms of defensiveness and about the clinical scales that most frequently had elevations are consistent with the prior MMPI-2 studies cited a number of times earlier in this chapter. The current results that showed higher mean scores for predivorce cases consistently fit well with the hypothesis that such parents were generally experience higher level of defensiveness and aspects of distress than postdecree individuals. However, it is important to keep in mind that we may be overly inclined to rely on intuition to conclude that a finding is meaningful and not spurious if it happens to agree with our preconceived notions (e.g., see Chapter 3).

In recent years, the development of the MMPI-2 RF has attracted interest in the broader field of psychological assessment. The interpretive guides by Graham (2011) and Greene (2010) provide good coverage of that content area. In particular, Graham provides a helpful perspective on the comparative strengths of the MMPI-2 versus MMPI-2 RF. There has been controversy about their comparative utility in child custody evaluation, as can be seen in recent articles by Butcher and Williams (2012) and Ben-Porath and Flens (2012). The MMPI-2 RF has been used to compare custody evaluation and parental fitness samples (Pinsoneault & Ezzo, 2012).

A number of other practical considerations are crucial for custody evaluators, to a degree of focus and concern beyond typical clinical practice. These considerations include adequate environmental comfort and monitoring in testing, cautions about the use of computerized test interpretation, and the need for external validity data specific to the custody evaluation contexts. See Chapter 8 on the PAI for more detail about these matters.

It is always important for evaluators to remain cognizant that, while appropriate psychological testing can be very useful, every test includes error variance. It is always necessary to integrate information from all the different sources of data collection and look for convergent evidence.

Chapter 11

OTHER PSYCHOLOGICAL MEASURES

PRACTICE CHECKLIST

____Know basic strengths and limitations of any psychological measure used.

____Do not rely on any psychological measure in isolation.

____Interpret measures in accordance with standardization sample norms, informed by available custody evaluation reference data.

____The Parenting Stress Index (PSI) 4th edition may be useful in identifying potential parenting problems, though the vast majority of extant research included only women and is based on a prior version.

____If there is reason for specific concern about the presence or potential for moderate or severe child physical abuse, the Child Abuse Potential Inventory (CAPI) may be useful, but it should not be used as a general screening measure.

____The Revised Conflict Tactics Scales can help obtain a comprehensive overview of reports related to domestic violence, but it is not a test and does not provide proof of the presence or absence of domestic violence.

____If there is concern about child dysfunction, the Conners 3 or Child Behavior Checklist can help obtain relatively comprehensive data.

____Do not use the Rorschach.

____Do not use the Millon Clinical Multiaxial Inventory–III (MCMI-III).

____Do not use the Bricklin Perceptual Scales.

____Do not use the Perception-of-Relationships-Test (PORT).

Note: This form is a guide to promote productive reasoning and good practice. It is not comprehensive or all-inclusive and does not replace adequate training and experience.

Additional information about psychological measures in custody evaluation is covered in this chapter. Because defensiveness occurs regularly, the first section brings together data on patterns of defensive responding by custody evaluation parents on the MMPI-2, PAI, and PCRI. The remainder of the chapter is devoted to briefly summarizing other psychological measures that, for the most part, are reported in recent surveys (Ackerman & Pritzl, 2011; Quinell & Bow, 2001) as regularly used in custody evaluation. Although most of the tests described below are regularly used, the MMPI-2 appears to be the only psychological test that is used in a majority of custody evaluations (Hagen & Castagna, 2001).

As described earlier in this book, evaluations of any type are more likely to be accurate when they include reliance on measures that are appropriate and have strong empirical bases (Garb, 1998). From a legal risk management standpoint, evaluators should have empirically based and objective information as central areas of focus (Woody, 2013).

DEFENSIVENESS

The statistical analyses carried out here included investigations of defensiveness scales. This section focuses on patterns of scores across different tests. The main MMPI-2 defensiveness scales, L and K, are described as representing somewhat different aspects of defensiveness, though as shown below, they are significantly correlated with one another. L is believed to represent primarily an active intention to create an unrealistically positive impression, whereas K is thought to mainly demonstrate limited insight about oneself as a type of self-deception (Graham, 2012; Greene, 2011). The PAI and PCRI each have one main scale that measures defensiveness, PIM and SOC, respectively.

There were 143 individuals in the current data set who completed both the MMPI-2 and the PAI. There were significant correlations between PIM and L ($r = .46$) and K ($r = .50$). In this section, all statistically significant correlations had $ps < .001$.

Of the individuals who completed the PCRI, 133 also took the MMPI-2. It is important to recall that lower scores on SOC represent greater defensiveness, in contrast to the other defensiveness scales reported here, and therefore a negative correlation simply represents that difference in the direction of scoring. There was a significant correlation between SOC and L ($r = -.29$), but the correlation between SOC and K was not significant.

There were 202 parents who completed both the PAI and PCRI. The significant correlation between PIM and SOC ($r = -.28$) is again in a negative direction because of the reversed scoring for SOC.

In years of reviewing test scores from this data set, it appeared that there might be a statistical relationship between the MMPI-2 defensiveness scales and the MMPI-2 Social Introversion (Si) scale, in that greater defensiveness appeared to be associated with lower Si scores. The Si scale has a somewhat unusual structure and interpretation in that higher scores are representative of greater introversion and lower scores of more extraversion. Although there was not a significant correlation between *Si* and *L*, the correlation with *K* was statistically significant ($r = -.35$). In the standardization sample (Butcher et al., 2001), the correlation between *Si* and *L* was not significant, but the correlation with *K* was somewhat stronger (-.56) than found in the current custody litigation sample.

Also, within the MMPI-2, *L* and *K* had a correlation of .36. That correlation is very similar to the data found in very large samples that were not associated with custody evaluation (Greene, 2011).

Therefore, it appears that PIM has an approximately equivalent, moderate correlation with both *L* and *K*. The overall correlations between those three scales in the current custody evaluation data set are quite similar to the respective correlations for the standardization samples reported in the PAI manual (Morey, 2007). The fact that SOC is significantly correlated with *L* but not *K* suggests that it may primarily represent active efforts at impression management. The relatively small size of the significant correlations between SOC and both *L* and PIM is likely due, at least in part, to the very restricted range of a large proportion of the SOC scores in the current data set. The fact that *K* and *Si* are negatively correlated suggests that self-reported extraversion is to some extent associated with self-deceptive defensiveness.

MEASURES OF ADULT PERSONALITY AND PSYCHOPATHOLOGY

Rorschach

The Rorschach is a projective measure that has been used clinically since its inception in the early half of the twentieth century, and the surveys noted above reported that it is used moderately frequently in custody evaluation. There has been controversy for decades about its use in any setting. At times, arguments about it take on an almost religious fervor.

In many clinical settings, its use mainly has been to generate hypotheses about numerous areas of psychological functioning to assist in treatment efforts. Under such circumstances, hypotheses generated from Rorschach responses tend to be gradually supplanted by other information that emerges during the treatment process.

In contrast, Rorschach use in custody evaluation, like other forensic procedures, is entirely separate from a treatment process, and is focused on providing information to the legal system about possible adult psychopathology and/or personality functioning that would be potentially relevant to the best interest of the child. Consequently, there is a much higher level of validity required for such a forensic use as compared to clinical hypothesis generation, and in almost all respects, the Rorschach manifests inadequate psychometric properties. Some scholars, including textbook authors (e.g., Anastasi & Urbina, 1997) maintained that the Rorschach is not structured in such a way as to even be considered a psychological test, with the possible exception of the Exner (2002) system of scoring and interpretation.

However, there have been numerous serious criticisms of the Rorschach even when the Exner (2002) system is used, especially within the forensic context. For example, independent research has found serious problems within the Exner data set; in addition, when the Rorschach has been independently administered to normal samples, and the Exner system has been used, the results showed a much higher level of psychopathology than should have occurred given the characteristics of that sample (Garb, Wood, Lilienfeld, & Nezworski, 2002). That is, the normal samples looked quite dysfunctional in their Rorschach responses. These results are of particular concern because only clear minorities of custody evaluation parents manifest significant psychopathology (though a number experience transient, divorce-related distress).

It is noteworthy that others (e.g., Weiner, 2013) have maintained that the Rorschach has good reliability and validity, and is appropriate for use in forensic cases, including child custody matters. However, one of the particular challenges in Rorschach use is its scoring, which inevitably requires a good deal of judgment on multiple types of scores and combinations of scores. The requirement of judgment in scoring contributes to a risk that different examiners may score the same response in somewhat different ways, leading to low interrater reliability and different conclusions about the overall patterns of responses. Although Weiner (2013) reviewed studies that showed good interrater reliability when the Exner system was used, there are good reasons for doubt about the applicability of that research to what takes place in actual practice.

For example, Wood, Nezworski, and Stejskal (1996) maintained that the Exner system did not include reliability data on summary scores, and argued that interrater reliability data collected within the controlled research context showed a level of agreement that was much higher than what can be seen in practitioners carrying out Rorschach assessments in the field. In response, Meyer (1997) agreed that there was more information needed on field reliability and acknowledged that at least some practitioners in the field neglected to carry out adequate rigor in their scoring. In an article on Rorschach interrater reliability based on a large sample, he and his colleagues also stated that practitioners needed to conscientiously attend to their scoring accuracy (Meyer, Hilsenroth, Baxter, Exner, Fowler, et al., 2002).

Rorschach data from a large sample of child custody litigants have been published in a book chapter (Singer, Hoppe, Lee, Olesen, & Walters, 2008), and those authors reported high levels of interrater reliability. Gender comparisons were also included.

Although the Singer et al. (2008) report has a number of important strengths, it also reflects significant questions. For example, it is important to keep in mind that the Rorschach purports to measure numerous personality characteristics, some of which appear to have questionable relevance for the concerns that are central to child custody evaluation; it is at least very debatable to what extent scores and concepts such as animal movement, inanimate movement, texture, shading, and introversive/extratensive are directly applicable to legal criteria and research findings about the best interest of children. There is also reason for concern that the authors described that only 10% of their sample manifested adaptive problem solving. Although poor problem solving is not necessarily synonymous with psychopathology, it would be reasonable to expect that the two would be significantly correlated with one another, and such a finding may therefore reflect the report of Garb et al. (2002) that the Exner system for the Rorschach led to excessively frequent findings of psychopathology in a normal sample.

I have serious doubts that practicing custody evaluators (as well as most of those who use the Rorschach in clinical practice) regularly review and practice correct scoring procedures that would increase the likelihood of an identical score being assigned to especially a multifaceted response, which occurs regularly. In addition, although Weiner (2013) described ways in which the Rorschach potentially offers personality information relevant to custody evaluation, he acknowledged that Rorschach findings alone must be accompanied by other relevant evidence, such as what might be observed directly in parent-child interaction and/or from collateral informants. In other words, there are significant questions about the incremental validity of the Rorschach, beyond what would be obtained through other evaluation procedures, including other tests that do not have interrater reliability challenges and that manifest more clear and relevant validity in terms of psychopathology and personality.

It should be noted that Garb et al. (2002) reported that there are some areas of adequate validity for the Exner Rorschach system. They involve scores for form quality and deviant verbalizations showing validity in the identification of psychotic features, and the oral dependency scale as valid for dependent personality traits. However, such psychological features very rarely present as important in custody evaluations. Overall, the numerous Rorschach reliability and validity problems lead to a conclusion that it should not be used in custody evaluation (Grove, Barden, Garb, & Lilienfeld, 2002).

MCMI-III

The MCMI-III (Millon, 2009) is an objectively scored measure of personality and psychopathology that is especially focused on the identification of personality disorders and related dysfunction. It appears to have been the second psychological test, after the MMPI-2, with a research reference sample specifically drawn from custody evaluation parents (McCann et al., 2001). Those researchers made a noble effort to expand the potential scientific basis of custody evaluation testing, but their results helped to shed light on a very serious problem when this measure was used in the custody evaluation context.

Their results indicated that many more women than men had elevated scores, at the levels of personality disorders and dysfunctional personality traits (Millon, 1994), on histrionic, narcissistic, and compulsive scales. More specifically, in the McCann et al. (2001) custody evaluation sample, over 50% of women had standardized Base Rate scores indicative of histrionic and compulsive traits. Upon examination of Base Rate scores representative of personality disorder, women had frequencies of elevations on histrionic, narcissistic, and compulsive scales that were 2.5 to more than 4.5 times the frequencies of men.

An investigation into the details of those results found that, on those three scales, the raw score to Base Rate score transformations led to considerably higher Base Rate scores for women than for men when the raw score for both genders was exactly the same. In addition, other scoring adjustments to Base Rate scores accentuated this difference. Furthermore, objective research data about the prevalence of those three personality disorders did not support the gender differences in transformations from raw to Base Rate scores (Hynan, 2004). Consequently, the conclusion was that there was no sound scientific basis for the much higher rate of dysfunctional scores for women than men on those personality scales.

Since my 2004 article on this matter, more comprehensive epidemiological evidence has been published on the prevalence of personality disorders. Those studies (Grant, Hasin, Stinson, Dawson, Chou, et al., 2004; Stinson, Dawson, Goldstein, Chou, Huang, et al., 2008) give additional support for the finding that there was no sound scientific basis for higher rates for women on the three relevant personality disorder scales of the MCMI-III. Perhaps obviously, custody evaluations generally compare women to men, and therefore it is extremely important to have gender fairness in all aspects of the evaluation process.

Since then, the MCMI-III has been restandardized, and the 2008 norms discontinued the different scoring procedures for women and men. There is now a single norm group (Millon, 2009). In contrast to the prior manuals (Millon, 1994; Millon, Davis, & Millon, 1997) that stated the test was appropriate for use in child custody cases, the current manual appears to be silent on the topic of use in custody evaluation.

However, the current manual (Millon, 2009) specifically states that the test is not to be used with normal populations, and that the score transformations and normative data are based only on individuals from outpatient or inpatient

treatment settings. The fact that the MCMI-III is now based totally on clinical 55-a
samples makes it clearly inappropriate for use in child custody evaluation.
Child custody samples are clearly very different from clinical samples, as can
be seen in part in psychological test data reported here and elsewhere (e.g.,
Bagby et al., 1999; Bathurst et al., 1997; Hynan, 2013b). The conclusion is
that custody evaluators should not use this measure.

Interestingly, despite this clear information in the current manual (Millon,
2009), a recent chapter by Craig (2013) described purportedly positive features
of the MCMI-III for use in forensic evaluations. Craig made no reference to
the concerns about gender fairness (Hynan, 2004), and likely associated with
his lack of any reference to the current manual (Millon, 2009), did not manifest
awareness of its statement of strong caution against using the instrument outside
of clinical settings.

PARENTING INVENTORIES

Parenting Stress Index (PSI)

The PSI (Abidin, 2012) is completed by parents and is directed toward the
assessment of the level of stress in parent-child interactions. As described in
Chapter 1, overall stress has been found to be a factor that influences the
well-being of children of divorce (Amato, 1993). Perhaps the main utility and
relevance of the PSI in custody evaluation is that research has found a
number of relationships between PSI scores and parental abuse, neglect, and
other aspects of relatively inadequate parenting.

Prior to the current, fourth edition, the PSI had a significant limitation in
terms of its use within custody evaluations because its standardization sample
included 13 times as many women as men. Also, the standardization sample
of its prior edition (Abidin, 1995) had significant gender differences on some
mean scale scores that led to difficulties in interpretation, especially in the
custody evaluation context. There has been PSI custody evaluation mean
and standard deviation data published in tabular form about the earlier, third
edition (Abidin, Austin, & Flens, 2013, p. 368), but there have been significant
changes in the PSI and those data did not include important gender
comparisons.

As indicated in the current PSI manual (Abidin, 2012), there are consistently
strong reliability data. There have been so many validity studies on the PSI
that they are largely not included in the manual, but can be found on the
website of the test publisher, Psychological Assessment Resources. However,
because the current version of the PSI was published quite recently, and earlier
versions have had inadequate samples of males, there needs to be caution

about the external validity of fathers' PSI scores, as the vast majority of PSI research subjects have been mothers. Abidin et al. (2013) stated that there are a number of studies that indicated the prior version of the PSI was able to predict dysfunctional parenting as well in males as females. It is to be expected that the PSI will continue to be used frequently as a research instrument, and therefore the current version is likely to have a growing research database that includes relevant information on fathers.

Overall, the recent improvements of the PSI make it potentially a very useful measure for custody evaluators to assess relevant dimensions of stress within the family system, and possibly to identify risks for abuse and/or neglect. As with every other such instrument or evaluation procedure, findings need to be integrated with information derived from other evaluation methods.

Child Abuse Potential Inventory (CAPI)

The CAPI (Milner, 1986) is a questionnaire completed by adults that was designed originally to be employed by child protective services workers in order to screen for physical child abuse. In particular, the goal was to identify the potential for moderate to severe physical abuse. That level of abuse was described by Milner (1989) as intentional physical action that resulted in injury to the child.

Because custody evaluators wish, to all extents possible, to eliminate or at least reduce the risk that a child would be abused, this type of measure has drawn considerable interest. Both the surveys cited at the beginning of this chapter indicated that the CAPI has been used by a significant proportion of evaluators. The Ackerman and Pritzl (2011) report stated that about 52% of evaluators used the test, but did not offer further information about the mean percentage of cases in which it was used. The earlier Quinell and Bow (2001) study reported that 21% of their sample used the test, and made use of it in an average of 50% of their cases.

These data suggest that the CAPI is used inappropriately frequently by many custody evaluators. Specifically, the test manual (Milner, 1986, p. 4) states that the inventory was constructed and validated with families who were involved in child protective services, with an estimated base rate of about 50% of parents who manifested physical child abuse. The accuracy of the test changes significantly when the base rate is quite different from the base rate in effect during the validation, and the manual offers a clear mathematical example of that phenomenon. Although concerns about child abuse of some type occur in a significant minority of custody evaluation cases, as can be seen in part in the chapters of this book on the PAI, PCRI, and MMPI-2, it is clear that the proportion of custody evaluation cases with moderate to severe child physical abuse (such as those in which children sustain injuries) is much smaller than 50%.

In other words, the CAPI should not be used as a general screening device within the custody evaluation context. However, it appears reasonable to use this instrument in custody and related cases in which there is an allegation of moderate or greater child physical abuse. Alternately, it would be reasonable to use it if there were evidence that such abuse may have occurred, or there is a considerable reason for concern that there is a risk of it potentially taking place.

The CAPI generally has shown very good reliability, both in terms of internal consistency and temporal stability. In addition, researchers found that when it is used with appropriate samples, its correct identification of moderate to severe physical abusers versus nonabusive controls is high (Hart, 1989; Melton, 1989). At the same time, even when it is not used excessively in custody evaluation as a general screening instrument, it is crucial to be cautious in its use and interpretation.

For example, perhaps not surprisingly, it has not been successful in identifying mildly physically abusive parents, and there have been questions about the effectiveness of this instrument to identify abusers who may already have received relevant treatment (Hart, 1989). In addition, Melton (1989) pointed out that the legal system characteristically has a presumption of innocence, and therefore it may not accept the identification of an individual as a physical child abuser when it is based at least in part on the findings of an inventory that presumes a high base rate of moderate or greater child physical abuse.

It is crucial that any conclusion about an individual, especially in a forensic context, not rely entirely on group-level data such as testing results. Melton (1989) asserted that such a concern is especially true for the identification of possible child abuse, which can have very significant ramifications for a family. Therefore, particularly in this arena, it is paramount to look to multiple sources of information regarding whether any individual is or is not likely to engage in child abuse.

Consumers of custody evaluations largely work within the legal system, and because they cannot be expected to know the intricacies of technical matters within psychology and child development, legal professionals sometimes look to test results as *the* answer. As a result, it is also crucial to convey in a report or any other communication the full picture regarding investigations of abuse, including evidence for and/or contrary to its possible occurrence.

PARENT/TEACHER REPORTS OF CHILD FUNCTIONING

In some cases, parental report or other information leads to concern about the psychological and related functioning of a child. A number of psychometric instruments can assist in obtaining more detailed perspectives about problems and strengths. Two instruments often used in custody evaluation, as reported by the surveys described above, both have useful format that can be completed either by a parent or a teacher. In addition, child self-report forms are available.

Conners 3

The Conners 3 (Conners, 2008) is the most recent, third edition of the Conners inventories that have been in existence for over two decades. It is focused primarily on common child behavior problems such as attention deficit disorders, limitations in executive functioning, learning problems, and other externalizing behavior problems. It includes a number of screening items, though not full scales, for internalizing problems such as anxiety and depression. There are items that ask about functional impairments with relationships, at school, and/or at home, as well as others that inquire about strengths and skills.

The Conners 3 Parent and Teacher forms are valid for children ages 6 through 18, and involve a revision such that they are no longer applicable for younger children ages 3 through 5. The child self-report form is applicable for ages 8 through 18.

The manual (Conners, 2008) is very detailed and shows numerous examples of good reliability and validity. The external validity data show strong levels of anticipated correlations with other tests, such as the Child Behavior Checklist, described below, and the ability to distinguish between groups with identified behavior problems versus a sample of the normal population.

Achenbach System of Empirically Based Assessment/Child Behavior Checklist

The Child Behavior Checklist has been revised a number of times from its earliest version (Achenbach, 1991) and incorporated into the larger Achenbach System of Empirically Based Assessment, which has numerous components. The measures that would likely be of most use to custody evaluators are the Child Behavior Checklist for ages 6 through 18 (Achenbach & Rescorla, 2001), and a separate Child Behavior Checklist for ages 1½ through 5 (Achenbach & Rescorla, 2000). Both have formats the can be completed by parents, caregivers, or teachers. The youth self-report format is for ages 11 through 18.

A main difference between the school-age Child Behavior Checklist and the Conners 3 is that the former has a somewhat broader area of coverage, including scales that focus on areas of competency and internalizing problems, and consequently somewhat less focus on attentional and externalizing problems. The Conners 3 includes very brief validity scales, whereas the Child Behavior Checklist does not have them. The authors of the latter measure have maintained that validity scales are actually not useful, and that concerns about such response styles are better addressed by examining other sources of assessment information (Achenbach & Rescorla, 2013).

In general, the Child Behavior Checklist manifests strong levels of reliability and validity. External validity data include expected correlations with other measures such as the predecessor of the Conners 3, and correspondence with whether or not relevant external criterion groups did or did not manifest relevant behavioral problems (Achenbach & Rescorla, 2013). However, psychometric properties are stronger for the school-age versions than the preschool versions (Flanagan, 2005).

It should be noted that both the Child Behavior Checklist and the Conners 3 have scales that were designed to measure problem areas that fit the diagnostic categories of *DSM-IV* (American Psychiatric Association, 1994). Of course, there has been a revision to *DSM 5* (American Psychiatric Association, 2013), with considerable controversy in the new version regarding diagnostic categories and criteria. Those controversies are beyond the intended scope of this book, but evaluators who use either of these instruments need to be sufficiently familiar with both the changes and the controversies, especially in terms of making use of information from the scales oriented to *DSM-IV*.

BRICKLIN MEASURES

In contrast to every other psychological measure discussed in this book, these measures created by Bricklin were designed specifically for use in child custody evaluation. Decades ago, when I first received supervision about conducting custody evaluations that was required by a local court program, the use of at least one of the Bricklin measures was considered essentially mandatory. An influential article (Brodzinsky, 1993) stated that the Bricklin measures appeared promising in custody evaluation use. Since that time, the use of these measures has been justifiably questioned and criticized, and I stopped using them long ago when I started a lengthy process of closely examining evaluative procedures. The recent surveys cited above indicated they are still used by a substantial minority of custody evaluators.

Bricklin Perceptual Scales

The goal of the Bricklin Perceptual Scales (Bricklin, 1984) is to provide information about a child's largely unconscious experiences of each parent, so as to determine which one would be best for primary residential custody. The child is presented with a card that contains a black horizontal line, with each end anchored with the phrases "very well" and "not so well." For each of the numerous cards, the child is asked how well each parent would carry out a specific type of parenting behavior. There are equivalent questions that pertain to the mother and the father.

Although many of the questions pertain to relevant aspects of parenting, this measure manifests numerous deficits. In particular, Bricklin (1984) maintained that test reliability is not relevant in this matter. For example, he argued that temporal stability is irrelevant because children's views of their parents change over time. The central conceptual flaw in that argument is that if the child's experiences of each parent can change so readily, such as when this measure is used, the results are meaningless in terms of the ongoing well-being of the child.

There has been essentially no independent research data on the reliability and validity of the Bricklin Perceptual Scales published in traditional sources. However, a doctoral dissertation described that the measure showed inadequate test-retest reliability over a seven-day period (Gilch Pesantez, 2001).

The sparse validity data Bricklin presented are highly inadequate both in terms of the small numbers on which they are based and external criteria that are not well-founded. Gilch Pesantez (2001) reported that, in terms of external validity, the measure did not show a statistically significant correlation with the criterion, the Children's Version of the Family Environment Scale. Heinze and Grisso (1996) reviewed a number of measures used in custody evaluation and did not include the Bricklin Perceptual Scales (1984) among the recommended ones. In addition, as noted elsewhere (Shaffer, 1992), there is no evidence that children experience largely unconscious perceptions about their parents that would translate into them making corresponding marks on the type of black line used in this measure.

As described above, consumers of custody evaluations within the legal system can be prone to place excessive reliance on test results. A particular danger in using this measure is that it may be seen by such consumers as *the* direct test that provides *the* answer as to custody. In fact, the Bricklin Perceptual Scales do not actually qualify as a test, as the measure does not meet criteria for test manuals established by the Standards for Educational and Psychological Measurement (AERA et al., 1999). In summary, the measure should not be used in custody and related evaluations.

Perception-Of-Relationships-Test (PORT)

The PORT was also created by Bricklin (1989) with essentially a similar objective as the Bricklin Perceptual Scales of clarifying child custody decisions. The PORT handbook indicated that it measures the extent to which a child experiences positive interactions and/or closeness with the parent, and dispositions to behave in certain ways to facilitate interactions with the parent. It involves a brief series of line drawings made by the child that mainly pertain to each parent, the child, and the overall family. One of the drawings has more obvious content in terms of the child making a choice between each parent.

Again, regarding the PORT, Bricklin (1989) contended that reliability in terms of temporal stability was irrelevant because there were likely to be changes in the child's perceptions. As described above regarding the Bricklin Perceptual Scales (1984), that argument is highly flawed. The validity data presented in the PORT Handbook are very lacking in numerous ways (Carlson, 1995; Conger, 1995). There appear to be no available independent research data regarding PORT reliability or validity.

With rare exception, projective drawings generally have been found to not have adequate reliability and validity (e.g., Anastasi & Urbina, 1997). In their review of measures commonly used in child custody evaluations, Heinze and Grisso (1996) did not include the PORT on the recommended list. In addition, the PORT (1989) Handbook does not meet the criteria for test manuals of the Standards for Educational and Psychological Measurement (AERA et al., 1999). Overall, the conclusion is that the PORT should not be used in custody and related evaluations.

OTHER MEASURES

In some cases, an evaluation family may include an adolescent who presents with possibly significant psychological difficulties. Although two instruments described above, the Conners 3 and the Child Behavior Checklist, may provide useful information (especially from parent and/or teacher viewpoints), the Minnesota Multiphasic Personality Inventory – Adolescent (MMPI-A) (Butcher, Williams, Graham, Archer, Tellegen, et al., 1992) also deserves consideration. Although many clinicians find a significant proportion of adolescents to minimize or deny problems, if there is good reason to anticipate that an adolescent will be reasonably open about his or her difficulties, the MMPI-A may provide helpful clinical assessment information. The test manual provides information about reliability and validity. A relatively recent study of the MMPI-A in forensic cases reported mixed findings in terms of convergent and discriminant validity (Handel, Archer, Elkins, Mason, & Simonds-Bisbee, 2011).

The Adult-Adolescent Parenting Inventory (Bavolek, 1984) is a brief measure of parenting attitudes and beliefs. It includes four scales that measure inappropriate developmental expectations, empathy for children, disciplinary style, and role reversal. Although a limitation is that much of its content appears quite obvious, a main strength is that its standardization research found that the empathy scale showed a statistically significant difference, with approximately a medium effect size, between normal parents and those who had engaged in child maltreatment. There are also a few other studies supportive of construct validity (e,g., DePanfilis & Dubowitz, 2005; Gallant, Gorey, Gallant, Perry, & Ryan, 1998). However, the Adult-Adolescent Parenting Inventory is no longer published. A revised version changed essentially all of the questions contained in the original and is only available online, associated with educational offerings by the authors focused on parenting. As a result, the practical utility of this measure persists only for those evaluators who still have test materials, especially if they are able to make use of relevant local norms (Stricker & Trierweiler, 1995).

As described in more detail in Chapter 12, the assessment of domestic violence is a very important concern in a significant proportion of custody evaluation cases. Numerous authorities on domestic violence have commented that different circumstances associated with possible domestic violence call for somewhat different assessment measures, especially with regard to self-report inventories. The Revised Conflict Tactics Scales (CTS2) (Straus, Hamby, & Warren, 2003) has important strengths and limitations in custody evaluation use. The original version of this measure (Straus, 1979) was not designed to be a comprehensive testing procedure regarding domestic violence, though appears to have been the most frequently used dependent variable in domestic violence research.

The CTS2 includes 78 items and five scales, which are labeled as Negotiation, Psychological Aggression, Physical Assault, Injury, and Sexual Coercion. The parent responds to each item by giving an estimate of how frequently within the past year the specific behavior has taken place, or whether it has occurred at all prior to the most recent year. The questions are arranged so that the parent, for each item, gives a response in terms of their own behavior, and a separate response regarding the partner's behavior.

In evaluation practice, the main benefit of this measure is to obtain reasonably comprehensive coverage of parental reports about positive and maladaptive means of dealing with conflict. As described by the authors, it can augment information provided in interviews and/or other assessments, and it is often important to follow up with parents after they have completed the measure to ask them clarifying questions. A major problem in many settings is the underrecognition of domestic violence, and the use of the CTS2 helps to facilitate a thorough assessment of such behaviors.

At the same time, it has significant limitations in terms of the sample on which it is based, reliability, and validity. It was constructed using a sample of college students instead of a larger and more traditionally structured standardization sample. Individual scores can be compared to percentiles drawn from the college sample, though it is unlikely that custody evaluators will find such comparisons very useful. In terms of reliability, internal consistency is generally good, but there are no data regarding temporal stability (Davidson, in press). Validity data are very limited. The authors provided evidence of concurrent validity with another measure they have created, but otherwise there do not appear to be validity data regarding extratest criteria (Davidson, in press; Vacca, in press).

Therefore, CTS2 should not be considered a test regarding domestic violence. Instead, it is a potentially very useful method of providing assessment coverage regarding domestic violence, verbal/psychological aggression that would not always be considered as domestic violence, and a sample of positive means of coping with conflict. Perhaps its utility in the future will expand further if there are relevant data collected in terms of temporal stability and correspondence with extratest criteria.

Chapter 12

DIFFICULT EVALUATION CHALLENGES: DOMESTIC VIOLENCE, CHILD ABUSE, SUBSTANCE ABUSE, AND RELOCATION

PRACTICE CHECKLIST

____Men and women perpetrate domestic violence, but men are more likely to initiate severe violence that results in injury.

____Know the differences between coercive controlling domestic violence, situational couples violence, separation-instigated violence, and violent resistance.

____Review potentially objective information about domestic violence aside from parental allegations.

____Child interviews about possibly having been abused need to be carefully carried out and preferably recorded.

____There are a number of relevant procedures for evaluating whether abuse has occurred, but there are:

    ____No tests that are valid by themselves in identifying whether an individual has carried out child abuse.

    ____No accurate profile of a sexual abuser.

    ____No set of behaviors or symptoms that are uniquely a result of a child having been abused.

____Ask detailed interview questions about substance use and history of use.

____If there is reason for concern about substance misuse, ask questions about effects on life functioning and relapse risks, and pursue relevant collateral information.

____Know general research findings on the effects of relocation on children.

____Investigate and analyze specific facts and circumstances of each relocation case individually.

Note: This form is a guide to promote productive reasoning and good practice. It is not comprehensive or all-inclusive and does not replace adequate training and experience.

As described in earlier chapters, a considerable proportion of custody and related evaluations include allegations of very significant parental problems such as domestic violence, child abuse, and/or substance abuse. There is an important knowledge base associated with each such problem area.

Parental wishes to relocate with the child or children outside the state of residence present a different type of challenge for evaluators. In my practice, there have been very few relocation cases that have not also included contested custody. The time-sharing schedule, of course, is typically influenced a great deal by a parent moving out of state, whether or not custody is contested.

DOMESTIC VIOLENCE

All too often, custody evaluators are beset with conflicting parental reports of domestic violence. It is an extreme example of interparental conflict, and witnessing it tends to have a very negative effect on any children (e.g., Jaffe, Baker, & Cunningham, 2004), including those going through the divorce of their parents. A significant proportion of parents who carry out domestic violence also reportedly engage in child abuse (Appel & Holden, 1998).

Associated with domestic violence allegations, one or both parents may pursue court protective Orders. Such Orders can be valuable in protecting individuals who have been victimized, but evaluators sometimes have described that it appears there is a race between parents to get to the courthouse to first obtain such an Order. It is very rare for evaluators to obtain similar reports from parents regarding what, if any, domestic violence took place, including agreement on the main initiator and the victim.

Gender factors frequently enter into divergent parent reports about domestic violence. A number of mothers assert that they clearly could not have been the main perpetrator because the father is bigger and stronger. Numerous fathers complain that the legal system is allegedly unfairly predisposed to assume they are the guilty ones.

In this section on domestic violence, I review relevant research and professional perspectives. The main purpose here is to provide the custody evaluation practitioner with a solid information base about the most important and relevant domestic violence factors. It is not an exhaustive review, which would likely require a multivolume treatise.

First, I summarize domestic violence research on reported incidence, rates of substantiation, gender factors, and typologies. Then, there is a focus on the assessment of domestic violence, including conceptual frameworks and methods. Finally, I describe further specific assessment considerations, such as statutory factors, gleaning relevant information from protective Orders and associated legal pleadings, and other deliberations aimed at ascertaining the truth about what, if any, intimate partner violence actually took place.

There is consistent evidence that allegations of domestic violence occur in a substantial proportion of separation or divorce cases. For example, Ellis (2008) stated that about half of such couples have reported at least one incident of physical aggression during the time that they were together. A 1991 data set that included 1,318 California families mandated for mediation or custody evaluation showed allegations of domestic violence in 39% of cases (Depner, Canata, & Simon, 1992), and a 1999 California data set of 18,000 child custody cases found allegations of domestic violence against 9% of mothers and 26% of fathers (Johnston, Lee, Olesen, & Walters, 2005). In a smaller sample of 120 high-conflict couples in the San Francisco area, Johnston et al. (2005) found allegations of domestic violence against 30% of mothers and 55% of fathers. A separate California sample of custody and access disputes reported that domestic violence allegations took place in 76% of cases (Kelly & Johnson, 2008). As can be seen in earlier chapters of this book focused on psychological testing, the percentages of cases from my practice data set with allegations or evidence of domestic violence (37 to 50%, depending upon the test used) are roughly similar to those published reports.

There are ubiquitous disagreements about what alleged domestic violence did or did not actually take place in contested divorces, and there have been efforts to identify what proportion of allegations are substantiated. Johnston et al. (2005) found, in their sample of high-conflict couples, that allegations the mother carried out domestic violence were substantiated 15% of the time, as compared to 41% when the allegations were that the father was the perpetrator.

The exact percentages of domestic violence allegations in the research studies noted here vary to some extent, and such variations appear to a result of factors such as different sample types and identification methods. Regardless of the differences, it is clear and important that a substantial proportion of custody evaluation cases include such allegations. Also, there is a mix of substantiated allegations and ones that are not categorized as substantiated. The unsubstantiated ones are not necessarily disproven, and there are questions about whether it is best to conceptualize them as cases that simply did not have the benefit of more objective evidence or as examples of false accusations.

Research evidence and professional experience indicates that, within separating and divorcing samples, more men than women are alleged to have carried out domestic violence. Beyond the realm of such samples, there has been a long-standing controversy over whether women or men actually carry out violence against their romantic partners more often. Understandably, this controversy and evidence marshaled in either direction are relevant for custody evaluation and efforts to accurately assess such allegations. Although it is crucial to assess each case individually, it is also important to have a competent grasp of relevant evidence regarding gender differences and physical aggression inclusive of domestic violence.

It is relevant to consider gender differences in aggression outside the realm of domestic violence. In general, research findings suggest that men are more likely to be physically aggressive than are women. Some, but not all researchers argue that the tendency for men to manifest greater physical aggression than women is ameliorated, to some extent, by the presence of provocation (Bettencourt & Miller, 1996; Eagly & Steffen, 1986). That is, there are indications that if provocation is experienced, the difference between male and female physical aggression is much less than if no provocation has occurred.

When the focus is narrowed to physical aggression between romantic partners, the research has yielded very different findings depending upon the source of the data. In brief, samples from female victims and law enforcement reports indicate males to be by far the most frequent perpetrators of physical aggression, and samples drawn from the community, including married, cohabiting and dating couples, show a fairly even frequency of physical aggression by each gender (Archer, 2000, 2002; Johnson, 1995; Kelly & Johnson, 2008). There are important though not always large differences in such findings depending upon factors such as the specific sample that was studied, the type of physical aggression, whether the violence led to significant injury, reliance on self-report versus that of the partner, and the dependent measures used.

Archer (2000, 2002) conducted meta-analyses of existing research that allowed comparisons between male and female physical aggression in heterosexual romantic couples. That research most frequently employed the Conflict Tactics Scales (CTS) (Straus, 1979) as a main the dependent measure. The CTS is a self-report measure that includes items about physical aggression. Archer (2000) conducted a comprehensive review that included many studies of noncohabiting dating samples. However, he also included married or cohabiting couples from the community or from military bases, as well as people from women's shelters and those in treatment programs for marital violence. Archer's (2000) general finding with the CTS was that there was a small yet statistically significant effect such that women were more likely to have been physically aggressive than men, especially when self-report was relied upon. That difference was considerably smaller but in the same direction, and was only marginally statistically significant, when the report of the intimate partner was relied upon.

In contrast, when the dependent measure was whether an injury was sustained as a result of the physical aggression, the result was that males had primarily carried out the aggression. In only those cases with injuries, the woman was the victim in 65%. When only those injuries that required medical treatment were looked at, 71% had a female victim. When only those studies that had couples with marital problems as research subjects were examined, 83% of those who required medical treatment were women (Archer, 2000).

Other differences in the Archer (2000) meta-analysis are relevant for custody evaluators. With few exceptions, custody evaluation involves parents who are or had been residing together, whether married or otherwise. When the researchers looked at married/cohabitating couples versus those who were single and essentially dating, there was a tendency for a higher frequency of female aggressive acts to occur in the dating sample. There was essentially no difference in the frequency of overall aggressive acts between women and men in married and cohabitating couples. When violence that resulted in injuries is examined, for both the total injury measure and the injuries that required medical treatment, the married/cohabitating group showed a larger proportion of men having been the perpetrators than the singles/dating group.

In a later meta-analysis, Archer (2002) used only CTS data, but conducted a separate analysis for each specific physically aggressive act covered by that instrument. The importance of that analysis is that it allowed a crucial distinction between generally less severe forms of aggression (e.g., slapping, pushing, or throwing something) versus more severe types (e.g., beating up, strangling, or threats or use of a weapon) that are represented in the CTS items.

In general, Archer (2002) found that the more minor acts of aggression tended to be carried out by women and relatively severe ones by men. However, the overall effect sizes were very small for some statistical analyses. The largest effect sizes were found for men to be more likely to engage in choking or strangling. In custody evaluation practice, a large proportion of allegations involve relatively minor acts of aggression such as pushing, shoving, and grabbing; on representative CTS items, gender differences were sometimes statistically significant, but the effect sizes (Cohen, 1992) were so small that they are generally seen as not of practical importance.

These meta-analyses are highly informative, and yet the author's descriptions of limitations, especially of dependent measures, are worth noting for evaluators who try to conceptualize these findings in such a way as to productively inform their work. Some of the CTS items are overly vague; for example, regarding a question about throwing something at one's partner, there is a huge difference between throwing a towel versus a brick. Archer (2000) also noted limitations in the accuracy of data that are found in crime surveys and police reports.

Typologies

A number of authorities have contributed to the understanding of domestic violence by proposing typologies based on specific aggressive behaviors, emotional/interpersonal experiences, and situational factors. For example,

Babcock, Jacobson, Gottman, and Yerington (2000) categorized male batterers into those who had overly preoccupied attachment to their partners and became violent only upon threat of departure versus those who became violent when the partner was demanding or demeaning. Others have classified domestically violent men according to whether they appeared more proactively controlling versus reactive in their aggressive behavior (Chase, O'Leary, & Heyman, 2001). One of the more influential domestic violence typologies in the literature categorized male batterers into those who carried out violence only within the family, borderline/dysphoric individuals, or generally violent and antisocial persons (Holtzworth-Munroe & Stuart, 1994).

Controversies about domestic violence in the divorce arena and broader society, together with advances in empirical knowledge and professional experience, led to the 2007 Wingspread Conference on Domestic Violence and Family Courts, cosponsored by the National Council of Juvenile and Family Court Judges and the Association of Family and Conciliation Courts. One of the productive consequences of that conference was an advanced framework for conceptualizing domestic violence that can potentially aid in assessment and intervention (Kelly & Johnson, 2008).

A central aspect of that framework was the development of a domestic violence typology highly relevant for the separation and divorce arena. Kelly and Johnson (2008) described the typology. Coercive controlling violence is a type of physical aggression against a romantic partner that is accompanied by intimidation, coercion and control. It is classically described by terms such as battering and wife beating, and has been the main type addressed by often-used intervention programs based on the Duluth Model, inclusive of the Power and Control Wheel as a conceptual framework and educational tool (Pence & Paymar, 1993).

Situational couples violence is described as a type of behavior that occurs in domestic violence cases that are not primarily based on power and control motivations. This type of domestic violence typically involves heated disagreements and arguments that escalate into physical aggression (Kelly & Johnson, 2008; Ver Steegh & Dalton, 2008).

Separation-instigated violence is a type of domestic violence that first emerges during the separation. Therefore, it is different from the other types that tend to be repeated or continuing. Domestic violence that is continuous during the separation is more likely to be situational couple violence or coercive controlling violence.

Violent resistance is a type of aggressive behavior that involves efforts to defend oneself against coercive controlling violence, with the objective of stopping it. In the past, a number of women's advocates have asserted that this type of violence is the only one carried out by women (e.g., Walker, 1984).

There have been more recently proposed modifications to the typology of domestic violence. Austin and Drozd (2013) proposed additional subtypes of substance abuse-associated violence and major mental disorder-associated violence.

These typologies of domestic violence are very helpful, and yet like others, they are not perfect and should not be considered the final word on the subject. For example, some instances of situational couple's violence appear to intensify into controlling couples violence (Kelly & Johnson, 2008), and therefore custody evaluators need to be diligent about the possibility of such transformations.

There have been efforts to identify gender differences associated with the different categories of domestic violence. In general, coercive controlling violence is mainly perpetrated by men and involves a greater severity of physical aggression than other types of domestic violence. Similar to the Archer (2000, 2002) meta-analyses, recent research has reported that domestic violence data drawn from police records, shelter agencies, and hospitals predominantly find coercive controlling violence with its relatively high severity of physical aggression. Community survey samples identify higher frequencies of situational couples violence, with a more even gender balance and lower severities of aggressive behavior (Johnson, 2006; Kelly & Johnson, 2008).

For custody evaluators, a solid grasp of this empirical and conceptual information is crucial. Of course, there needs to be an integration of such knowledge with the particular facts and circumstances of each individual case so that recommendations can be made that promote children's best interest. A very useful framework has been proposed by a number of leading authorities in the field (Jaffe, Johnston, Crooks, & Bala, 2008) that integrates a domestic violence typology, relevant dimensions of violence, credibility considerations, and proposals for appropriate parenting plans. Those authors propose that three domestic violence factors be strongly considered: potency; pattern; and primary perpetrator. Screening for them includes a number of questions to address under each of the three categories, and custody evaluators can use this format as a conceptual guide to help consider important factors to assist in reaching productive conclusions and recommendations.

Assessment Instruments

There are a number of other methods and instruments for assessing domestic violence. Many can be helpful and none are perfect. Numerous individuals in the domestic violence field have remarked that it is difficult for any single instrument to be optimally useful in a variety of different settings in which domestic violence needs to be a focus area. As described above, the CTS (Straus, 1979) has been the instrument mainly used in academic research.

However, it was not designed to primarily and comprehensively investigate details of domestic violence, and over the years that it has been used, a number of deficits were identified.

A revised version of the CTS (Revised Conflict Tactics Scales) (CTS2) (Straus, Hamby, Boner-McCoy, & Sugarman, 1996) has been published with a number of important improvements. Those include item content, number of questions, coverage of relatively severe and minor aggressive acts, and scales for sexual coercion and physical injury that results from aggression.

Ellis (2008) described having investigated over 25 different instruments aimed at assessing domestic violence. However, he needed to create a different one, DOVE (Domestic Violence Evaluation) in order to have specific focus on mediation.

Drozd (2008) compiled a series of questions aimed at helping an interviewer cover important facets of conflict resolution efforts, inclusive of domestic violence. The author emphasized that this protocol is not a test and is meant as a guide especially focused on child custody cases.

The Spousal Assault Risk Assessment (SARA) (Kropp, Hart, Webster, & Eaves, 1999) is another instrument intended as a guide to assess domestic violence. However, its main validity data involve men who were incarcerated or on legal probation. Therefore, custody evaluators may reasonably wonder about its degree of applicability to child custody evaluation parents.

Regardless of any instrument used to try to clarify the possible presence of domestic violence in evaluation cases, it is likely that follow-up interviewing will be necessary in many instances. In carrying out such follow-up interviewing, it may be useful to make use of checklists and other guides (e.g., Austin & Drozd, 2013; Nichols-Hadeed, Cerulli, Kaukeinen, Rhodes, & Campbell, 2012) to assist with reasonably comprehensive coverage of intimate partner violence and relevant other behavior problem areas.

Of course, allegations of domestic violence are routinely disputed, particularly within the context of child custody evaluations. The typically very private nature of domestic violence makes such credibility assessments a significant challenge. In a number of cases, however, relatively objective evidence exists that can help shed light on the matter.

Collateral Information

As described previously, allegations of domestic violence frequently are accompanied by one or both parties pursuing protective Orders (although such Orders can be requested and issued for reasons other than domestic violence). At times, some of those Orders can provide useful information about the validity of the allegations, depending upon the circumstances. Perhaps obviously, different states have different formats and procedures regarding protective Orders. In Illinois, there often are two main steps, beginning with a parental request for an Emergency Order of Protection, which usually lasts for only a very limited time. Characteristically, one parent is present in court, and associated with having completed a relevant Petition, requests that the judge issue the Emergency Order of Protection so that the other parent will not be able to make contact with him or her. In the past, the judiciary had informed local evaluators that such Emergency Orders are largely granted as a safety measure in what is perceived to be a time of crisis. In other words, under such circumstances, judges generally prefer to be on the safe side, and as a result, evaluators should not infer that judges believe they have had ample opportunity to decide whether there is a sound reason for such an Order. Depending upon the circumstances, that parent may petition for a much longer-duration Plenary Order of Protection. There is a hearing before a judge in order to determine whether a Plenary Order of Protection is justified. Therefore, the judiciary has advised that if a judge has issued a Plenary Order of Protection in response to a domestic violence allegation, it is reasonable for evaluators to conclude the judge believed there was adequate evidence that the domestic violence actually took place. At the same time, it may be productive for evaluators to request to obtain a transcript of the hearing for relevant details.

Police reports about alleged domestic violence incidents at times provide useful information about the accuracy of allegations. For example, because calls to the police often occur during or soon after an incident, a reporting officer may obtain a more accurate description from one or both parties, as compared to what may be related to an evaluator weeks or months later. Also, because police reports are made relatively contemporaneously, and are made by trained, objective individuals, they are more likely to be unbiased than a report given by a parent during an evaluation interview. At other times, however, police reports may simply record the opposing statements of each parent.

Medical records are available in some cases that might provide corroborating information about domestic violence allegations. Perhaps obviously, it is important to read the details of any such record that is reviewed. A parent may go to an emergency room and report having been the victim of a domestic violence incident, whether or not such an incident actually occurred. If a parental trip to an emergency room provides clear evidence of injury that is consistent with the parental report of what transpired, and perhaps also consistent with a police record, then there is a significant degree of consistency in the evidence that the allegation is valid. In contrast, if an emergency room visit leads to a record that shows no evidence of any injury, and just reports that the parent came for service because they wanted a record of the alleged incident, it raises the possibility that the parent might be carrying out a strategy to create a set of documents that appear favorable to him or her.

Somewhat similarly, parents sometimes submit photographs of what they state are injuries they have received as a result of the other parent's aggression toward them. Such photographs, in some cases, may provide useful supplementary information if they are corroborated by police reports, medical records, or other objective sources of data. However, in some cases parent submit photographs that are questionable. For example, some parents have submitted photographs of apparent bruises, though there was no evidence in any of the photographs that the subject of that picture was actually the parent who submitted them. Also, aside from the parental assertion, there was no other indication that the bruises were the result of physical aggression by any other individual.

It is important to collect information from other sources of probably objective information about allegations of intimate partner violence. In a number of cases, children have been witness to relevant incidents. However, it is crucial to interview children about such matters in a way that maximizes the likelihood of them reporting information accurately. See Chapter 7 for details.

It is fairly rare to find individuals who are both reasonably objective and who can provide useful information other than immediate family members. However, when such interviews take place, it is important to clarify with such collaterals what relevant interactions they had directly observed.

There are other behavioral features periodically correlated with intimate partner violence that are often useful to clarify. For example, perpetrators of domestic violence generally are more likely than most individuals to manifest substance misuse, major psychological disorders, and/or past physical aggression outside the intimate relationship (Austin & Drozd, 2013). However, for each particular case, it is important to keep in mind that the presence of features such as substance abuse or psychological disorder does not lead to a certain conclusion that the relevant individual is a domestic violence perpetrator.

CHILD ABUSE

Child abuse and neglect are unfortunately common in the United States. It is estimated that 1.25 million children experienced maltreatment of some type according to the most recent federal government data. More specifically, about 323,000 children experienced physical abuse and 135,000 sexual abuse. Approximately 295,000 children experienced physical neglect, and the remainder experienced other forms of maltreatment (Sedlak, Mettenberg, Basena, Petta, McPherson et al., 2010). At the same time, it is noteworthy that Kuehnle and Kirkpatrick (2005) previously maintained that national surveys do not provide reliable approximations of the incidence of child sexual abuse.

A significant minority of custody evaluation cases include an allegation or evidence of abuse or neglect. In the data set from my practice that I relied upon for psychological test data, allegations or evidence of child abuse occurred in 27 to 33% of cases, depending upon the test used. As in the national sample, most of the abuse allegations pertain to physical abuse.

There has been controversy over whether, and how much, allegations of abuse, especially sexual abuse, may occur more frequently in the context of child custody evaluation than in other settings. Earlier studies (McIntosh & Prinz, 1993; Thoennes & Tjaden, 1990) reported that allegations of child sexual abuse occurred in less than 2% of all divorces in which custody was disputed. Although it is obviously a very small percentage, Poole and Lamb (1998) pointed out that the rate of allegations in national statistics generally was about one-sixth that rate. Ceci and Bruck (1995) maintained that rates of false allegations are higher in custody cases than in other arenas. Poole and Lamb also stated that there is a consensus that false allegations are more common when the complaints are initiated by parents as opposed to children, and that a considerable proportion of those allegations are results of sincere concern by a parent that abuse may have taken place.

Perhaps obviously, evaluators need to have adequate training in the area of assessing child abuse to do a competent job. Individuals who do not have adequate background should not serve as evaluators in such cases. A lack of relevant expertise is one of the harbingers of doom in custody evaluation described by Woody (2000), who is both a psychologist and attorney. The information in this section is intended as a useful summary for evaluators, and may serve as a springboard for further professional development in this arena. It is by no means comprehensive, which would likely require, as in the domestic violence area, multiple volumes. A good general source for information and training in this area is the American Professional Society on the Abuse of Children. For example, that society has published or sponsored books on the assessment of sexual abuse (e.g., Faller, 2002; Quinsey & Lalumiere, 2001). Also, a book by Kuehnle (1996) on sexual abuse assessment contains a great deal of relevant information.

The child interview is a main method of assessing whether abuse has occurred. Child interviews can supply generally useful and accurate information if the interviews are carried out at a high level. However, it takes considerable focus and effort to plan and carry out good-quality child interviews. Also, it is important to note that prior interviewing, sometimes done informally by parents or others, can interfere with the later accuracy of a well conducted professional child interview. When an evaluator is aware in advance that a child interview will be focused, at least in part, on assessing possible abuse (in some cases, statements about abuse arise unexpectedly during interviewing about other matters), it would be productive to include electronic recording of the

interview. Chapter 7 contains a summary of research background and important recommendations for conducting the child interview, but it should not be
seen as adequate training in itself. Kuehnle and Kirkpatrick (2005) described
their preferred methods of integrated home-based parent-child observations
and interviews, combined with separate child-only interviews in an office
setting.

When there are allegations that a parent has been abusive, it is also important
to carry out relevant procedures with the alleged perpetrator. In the literature,
the primary focus has been on alleged sexual abuse. Sachsenmaier (2005)
summarized assessment methods primarily focused on potentially identifying
parents who carried out sexual abuse. She emphasized that, although a
number of procedures may be potentially relevant for such an assessment,
there are no evaluation procedures of any type, including psychological or
physiological tests, which are valid in clearly identifying whether or not an
individual has or has not carried out a sexually abusive act. Somewhat similarly, she pointed out that there is no accurate profile of a sexual abuser, and
that there is no set of symptoms or behaviors that is uniquely a result of the
child having been abused, a point also made in a number of other important
reviews (e.g., Ceci & Bruck, 1995; Poole & Lamb, 1998).

When the question of abuse has been raised in a substantive manner prior
to the custody evaluation, a child protective services agency may already
have had involvement, including having conducted a child interview. It
would be important for the evaluator to try to obtain the records of that investigation, though depending upon the jurisdiction, they may not be available
without a subpoena or Order. Also, the quality of work by a child protective
services agency can be variable.

In the state where I practice, Illinois, I have seen the work product of the
child protective services agency vary between excellent and inadequate. All
too often, such agencies are underfunded, as they seldom are political priorities.
In a fairly recent case, prior to the Order for a custody evaluation, the agency
appropriately coordinated with the local state attorney in conducting a video-
taped child interview carried out by a trained staff member. However, because of inadequate funding, the videorecording equipment was not working
well, and therefore the most crucial part of the interview did not get clearly
recorded. In another case, the agency decided that sexual abuse of a very
young child, who had understandably very limited verbal development, had
taken place because she responded affirmatively when asked a specific question
about whether she had been touched inappropriately. However, an evaluation
included further interviewing that revealed she responded affirmatively to
essentially every question asked of her, including whether there was a dog
present in the interview room when there actually was none. In a separate
case, an older child disclosed that a parent had been repeatedly physically

abusive toward him, even though he previously had informed a child protective services interviewer that no such abuse had taken place. When he was asked about that discrepancy, he replied that the child services worker had interviewed him in the kitchen of his relatively small home, and he was afraid that the parent who had abused him would easily be able to hear from the next room, a highly understandable concern.

When child physical abuse has been alleged, the Child Abuse Potential Inventory (CAPI) (Milner, 1986) may be appropriate to administer to the person alleged to have carried out the abuse. That instrument is designed to identify moderate or higher levels of child physical abuse. Milner (1989) described child injury as the criterion for identifying whether physical abuse has been at a moderate or higher level. Also, the CAPI is most likely to be accurate when used in settings in which the base rate for moderate or higher physical abuse is approximately 50%. In my experience, the solid majority of allegations about physical abuse that arise in child custody practice pertain to relatively mild or minor physical abuse. Therefore, it would be very appropriate to use it in custody evaluations when the allegation is about moderate or greater physical abuse, but it should be used only for that purpose for which it is validated and not regarding mild abuse or as a general screening device.

In cases of alleged abuse or neglect, it is important to try to obtain information from objective collateral sources. Such sources may include, but are not limited to police records, medical records, behavioral histories of alleged perpetrators, and statements from other individuals who may have witnessed relevant actions and/or statements. See Chapter 5 and the section above on domestic violence for further detail about collateral information.

Substance Misuse

The World Health Organization (2007) estimated that the lifetime prevalence of any substance use disorder in the United States was approximately 21%. The 12-month prevalence was approximately 4.5%. As described in the chapters of this book that include psychological test data, concerns about substance misuse are present in a significant minority of the current evaluation cases.

In recent decades, there has been a great deal of concern about how substance misuse by parents influences children throughout the lifespan. For example, young adults who were children of alcoholics, compared to those who were children of nonalcoholic parents, manifested more substance abuse problems, psychological difficulty, and lower academic achievement (Sher, Walitzer, Wood, & Brent, 1991). A longitudinal study that began with adolescents who had either an alcoholic parent or no alcoholic parent, and followed up over 5 to 7 years later, reported that those who grew up with an alcoholic parent had higher levels of substance abuse and mood problems than others (Chassin, Pitts, DeLucia, & Todd, 1999).

Also, it is commonly observed that there frequently is a link between substance abuse and domestic violence. A longitudinal study over two years found that problem drinking appeared to prevent marital couples from coping adequately with disagreements, and that marital problems seemed to contribute to alcohol consumption as a maladaptive form of coping (Keller, El-Sheikh, Keiley, & Liao, 2009).

There are often practical and important health questions about what constitutes substance misuse versus healthy use. The answers can be very relevant for parenting and parent-child relationships. In general, any illicit drug use can accurately be seen as the misuse of a substance because it violates the law. Because marijuana is legal, at least under some circumstances, according to a number of state statutes, it is important for evaluators to be knowledgeable about such local facts.

Obviously, alcohol is legal and yet is frequently misused. The Centers for Disease Control (CDC) (2012) describe the upper limit of moderate drinking as no more than two normal-sized drinks per day for a male and one for a female. Accordingly, heavy drinking is described as any amount larger than moderate drinking. Binge drinking is defined by the CDC as five drinks or more per episode for a male and four or more for a female. Alcohol abuse is also described by that agency as resulting in a significant problem in life functioning, such as family, work, physical functioning, and/or psychologically. Alcohol dependence is described as characterized by craving alcohol, an inability to limit or stop drinking, and continued use despite repeated problems.

For evaluators, an important consideration is obtaining a clear picture of parental substance use. As described in Chapter 5, such questioning should be a routine part of structured clinical interviews of parents. It is interesting that many parents seem quite unaware that their alcohol use regularly exceeds moderate, healthy levels. A number of parents, when first asked to describe their alcohol use, replied that they did not drink. In such circumstances, an additional inquiry is useful, such as asking "not at all"? In most of these cases, after that type of follow-up question, parents acknowledged alcohol use, though often at a mild to moderate level.

When there is information from any source that an individual's substance use may have been heavy at any time, it is crucial to ask detailed questions about it. For example, the parent should be asked about not only recent or current use, but about the heaviest period of use, including frequency, amount, other use patterns, and consequences. It is important to obtain a full history from that individual of any relevant treatment they may have had, as well as involvement in 12-Step or similar self-help organizations. The parent may be asked if they have had other experiences, not covered by the questions noted above, that fit with relevant diagnostic criteria. Schleuderer and Campagna (2004) suggested interview questions, based in part on their experiences, focused especially on alcohol and marijuana use, which are the substances most frequently misused.

In some cases, a parent will acknowledge having had a period of time of substance misuse. It is likely to happen only extremely rarely that a parent will state that they are regularly misusing a substance at the time of the evaluation. For those parents who described that they have had a history of substance misuse, it is often very productive to ask them about their plans for continuing recovery. Substance abuse and dependence are disorders that have very substantial relapse rates, regardless of the particular substance or substances misused (though there are reported differences in relapse rates between a number of different substances). Active and sincere involvement in ongoing treatment and/or appropriate self-help generally leads to lower relapse rates. If an individual's response indicates that they are not involved in such recovery activities, while there can be no certain predictions made, the risk of relapse is generally higher. In addition, with parents who have had substance misuse problems, I routinely ask them what they perceive to be risk factors for relapse. Individuals who respond that they do not need to be concerned about possible relapses manifest denial about the nature of their problem. The more common general risk factors include associating with others who are likely to be using, being in situations in which substance use is likely, and/or experiencing emotional states (usually but not always negative) likely to lead to cognitions or even craving for substance use.

If there is a concern that the use of any illicit substance might be ongoing, it may be useful to consider a toxicology screen. Urine screens are the most common, though a limitation is that most substances of abuse can only be detected if they have been used a very short time prior to an individual leaving the sample. For many substances the estimated detection time is only about 1 to 3 days, and for alcohol it is only a few hours. A few substances, such as marijuana and benzodiazepines, remain in the body much longer and therefore can sometimes be detected for a few weeks. Laboratories that conduct the toxicology screens typically have certain panels of drugs for which they test, and a relatively basic panel will cover most substances of abuse. However, especially with increased use of prescription pain medication, it is important to specify the substances for which testing is needed. Also, some substances change very rapidly in the body and therefore may show up as positive in a urine screen, but in a different form. In that regard, if the testing takes place a short enough time after the ingestion of heroin so that a positive result is found, it is likely to be identified as morphine in the urine sample. Evaluators who make use of urine screens should develop basic working knowledge about them (e.g. Standridge, Adams, & Zotos, 2010; U. S. Library of Medicine, 2013).

An alternate means of testing for possible drug use is hair analysis. A reported advantage of hair analysis is that there is a much longer period of time that evidence of drug use shows up in hair analysis as compared to urinalysis. However, I have heard numerous informal anecdotal reports that there are various ways to treat hair that are likely to overcome the ability of hair analysis to detect drug use. Although there are also ways that individuals try to defeat urinalysis, such as by smuggling into the lab someone else's urine to use as the sample, adequate monitoring of the urine drop usually prevents of such efforts. In contrast, if an individual expects that they may need to leave a hair sample, the efforts to defeat such an analysis can be carried out at the individual's home without likely means of detecting it.

Although there are psychological testing scales designed to identify actual or potential substance misuse problems, in practice I have found them rarely useful. The MMPI-2 has a number of supplementary scales focused on alcohol problems. Although I did not statistically analyze any supplementary scale data, the ones focused on alcohol use very rarely showed any elevation, even when there were other consistent indications of heavy alcohol use by that parent.

The PAI has main clinical scales designed to measure drug (DRG) and alcohol (ALC) problems that were included in the statistical analyses. In the cases that were identified as including an allegation or evidence of substance misuse, there were statistically higher ALC but not DRG scores as compared to cases without any indication of substance misuse. However, even in those cases with the allegation or evidence of substance misuse, the mean ALC T-score was below average. Schleuderer and Campagna (2004) also noted that psychological testing scales focused on substance misuse were rarely effective, and were less productive than interviews together with relevant collateral information.

The assessment of possible substance misuse by a caregiver needs to consider collateral information, to the extent that it is available. As described elsewhere in this book, primary considerations regarding collateral information include source credibility, obtaining interview descriptions that contain direct observations of relevant behaviors, and making an effort to obtain potentially relevant documents such as DUI histories and other police records that might exist. In addition, in some cases, parents who are alleged to have been engaging in substance misuse identify collaterals to interview. Such collaterals routinely assert that the parent has no problem with substance misuse. In the vast majority of these cases, the focus has been on possibly excessive alcohol consumption. In a number of interviews, when the collaterals have been asked to describe what alcohol consumption they observed by the parent, they reported the parent routinely consumed a number of drinks per occasion that falls in the heavy drinking category. Obviously, the collaterals were unaware that what they had described was heavy drinking. At times they belonged to a social group with the parent that engaged in frequently heavy alcohol consumption, and they believed it was within the normal drinking range.

RELOCATION

It is essential that evaluators be thoroughly familiar with the legal criteria for relocation in the state in which they are working (for a few examples of different state criteria, see Austin, 2008b; Duggan, 2007; for California case law and Arizona statute, see Stahl, 2013; for Illinois criteria, see Chapter 2, Case B). Also, relocation criteria likely differ considerably from those regarding custody or visitation. In general, however, many questions about relocation focus on the child's best interest, especially promoting positive relationships with both parents, considerations about stages of children's development and other aspects of their lives, and possible major life changes for a parent such as marriage and/or work that are likely to impact children.

Austin (2008a) reviewed research literature on relocation and concluded that there is considerable evidence that it generally leads to worse outcomes for children. The poorer outcomes for children who relocate are found whether or not they involve intact or separated-divorced families. However, there are lower rates of relocation by intact families as compared to others. More frequent relocations appear to generally lead to increasingly worse child outcomes. The effect for poor outcomes associated with relocation is strong even after controlling for family income. It is noteworthy that Stahl (2013) questioned the degree to which extrapolations from this body of research are applicable to legal petitions for relocation.

In one representative study of actual postdivorce relocation, college students with divorced parents were divided into groups based on whether moving away had taken place. When parents had moved, it generally led to worsened child outcomes (Braver, Elman, & Fabricius, 2003). Concern has also been raised about the impact of relocation especially on very young children. For example, when relocation takes place that decreases the frequency of contact between a very young child and a parent, it would have a risk of interfering with the development of attachment security (Kelly & Lamb, 2003).

However, as described by Austin (2008a), it is crucial that evaluators not use these general research findings to develop a bias against relocation. Although it is important to be familiar with such research data, each case needs to be examined according to its own unique facts and circumstances. Although relocation cases can be especially challenging, for some children and family circumstances, a relocation is likely to lead to improved outcomes. It important to keep in mind that the United States is a nation of historically significant residential mobility, and that there is a danger of trying to excessively predict individual case outcomes only on the basis of general, group-level research data.

Accordingly, Austin (2008b) described a number of factors to be considered in relocation evaluation specific for each case. Within each factor, there are multiple layers of conceptual and factual consideration. One of those factors, the involvement of the nonresidential parent typically left behind in relocation is frequently of central importance in an evaluation. For each case, an important consideration is the amount and quality of interaction between the child and the nonresidential parent prior to a possible move. In general, research has found that the quality of parenting by a nonresidential father is an important determinant of child outcomes (Amato & Gilbert, 1999). A particularly strong area of focus is the relationship between the child and the nonresidential parent that would be able to take place after a potential relocation. Although research has not identified a statistical relationship between the frequency of visits and child outcome, there clearly needs to be an adequate amount of contact to permit good-quality parent-child relationships, and there is a general risk of involvement by a nonresidential parent dropping off or discontinuing if the child relocates 75 miles away or more (Austin, 2000b).

Other factors described by Austin (2000b) that need to be considered on an individual case basis also require careful deliberation. Those factors are child age; relocation distance and travel time; the psychological functioning of the potentially relocating parent; the parenting effectiveness of both parents; individual differences in child/family resources, child temperament, and special needs; levels of support and/or nonsupport for the relationship between the child and the other parent; interparental conflict and domestic violence; and how recently the marital separation had taken place. Recently, Stahl (2013) described very similar factors that should be considered by evaluators.

From a judicial perspective, Duggan (2007) reviewed relevant statutory and case law. He identified 36 different factors that have been considered in relocation cases and statutes.

Perhaps obviously, there are almost innumerable combinations of different factors that may be relevant for different cases. Such individual family complexities require careful case-by-case analysis. One method for structuring a relevant analysis that promotes necessary deliberation is described in Chapter 2. It involves staying cognizant of legal criteria and scientific evidence, while also specifically noting the assertions of each party, as well as other hypotheses that might be developed by the evaluator, and recording evidence of that both supports and contradicts each assertion or hypothesis. Evidence that is most objective would need to be highlighted. Thorough analysis with a focus on empirically-based information, sound reasoning, and relevant legal statutes and/or case law facilitates the likelihood of a quality assessment, and it also provides a solid foundation for risk management (Woody, 2013).

Chapter 13

PARENTAL ALIENATION AND GATEKEEPING

PRACTICE CHECKLIST

Children can become alienated from a parent for a number of reasons and combinations of reasons, including:

_____A purposeful campaign by a parent to lead a child to despise and avoid the target parent.

_____Abusive, neglectful, and/or other negative behavior by the target parent.

_____Fear and worry by a parent that the target parent has carried out highly negative behavior or is a high risk to do so.

_____Child enmeshment with the aligned parent.

_____A child's fear of upsetting a parent by leaving him/her alone to visit the other parent.

_____Normal separation anxiety in very young children.

_____Distress associated with transitions between parents in very children.

_____Strong child dependence on the aligned parent.

_____Child psychological problems.

_____Inadequate warmly involved parenting by the target parent.

_____The target parent's psychological and/or social problems.

_____The presence of intense marital conflict.

_____Heated and/or protracted divorce-related litigation.

_____Contributions of mild to moderate parenting limitations by the target parent.

_____Psychological testing has not effectively distinguished between alienating and nonalienating parents.

_____Intervention efforts should be carried out by highly experienced and well-trained practitioners.

Note: This form is a guide to promote productive reasoning and good practice. It is not comprehensive or all-inclusive and does not replace adequate training and experience.

Parental alienation has perhaps been the most heated and controversial issue in the child custody realm. In brief, parental alienation refers to one parent turning a child against the other parent, or at least attempting to do so. A significant proportion of the evaluation cases include allegations of some type or degree of parental alienation.

In recent years, there has been increased focus in the literature on parental gatekeeping, a broader concept that partially overlaps with parental alienation. Parental gatekeeping has been described as behaviors by either parent that influence the involvement and relationship of the child with the other parent, and has its origins in research on maternal actions that restricted father involvement within intact families (Allen & Hawkins, 1999). Within the divorce and child custody context, gatekeeping is seen potentially as either restrictive or facilitative, and at least some aspects of highly restrictive gatekeeping have more typically been described as parental alienation (e.g., Austin, Fieldstone, & Pruett, 2013; Austin, Pruett, Flens, & Gould, 2013; Pruett et al., 2007).

In the remainder of this chapter, there first is a focus on parental alienation and the main controversies associated with it. Those controversies include matters of definition, sociopolitical positions, etiological factors, research, and professional considerations. Second, there is a discussion of the parental gatekeeping concept, including its potential contributions to the field as well as possible difficulties associated with semantic and conceptual clarity. Then, information from various sources is integrated into considerations for practicing evaluators.

Whether one is considering parental alienation or restrictive gatekeeping, there potentially are numerous complications involved, and it may be useful when considering each case to keep in mind three basic questions. The first is to consider evidence of the degree to which a child has or has not veered away from or rejected one parent and become aligned with the other. The second is whether either parent has carried out communication and/or other action that would potentially limit the child from involvement with the other parent. Also, a central challenge in a number of these cases, especially when one parent has worked to limit child contact with the other, is to what extent there is good reason for that contact to be restricted. Clearly, some parents engage in child maltreatment, inadequate care, domestic violence, and/or have other very significant individual problems that warrant protection for the child, inclusive of limitations in contact.

PARENTAL ALIENATION

Although an earlier report (Wallerstein & Kelly, 1976) described that, associated with separation and divorce, some older children were resistant to see one parent and aligned with the other (a form of triangulation noted by early family therapy scholars), within the child custody field, the term and concept of parental alienation was first popularized by Gardner (e.g., 1992), a psychiatrist. He argued that the parental alienation syndrome had a set of common symptoms and therefore was a distinct disorder. Gardner's view of the parental alienation syndrome was that a child, without justification, manifested an extremely negative attitude and denigrating behavior toward a target parent; the alienation resulted from brainwashing behavior by an angry, alienating parent, plus child additions to the disparagement.

There were both highly favorable and unfavorable reactions to this view of parental alienation. In most custody cases mothers have been the primary caregivers, and as a result, in cases in which parental alienation has been alleged, fathers mainly have been the target parents. Accordingly, fathers' rights groups, which have often argued that the legal system favors women, tended to show considerable positive regard for Gardner's (1992) parental alienation stance. Women's rights organizations at times maintained that allegations of parental alienation were aimed at covering up or avoiding abusive, violent, or otherwise coercive behaviors by fathers. Recently, there has been controversy (e.g., Bernet, 2008; Walker & Schapiro, 2010) about possible inclusion of the parental alienation syndrome as a disorder in the revised Diagnostic and Statistical Manual (DSM5) of the American Psychiatric Association (2013). The DSM5 committee reportedly considered the proposal but did not include parental alienation as a disorder.

A number of practitioners and researchers perceived that, while children sometimes did become alienated from parents, and that some parents did actually carry out campaigns to diminish and interfere with the relationship between the child and the other parent, the Gardner (1992) position on parental alienation contributed to significant problems. In part, in some highly contested custody cases, parents and/or attorneys would lump together various child and parent attitudes, statements, and behaviors as alleged parental alienation, without considering numerous other factors.

In order to address such complex matters and potentially advance the field toward a more accurate and useful understanding, Kelly and Johnston (2001) proposed an influential reformulation of the parental alienation concept. I recommend that anyone involved in working with alleged or actual parental alienation read the article in full. The main points are briefly summarized here.

Kelly and Johnston (2001) pointed out there are multiple problems with the Gardner (1992) definition of parental alienation. Those problems include evidence that children can become alienated for reasons other than actions of the supposedly alienating parent. Also, the Gardner hypothesis of alienation causation is not one that lends itself to productive research, and the majority of

Gardner's writings have not been peer reviewed. Kelly and Johnston maintained that it is more objective and scientifically productive to have an initial point of focus on the alienated child. Also, they asserted that because such children provide considerable challenges for almost everyone involved, it is important to place them at the center of efforts to understand relevant phenomena.

In that regard, Kelly and Johnston (2001) pointed out that there are reasons other than actively alienating behaviors by one parent that can lead children to avoid or resist visitation with the other parent. Those reasons can include phenomena such as a child's worry about leaving a highly distressed parent alone to visit the other parent, a very young child's relatively normal separation anxiety, child distress associated with the transition between parents, and concerns about interactions with a parent's new spouse or significant other. The authors also recognized that children can avoid and resist visits with a parent for healthy reasons, when that parent has actually carried out highly negative actions, and they labeled children's responses under such circumstances as estrangement, not alienation.

The authors described that the relationships between the child and each parent are best viewed as being on a continuum. On the healthiest end of the continuum, the child has a positive relationship with both parents. A modest step away from that optimal circumstance involves the child experiencing an affinity with one parent but wanting to have regular contact with both. The next step away from the healthiest end involves a child who is allied with one parent and wants only limited contact with the other parent after the separation or divorce. At this point, the child experiences ambivalent feelings toward the nonpreferred parent. In a number of these cases, the child is estranged from the nonpreferred parent for good reasons; they may include that parent's pattern of abusive or violent behavior, inadequate or harsh parenting, and/or other significant problems such as substance misuse. At the least healthy end of the continuum is the alienated child, who manifests highly entrenched negative attitudes and behaviors toward the target parent, often refusing any contact at all.

When a child is clearly alienated, Kelly and Johnston (2001) indicated there are a number of factors that can contribute toward that alienation. Such factors include the presence of intense marital conflict, high-conflict litigation, the aligned parent's experiences of humiliation associated with the divorce, and contributions of other individuals such as extended family, new romantic partners, and/or misguided or unaware professionals.

The parent who is aligned with the alienated child at times manifests certain attitudes and/or behaviors. According to the authors of the reformulation, such parents can tend to believe that the other parent is not necessary for the child's life, and that he or she is not worthy of involvement with the child. It commonly occurs that the aligned parent believes that the target or rejected parent never really cared for the child. A number of aligned parents believe that the other parent is dangerous or at least incompetent. Also, aligned parents can tend to manifest individual psychological problems associated with not maintaining adequate personal boundaries with the child.

As emphasized above, sometimes a parent is rejected for sound reasons by a child, such as abusive, neglectful, and/or other dysfunctional behaviors. Kelly and Johnston (2001) described that there can be other behaviors by a rejected parent that inadvertently contribute toward alienation in a child. For example, some rejected parents have had a history of passivity and withdrawal in the midst of conflict with the aligned parent, and therefore have had relatively little positive contact with the child. Other rejected parents responded by manifesting a type of retaliatory rejection toward the child. A number of target parents may have manifested more moderate parenting limitations such as rigidity, self-centeredness, limited empathy or excessive criticism.

Kelly and Johnston (2001) asserted that there are a number of developmental factors that can influence a child's response to a parent. For example, it is rare to see a stance of thorough and crystallized alienation by a child younger than approximately the age of seven, perhaps associated with young children having relatively shifting internal representations of parents which rely a great deal on current or most recent experiences. However, Ludolph and Bow (2012) described that younger children can be alienated, especially in cases in which an older sibling is thoroughly alienated from the target parent. A number of children may be highly dependent on the aligned parent and may have experienced threats of banishment if they express positive attitudes about the target parent. A child who experiences significant psychological problems may be more susceptible to dysphoria associated with conflict, and therefore may be more likely to align with one parent as a way of moderating his or her emotional discomfort.

In addition, Kelly and Johnston (2001) pointed out that if there have been allegations of sexual abuse directed toward the target parent, that individual may consequently have very limited visitation time with the child, which potentially can lead the child to feel rejected. Also, it would at least diminish opportunities for positive experiences with that parent.

A number of criticisms have been directed toward the Kelly and Johnston (2001) reformulation. For example, Gottlieb (2012), writing from a therapist vantage point, reported having worked with numerous children who persistently and thoroughly rejected a good parent without any sound rationale at all. She summarized material from a number of relevant cases. However, as noted above, Kelly and Johnston clearly stated that active parental alienation can and does occur in a number of cases, though their experiences, especially in the clinical research of Johnston and her colleagues summarized below, demonstrated that there can be a much broader range of factors, and combinations of factors, which lead a child to reject a parent. Also, Kelly and Johnston described that they perceived clearly alienated children to manifest the same types of behavior patterns described by Gardner (1992) and Gottlieb (2012).

Research

For a number of reasons, parental alienation is difficult to research. For example, in most cases in which alienation is alleged, there is vigorous disagreement by parents and attorneys as to whether or not it has occurred, or to what degree. Parents do not volunteer to come forward for research studies and identify that they have carried out campaigns to try to have their children despise the other parent. Therefore, in order to objectively identify cases in which some intensity of parental alienation has occurred, it is often necessary to closely examine many potential cases, and it is a challenge to collect sufficient numbers of cases that would allow for statistical comparisons as well as provide a basis for conclusions that would have a reasonable chance of generalizing beyond the specific sample.

Consequently, as pointed out in a recent review of parental alienation research (Saini, Johnston, Fidler, & Bala, 2012), there are significant methodological limitations in the research that has been conducted. However, some of these limitations are probably inevitable given the reality of the parental alienation phenomenon. For example, a common criticism of Saini et al. (2012) involved research studies not having drawn participants from a random sample, but it is difficult to imagine how there possibly could be a random sample of parental alienation cases, given the realities noted in the paragraph above.

Although it is important to maintain awareness of the research limitations, it is also crucial to note that the amount and quality of information derived from much of the relevant research constitute major steps forward beyond reliance on informal observation and case anecdotes. The research studies reviewed here are selective and not comprehensive. They include those that appear to have considerable relevance for evaluators.

A number of research studies have been carried out by Baker and her colleagues, focused on collecting information from individuals who reportedly had experienced parental alienation. Baker and Darnell (2006) surveyed parents who felt that they had been targets of alienating actions and statements by the other parent. A main objective was to identify behaviors used by the alienating parent. The survey respondents indicated that alienating parents frequently made negative statements about them to the children, restricted visits and phone contacts, and engaged in numerous types of emotional manipulation of the children. The authors concluded that the types of behaviors manifested by the alienating parents generally endorsed Gardner's (1992) description of the parental alienation syndrome.

In addition, Baker (2005a, 2005b) collected qualitative interview information from 40 adults who described that, as children, they had experienced an alienating parent having turned them against the other parent. Those individuals identified a similar pattern of behavior by the alienating parent as described in Baker and Darnell (2006). In addition, the research participants reported frequent negative personal consequences even in adulthood, including low self-esteem, depression, substance misuse, difficulties trusting others, and alienation from their own children.

Johnston and her colleagues have conducted more broadly-focused research, consistent with a primary focus on the alienated child (Kelly & Johnston, 2001), and with a frequent objective of trying to clarify the factors that contribute toward a child rejecting a parent. In a relatively early study (Johnston, 1993), investigated two samples of court-involved families who had not settled custody-related conflicts. Children resisted visitation in most of these cases. A main objective of the research was to identify what contributed toward the avoidance of visitation with one parent and a strong alignment with the other. There were a number of factors that appeared to contribute toward the visitation resistance, including long and intense parental conflict, children's exposure to violence and abuse, separation anxiety in very young children, enmeshment with dysfunctional parents, counterrejection by the nonpreferred parent, and children's inability to cognitively process opposite points of view in parents.

In a later study, Johnston (2003) looked at a community sample going through dissolution and court-referred families who manifested high conflict levels. There was a total of 215 children. The main objectives of the research were to obtain an estimate of the prevalence of visitation resistance/alignment with one parent, and to statistically test factors hypothesized to contribute to alienated child behaviors. Johnson reported that 20% of the court-referred children and 15% of the community children showed that they were very aligned with one parent against the other. Both mother-child and father-child alignments were identified, though in the court-referred group, there was a much higher proportion of alignments that involved the mother. In addition, the study found that multiple factors influenced rejection of a parent. More specifically, rejection of a mother or father was most strongly correlated with that parent manifesting relatively low levels of warmly involved parenting. Also, rejection of a parent of either gender was associated with child separation anxiety from the aligned parent. Rejection of a father was associated with negative maternal behaviors such as sabotage of child-father interactions and using the child for her own emotional support. Rejection of mothers was correlated with child behavior problems. In addition, there were important relationships between a number of variables. For example, for both mothers and fathers, low levels of warmly involved parenting were correlated with the presence of parental psychological/social problems and low levels of child social competence.

Johnson, Walters, and Olesen (2005b) studied a group of 125 court-referred children with the objective of shedding light on four hypotheses as to the reasons that a child would reject a parent. The hypotheses were as follows: an alienating parent teaches the child to despise the other, good-quality parent; the rejected parent had carried out child abuse and/or domestic violence; there were inadequate boundaries and role reversal that involved the aligned parent; or there was a combination of the first three factors. The authors found that there was extreme rejection of 7% of the mothers and 11% of the fathers. They also found that a combination of the first three hypotheses functioned as the best predictor of rejection of a parent. In addition, in some cases, both parents were engaged in carrying out potentially alienating behaviors.

In a separate article, Johnston, Walters, and Olesen (2005a) investigated whether alienated children manifested more psychological problems than children who did not experience alienation. Using a court-referred sample, information obtained from the aligned parents, who completed a well-standardized psychological measure, showed that alienated children tended to manifest more serious psychological problems such as depression, withdrawal, and aggression, as compared to children who were able to maintain relationships with both parents.

A small number of studies have investigated the MMPI-2 scores of parents who manifested alienating behaviors as compared to those who did not do so. For example, Siegel and Langford (1998) compared the validity scores of a small number of mothers who engaged in parental alienation to those of mothers who did not. They found statistically significant differences such that those who manifested manifested alienating behaviors had higher scores on Scale K and lower ones on the Scale F and those who did not manifest alienating behaviors. Such scores suggest higher levels of defensiveness and lower admission of psychological problems. However the differences between mean scores were small, well within the standard error of measurement, and therefore not clinically significant. Consequently, the differences are not practically useful for evaluative purposes.

As described here and elsewhere, when a child does become alienated from a parent, there is often a great deal of entrenchment of the rejecting attitudes and behaviors, and while there does not appear to be any solid empirical evidence about the effectiveness of relatively traditional individual and/or family therapy, clinical experience indicates these are often very difficult cases. Relatively intensive interventions have been reported by Sullivan, Ward, and Deutsch (2010) and Warshak (2010). Both reports involved small numbers of families and a camp or intensive workshop experience.

Both are preliminary studies of novel interventions, and give indications of potentially promising avenues for future research, but many questions remain about how to intervene effectively with children who reject parents without reasonable bases.

GATEKEEPING

The gatekeeping concept in parenting relies on the *gate* metaphor in that an open gate represents a parent facilitating and promoting the relationship between the child and the other parent, whereas a closed gate restricts or blocks such positive interactions. As noted above, the gatekeeping concept primarily has been used in academic studies of intact families and has focused on restrictive maternal behavior.

In many ways, within the divorce and child custody field, the concept of gatekeeping overlaps to a considerable extent with coparenting. Although I do not believe there has been any formal count, within the child custody field, the term and concept coparenting appears to have been used much more frequently than gatekeeping. Perhaps obviously, coparenting refers to parenting with another individual, typically the other parent. Recent articles that have focused on gatekeeping within the divorce context (e.g., Austin et al., 2013; Austin, Pruett et al., 2013; Pruett et al., 2007) have noted that there is considerable overlap between gatekeeping and coparenting.

There are nuances in terms of different connotations when using the term gatekeeping versus coparenting. For example, because most gatekeeping research has been on the restrictive type, that term may have a somewhat negative connotation. In contrast, coparenting may have a modestly positive connotation because it suggests cooperation between parents, which is positive for children. At the same time, as pointed out in the gatekeeping articles cited above, gatekeeping can be facilitative and thus much the same as good coparenting. Although the term negative coparenting does not seem to be used much, it clearly conveys parents not working well with one another regarding children. Also, at least in some contexts, coparenting seems to have broader meaning than gatekeeping.

It is important to note that a well-designed research study (Pruett, Insabella, & Gustason, 2005) of a multifaceted intervention aimed at parents going through the divorce process found a number of successful outcomes, and used the gatekeeping concept as an important component of the parent education. However, because the study understandably looked at larger outcomes such as reported levels of parental cooperation and how long it took to complete the divorce process, it did not specifically investigate the use of the gatekeeping concept as compared to other terminology such as coparenting.

A number of state statutes include what are sometimes referred to as friendly parent provisions, which can pertain to gatekeeping (Austin, Pruett et al., 2013) and coparenting. Similarly, statutes that indicate considerations about joint custody need to consider the ability of the parents to cooperate with one another can be seen as relevant to gatekeeping and coparenting.

Because of the relative success of the Pruett et al. (2007) collaborative divorce project, which employed gatekeeping in educational efforts with parents, the gatekeeping concept may be a valuable one within such highly structured contexts. It is positive that Austin, Pruett et al. (2013) encourage individuals to consider gatekeeping as a continuum as opposed to a dichotomy, and also to focus on specific relevant behaviors. The same hold true for coparenting.

As noted elsewhere in this book, especially within the context of custody litigation, all too frequently there is confusion about the meaning of important terms such as custody and parental alienation. When such confusion occurs, it mainly is to the detriment of parents going through extremely difficult circumstances who have no reason to know about the multiple usages of such terms. As there continues to be attention given to gatekeeping within the divorce and custody arena, it would be useful for scholars and practitioners to consider what unique value the gatekeeping terminology and concept bring to the field, especially when there is child custody litigation, beyond the language and conceptualizations that have been in use over longer periods of time.

CONSIDERATIONS FOR PRACTICE

Clearly, there are cases in which a parent engages in actions and statements that that lead a child to become alienated from the other parent. There are other cases in which a child resists seeing a parent for healthy, constructive reasons, such as highly negative and perhaps dangerous actions in which that parent has engaged. Also, as explicated by Kelly and Johnston (2001), there are a number of other factors that can contribute toward a child's resistance to see a parent. Evaluators need to be familiar with and consistently consider these various possible etiologies and multiple factors in relevant cases.

The research findings summarized here, together with the relatively broad conceptualization of the alienated child, shed useful light on a phenomenon sometimes seen in evaluation practice. That is, although a child may reject a parent without sound reason, that parent may manifest mild to moderate difficulties that are significantly exaggerated by the child and the aligned parent. For example, the rejected parent may have had a history of yelling somewhat too frequently, but the aligned parent and child describe that parent as routinely out of control and potentially dangerous, a great exaggeration. Further complicating the evaluative picture, the aligned parent may seem especially attractive to the child because of other reasons, such as doing a great deal for the child, being relatively lax in limit setting, and/or sharing common interests.

In some cases, there is clear evidence that a parent has made numerous efforts to negatively influence a child's attitude toward the other parent, but the child nonetheless exhibits a primarily good relationship with the target parent. In some cases, the good relationship with the target parent has a foundation in the positive direct experiences the child has had with that parent. In other cases, it may be due to the child being very young, and therefore generally unlikely to consistently adopt the negative attitudes toward the target parent. In such cases, evaluators need to be cognizant that such efforts by the potentially alienating parent might continue with the consequence of eventually having a significant impact on the child.

A different, very challenging circumstance arises in a very small proportion of cases in which there is a parent with a serious psychological disorder whose behaviors have a significant impact on the children. In a clinical setting as opposed to a custody evaluation, an appropriate therapeutic recommendation would include children learning age-appropriate educational information about the problems experienced by the dysfunctional parent, so that they can use such understanding to cushion their own emotional reactions, and potentially learn useful coping and problem solving. However, it becomes very complicated when there is a contested custody matter, as the healthy parent may wish to help the children as much as possible while also avoid making negative communications about the spouse. There clearly are no easy answers for this type of tragically difficult dilemma. It may be most useful to have the children enter into therapy with a provider who is skilled and reasonably experienced both with the problems experienced by the parent and the dilemmas associated with the divorce process.

Often, evaluators are expected to make recommendations, in cases that involve alienated children or highly restricted gatekeeping, not only about the main topics of dispute, such as residential custody, but also about how to try to ameliorate problems such as child resistance to see a child. Evaluators would need to consider numerous specific facts and circumstances relevant for each case, including, but not limited to what factors appear to have contributed toward the alienation of the child. Of course, if a child is estranged from a parent, and resistant to visits for good reasons, the parental problems would likely need to be addressed in the recommendations, also.

It commonly occurs that there are recommendations for interventions such as parent education and/or family therapy. However, a very generally worded recommendation is at a very high risk of being useless for children of divorce, especially when there are reasons for concern about an alienated child and/or a parent (either aligned or rejected) who has exposed the child to highly negative behavior. For example, I have seen numerous cases in which parents are directed simply to obtain therapy for the child and themselves, seek out a general mental health practitioner who may be referred through their insurance, and find themselves with a provider who has neither the training nor experience to be helpful in the matter. It is not easy to find therapists who are well trained and experienced in such highly complex cases, as also noted by Ludolph and Bow (2012). Therefore, recommendations are more likely to be useful if they include relevant specifics, including a requirement that the intervention takes place with adequate frequency and duration to give it a reasonable chance of being successful.

Chapter 14

REPORT WRITING

PRACTICE CHECKLIST

____Large majorities of judges and attorneys want recommendations included in reports.

____Clearly describe the purpose(s) of the evaluation, and cite the relevant Order or agreement.

____Clearly summarize the information that was collected.

____Clearly describe an analysis of the reasons for the recommendations.

____Use a report format that is organized logically and useful for consumers.

____Remain cognizant that the report is often an important settlement tool.

____The report is the main representation of all the work carried out in the evaluation.

Note: This form is a guide to promote productive reasoning and good practice. It is not comprehensive or all-inclusive and does not replace adequate training and experience.

In the vast majority of cases, because most cases do not require trial or deposition testimony, the evaluator's final work product is the report. Any professional report needs to strongly consider the needs of consumers of the report, and in forensic matters such as child custody and related evaluations, the judge and attorneys are generally acknowledged to be the primary such individuals (e.g., Grisso, 2010; Melton, Petrila, Poythress, & Slobogin, 2007). At the same time, I have heard a number of judges comment that they read the report only if there is a specific need to do so, such as if the case does not settle and they must preside over a trial.

Over my decades of practice, there has not been a highly agreed-upon structure and format for reports. Most of the time when I asked report consumers what they wanted, they replied they did not have specific criteria and made general references to whatever was deemed customary in the field.

It is essential for evaluators to stay mindful that there is considerable overlap between the collection and cognitive processing of evaluative information and the contents of the report. In other words, the report is built on the foundation of the evaluation that preceded it. For example, Martindale and Gould (2013), in an article written for attorneys about how to examine and critique evaluation reports, focused a good deal on evaluation procedures and evaluator thinking about the information that was collected. Therefore, the evaluation procedures, the cognitive processing of data, and the creation of a useful report are inextricably linked.

In the remainder of this chapter, I first describe results from survey research regarding judge and attorney preferences for reports. Second, I review positions of authorities in forensic psychology about important elements of reports and comment on a recent article about custody evaluation reports. Third, there is a discussion of interview formats. The chapter concludes with a number of points for consideration by evaluators.

James Bow and his colleagues have conducted surveys of individuals in the legal profession that have helped shed light on their perceptions about custody evaluation reports. A survey of experienced family law judges and attorneys in Michigan was carried out by Bow and Quinell (2004). Because there were no significant differences in the responses between the judges and attorneys, the data from the two groups were combined in the reporting of results. The respondents were asked to rate the importance of 15 different potential components of reports, and all were rated as relatively important. The three components rated most highly in importance were the strengths and weaknesses of the parents, child interviews, and recommendations for custody. In response to a question about the optimal length for reports, the average was approximately 10 to 12 pages. A later national survey of attorneys (Bow, Gottlieb, & Gould-Saltman, 2011) reported a number of similar findings, such as all potential report components having been rated as important. However, the later survey described that the most highly rated components of reports were descriptions of the procedures utilized, the best interest criteria, and parent-child observations. Also, the average optimal report length was described as 22 pages.

There has been controversy about whether child custody evaluators should make "ultimate issue" recommendations to the court about matters of custody and visitation (e.g., Grisso, 2005; Tippins & Wittmann, 2005). Both surveys cited in the prior paragraph found that a considerable majority of judges and attorneys indicated that such recommendations should routinely be made in reports.

Bow et al. (2011) described attorney complaints about custody evaluation reports. The most common category of complaint was that conclusions and recommendations either lacked logic, manifested indecisiveness, or were simply absent. The complaint regarding the lack of logical connection between the body of the report and recommendations is one of the main ones that I have heard over the years in meetings or informal conversations with attorneys. Also, it is noteworthy that the survey authors reported that the vast majority of attorney stated that a relatively detailed report is more likely to assist in arriving at an eventual settlement.

The authors of a major work on forensic psychological evaluation (Melton et al., 2007), a combination of attorneys and psychologists, made a number of recommendations for reports, not limited to the child custody field. Those authors emphasized the important differences between forensic and traditional clinical reports, including objectives, data collection, confidentiality, and levels of potential external scrutiny. Others, such as Gould and Martindale (2007), have made somewhat similar distinctions. The main recommendations put forth by Melton et al. (2007) included separating fact from inferences, staying within the scope of the referral questions, avoiding information overkill and "underkill," and minimizing clinical jargon. Grisso (2010) offered guidance for forensic psychological reports, based both on consensus from the literature and research of actual reports. His recommendations are generally applicable for child custody evaluation reports, though they comprised only a very small proportion of his research sample. He made a number of important points, some of which reflect the inevitable overlap between how evaluative information is collected and processed and how it is communicated in the report. Grisso emphasized the importance of looking for convergent information from different data sources, including self-report, the report of others, psychological test data, and collateral information. Accordingly, he maintained that it is important for the report writer to describe the data, indicate how inferences are drawn from the data, and explicate the reasoning that supports the opinions or recommendations.

The research reported by Grisso (2010) was based on reviews of 62 forensic reports. He described that the two most frequent faults, which occurred in most reports, involved opinions having been stated without adequately explaining their bases in data or logic, and that the forensic purpose of the evaluation was not clearly or accurately stated. Between 30% and 40% of the reports included disorganization, irrelevant data or opinions, and the failure to consider alternative hypotheses for interpretations or recommendations. Between 20 and 30% of the reports manifested inadequate data, interpretations and data mixed together, and overreliance on just one source of data. The other main problems, which occurred between 10 and 20% of the time, included language problems such as jargon or pejorative terms and improper test usage.

Recently, Pickar and Kaufman (2013) focused specifically on child custody evaluation reports. A number of points they made have substantive overlap with recommendations about forensic reports generally (e.g., Grisso, 2010; Melton et al., 2007). They also emphasized that the report has multiple consumers, and maintained that the parents should also be considered as primary consumers in part because reports can frequently serve a settlement function. There are a number of positive aspects of considering parents to be consumers, including that recommendations for intervention such as therapy and/or parent education are essentially focused on the family, and according to the surveys of legal professionals summarized above, appear to be valued by attorneys and judges. Although the potential settlement function of the report is an important reality, it is also vital that evaluators not primarily aim reports with an objective of having the parties reach a settlement. Although a reasonably good settlement is clearly a positive development, in a number of cases individuals in the legal system can try too hard to reach settlement by holding out a version of joint custody as a compromise even when the level of conflict has consistently been so high that it is unlikely the parents can cooperate well enough to make joint parenting successful.

There are a number of different potential formats for custody evaluation reports. Grisso (2010) and Melton et al. (2007) both emphasized that report should have organized formats that are logically coherent and useful to readers, though there is flexibility in how to achieve those objectives. Melton et al. offered an example of a format that is focused in large part on each adult participant.

A number of years ago, I was a member of a committee that included a judge and attorney, which had an objective of developing a custody evaluation report format. The overall recommended format appropriately relied a great deal on the preferences of the judge and attorney, as such individuals are routine reports consumers. Over the years, I made relatively modest modifications based on my experiences of what is helpful in organizing and communicating relevant evaluation information.

A brief overview is offered here. The format begins, like most others, with a listing of basic information such as case name and number, parent and child names, and the judge and attorney names. Then, there is a list of evaluation procedures carried out. The next section includes background information, including summary information about the Order for the evaluation that usually includes its objectives. That section also describes other basic data agreed upon by the parents. The following comparatively lengthy section summarizes the main information disputed by the parents that they assert to be relevant for the objectives of the evaluation. The next sections are focused on each parent, primarily as individuals. Those individual parent sections include self-reports of psychological functioning and substance use, results of psychological measures, reports of parent-child observation sessions, and child care plans. When there are other adults who live in the home with the child, or who would be likely to do so in the future, such individuals participate in person in the evaluation, and there are corresponding individual sections of the report focused on them. Sections on the children follow. They focus on interviews and characteristically include summaries of school and medical records. Afterward, there is a summary of other information, which typically includes topics such as relevant documents and telephone contacts with collateral individuals.

Recommendations follow in accordance with what has been identified in the Order as the areas of focus of the evaluation. Other recommendations may be offered when they appears to be important and appropriate, such as for therapy. A final section lists the rationale for recommendations in accordance with relevant statutes and/or case law. The rationale for recommendations was added to this format after the presiding judge of a local domestic relations division stated that he would find an analysis of the recommendations according to the relevant statutes to be very useful. This final section both explains the bases for the recommendations and explicitly ties them to the relevant legal criteria.

The fact that this format appears to been well received over number of years is not surprising, because it follows the preferences of regular consumers of custody evaluation reports. At the same time, as described above, it is likely that numerous specific formats might be very useful, as long as they are organized, follow a logical sequence, and include essential content.

There are a number of specific points raised by those who have written about evaluation reports that may provide particular challenges for custody evaluators. The recommendation to include only those data that are relevant to the referral question is especially challenging because most referrals pertain to child custody. Many states rely on a derivation of the UMDA (NCCUSL, 1974), which indicates that custody needs to be determined in accordance with the best interest of the child and lists a broad range of relevant factors. For example, in Illinois, the relevant statute (Best Interest of the Child, 2007) states that the court must consider *all relevant factors* (emphasis added) and then lists a number of factors. One of the UMDA factors present in the Illinois statute is particularly broad in that it covers the relationships of the child with the parents, siblings, and any other individual who may significantly influence the child's best interest. Therefore, custody evaluations require consideration of potentially a very broad range of information. Put somewhat differently, it is perhaps much easier to identify information that would not be relevant as compared to attempting to specify limits to what data would be potentially relevant.

However, consideration of case material may be helpful in offering relevant examples of materials reported by parents that may or may not be relevant to the referral question of child custody. A considerable proportion of parents have complained in interviews of alleged poor financial management by their spouse or partner. Although financial matters by themselves are usually not considered relevant in child custody determinations, if the evaluator asks the complaining parent about the possible relevance, the response, depending upon the details, may or may not demonstrate that the concern about such matters pertains to the best interest of the child. For example, one parent might reply that they do not know whether it relates to the child's best interest at all. Another parent might respond that the alleged financial mismanagement is one consequence of the other parent often acting impulsively, not being able to contribute to an adequately stable household, and behaving without regard for the impact on the children. In that second example, there is clear relevance regarding best interest factors, including the mental health functioning of all relevant individuals.

A pair of evaluation reports that I reviewed offers a different type of relevant contrast about this matter. Both reports included unusually extensive material about parental interactions prior to the children's births, and even prior to having lived together and/or having had their wedding. In both reports, those early parental interactions included considerable verbal conflict with one another. In one of the reports, that material was not integrated in any meaningful way with the rest of the report, including the reasons for the recommendations. In the other report, the evaluator stated that one of the parents voiced a belief that such very early conflict was relevant because it showed a consistent history of the parents not having been able to cooperate or otherwise manage conflict well, which allegedly continued in many disputes about important decisions regarding the children. Therefore, in that second example, there was clear relevance pointed out in terms of the Illinois joint custody (Joint Custody, 2010) statutory factor that pertains to the ability of parents to cooperate effectively and consistently with one another about the children.

An additional area of challenge for custody evaluators often involves efforts to avoid technical jargon while at the same time clearly distinguishing between data that were collected and inferences based on those data. For example, Grisso (2010) described that evaluation reports should include explanations of the normative meanings of psychological test scores. An explanation of such normative implications of test scores is a type of inference, albeit a relatively low-level one (for a discussion of different inference levels in child custody evaluations, see Tippins & Wittman, 2005). More specifically, a description of test scores together with the normative meaning combines data and inferences about those data. Somewhat similarly, when I describe direct observations of parent-child interactions in relevant sessions, I often include comparatively low-level inferences such as the levels of positive reinforcement offered by a parent and manifestations of positive mood or defiance by a child. Such low-level inferences appear to offer more meaning to the report consumer, beyond a mere description of behavior. In most reports sections, I first describe whether that section summarizes reported information without the inclusion of inferences, or whether certain types of inferences might be included. In general, Grisso (2010) and Melton et al. (2007) appeared to emphasize a clear separation of the data from the comparatively high-level inferences, such as inferences that pertain to overall parent-child relationships and recommendations based on appropriate legal criteria.

In general, evaluators encounter significant final hurdles when they complete each case by creating a good-quality report. Reports are more difficult to complete when there are larger volumes of data to consider, which clearly appears to have occurred in about the last 10 years, as represented in my own practical experience and the reports of others. Surveys of legal professionals (Bow & Quinell, 2004; Bow et al., 2011) indicated that the optimal report length approximately doubled in recent years, and Pickar and Kaufman (2013) commented on the increased amount of data seen in reports in recent years. While it is logical that larger volumes of data lead to longer reports, it is also essential that the reports include appropriate analysis (e.g., Grisso, 2010; Melton et al., 2007; Stahl, 2011) so that recommendations are made in a clear and logically coherent manner. All these report writing responsibilities take very large amounts of time and effort. From a risk management standpoint (Woody, 2013), a high-quality, balanced report is likely to decrease the likelihood of negative consequences such as complaints to the relevant professional board. Most importantly, a high-quality report that follows a very competent evaluation is likely to provide the most benefit during a very difficult time to a child and family going through the divorce process.

Chapter 15

ETHICS, GUIDELINES, RISK MANAGEMENT, AND IMPROVING PRACTICE

PRACTICE CHECKLIST

_____Read all ethical standards and practice guidelines for your discipline relevant for child custody and related evaluations.

_____Keep relevant documents on ethics and guidelines handy for reference.

_____Proactively consider ethics, guidelines, and risk management principles.

_____Participate in continuing education on ethics, guidelines, and relevant content.

_____Use sufficiently detailed informed consent and fees statements.

_____When psychological tests are administered, do not rely primarily on computerized test interpretation.

_____The best interest of the child needs to be the primary objective in every relevant evaluation regardless of who makes payment.

Note: This form is a guide to promote productive reasoning and good practice. It is not comprehensive or all-inclusive and does not replace adequate training and experience.

Child custody evaluation has, over many years, repeatedly been a top category of the types of cases opened for investigation by the APA Ethics Committee (e.g., APA Ethics Committee, 2001; 2013). Kirkland and Kirkland (2001) reported that many custody evaluators have needed to defend themselves in relevant professional licensing board hearings. A series of articles (Benjamin, Ally, & Gollan, 2009; McGarrah, 2009; Zimmerman & Hess, 2009) on ethical challenges in child custody and related divorce cases all referred to the area of practice as a minefield. Perhaps obviously, it is essential for evaluators to learn about appropriate ethical standards, practice guidelines and risk management principles. It is also crucial to maintain strong levels of expertise in these areas.

In Chapter 3, it was described that careful deliberation tended to be more accurate than intuition, but that it is very common for humans to make quick intuitive decisions. Kahneman (2011) emphasized that decision makers first need to recognize when they are in a cognitive minefield, and then put into effect deliberative steps that increase the likelihood of productive judgment. When there is a reasonable concern both with keeping out of trouble and simultaneously carrying out high level work likely to benefit families, relevant deliberative steps would include staying cognizant of relevant ethical standards, guidelines, and models for practice.

There are numerous documents of this type. The primary focus in this chapter will be on relevant APA documents. The most comprehensive one, the Ethical Principles of Psychologists and Code of Conduct (APA, 2002) (hereafter referred to as APA Ethics Code) is mandatory for psychologists. There are two sets of relevant APA guidelines that are aspirational in nature. The Specialty Guidelines for Forensic Psychology (APA, 2013) (APA Forensic Guidelines) pertains to all psychological practice that involves applying relevant psychological knowledge to the law. The most specifically applicable APA document is the aspirational Guidelines for Child Custody Evaluations in Family Law Proceedings (APA, 2010) (APA Child Custody Guidelines).

There are a number of relevant documents in the psychiatry field. The Principles of Medical Ethics with Annotations Especially Applicable to Psychiatry (American Psychiatric Association, 2013b) are mandatory. The American Academy of Child and Adolescent Psychiatry (1997) published the Practice Parameters for Child Custody Evaluation. That document is aspirational and reportedly undergoing revision. The American Academy of Psychiatry and Law (2005) Ethical Guidelines for the Practice of Forensic Psychiatry is also aspirational. A relevant aspirational document directed toward clinical social workers is the Practice Guidelines in Child Custody Evaluations for Licensed Clinical Social Workers (Luftman, Veltkamp, Clark, Lannacone, & Snook, 2005). The AFCC, a multidisciplinary organization of individuals from legal and mental health professions, has published an aspirational document, the Model Standards of Practice for Child Custody Evaluation (AFCC, 2006) (Model Standards). The American Academy of Matrimonial Lawyers reportedly has relied on the Model Standards in making recommendations to its members when they are involved in cases in which custody evaluation takes place.

Because the custody evaluation area is such a minefield, it would be easy to exhort the reader to essentially memorize whichever of these documents were relevant for their profession and work. However, such a recommendation would be impossible to carry out, or at least extraordinarily impractical.

In practice, it is reasonable and useful to study and periodically review the relevant documents. I find it practically helpful to keep copies nearby so that I can check relevant sections when I deliberate about a potential ethical or related dilemma. Especially in the custody evaluation field, which covers a broad range of content areas and includes multiple means of gathering data, there is a significant risk of information overload, especially when ethical standards and aspirational guidelines also need to be actively considered. Having the relevant documents at arm's length can be a useful way to manage the risk that is often associated with potential or actual information overload (Woody, 2013). Similarly, regularly taking part in continuing education regarding relevant ethical matters can keep any practitioner cognizant of important considerations and aware of relevant developments.

A number of features of the relevant APA and AFCC documents are highlighted here. Sections that are not discussed here should not be ignored. Each evaluator should read the documents relevant to his or her own discipline at a minimum. Even though most of them are aspirational, and not mandatory and enforceable, in actual practice professionals of various disciplines will expect a competent evaluator to have good familiarity with relevant documents. Many attorneys who carry out cross-examinations of evaluators will test to see if they are familiar with relevant documents and whether they have applied principles to their evaluation work.

The APA Ethics Code (APA, 2002), for the most part mandatory, includes general principles that are aspirational and can provide motivation and direction likely to steer psychologists toward positive practice and away from possible ethical errors. For example, the principles of beneficence and nonmaleficence potentially guide and inspire custody evaluators to carry out in practice the many very difficult tasks that constitute good-quality evaluations likely to benefit families. The mandatory ethical standards include a section that requires psychologist to develop and maintain specialized competence. As can be plainly seen in much of the content of this book, it takes considerable specialized competence to conduct custody evaluations well. In many ways, evaluators need to be both generalists and specialists. Routine expenditures of time and effort are needed to acquire and improve one's skills, and doing so helps to limit and manage risk (Woody, 2013).

According to the APA Ethics Code and other relevant documents, it is crucial to avoid bias and unfair discrimination. For custody evaluators, I believe the greatest risk is an inadvertent type of bias based on assumptions that evaluators may not fully recognize in themselves. For example an evaluator may have a largely unrecognized bias about gender, race, socioeconomic status, or preference for public versus private schools. There is also risk in making use of a procedure such as a psychological test that inadvertently contains an element of bias.

All three of the APA documents discussed in this chapter emphasize the importance of informed consent. It is advisable to have a relatively detailed informed consent, and to be sure to cover relevant information about fees. The one I use is four single-spaced pages. In such a document, a number of areas of potential risk or challenge can be covered prior to the first session, and therefore it can serve important functions of transparency, education, and risk management. For example, within the informed consent statement it is very advisable to cover any limits on confidentiality, matters pertaining to collateral information, and ensure there is no conflict of interest of any type. Fees arrangements should be spelled out as clearly as possible and include any division of fees specified in an Order or by agreement.

The APA Ethics Code has an entire section on assessment that includes considerable centrally important information. An area all too frequently overlooked by custody evaluators is reliance on computerized psychological test interpretation. As described by Flens (2005), reliance only on computerized interpretation carries a significant risk of constituting an ethical violation. For more detail, see Chapter 8.

As noted above, there are significant areas of overlap between the mandatory APA Ethics Code (2002) and the aspirational APA Forensic Guidelines (2013) and Child Custody Guidelines (2010). Both the latter documents refer to the Ethics Code as a foundational source of information and direction. The APA Forensic Guidelines emphasize that evaluations need to focus on legally relevant factors and make use of appropriate assessment procedures. Also, the APA Forensic Guidelines note the importance of distinguishing observations from inferences in forensic reports.

The APA Child Custody Guidelines (2010) appropriately emphasize that the best psychological interest of the child needs to take precedence over all other considerations in every evaluation. Those guidelines also point out that evaluative data need to be considered within the context of the child custody dispute. That point is particularly relevant when there are relevant descriptive statistics for psychological tests with custody evaluation reference groups that may have scales that show significant differences from the normative standardization samples. Of course, as described above, both sets of APA guidelines cover a broader range of detail, and any psychologist custody evaluator should be familiar with them.

The AFCC Model Standards (2006) appear to be relied upon primarily in geographical areas where AFCC has relatively large numbers of members and consequently greater influence. On a practical basis, evaluators would do well to informally assess how much the Model Standards are relied upon in the jurisdictions in which they practice. There is considerable general overlap in the concepts covered by the APA documents, described above, and the Model Standards. Two interesting features of the Model Standards are the specific categories of recommendation regarding training and continuing education.

In addition, it is interesting that the AFCC Model Standards (2006) strongly encourage evaluators to use references to peer-reviewed published materials in their evaluation reports. Although the use of such references may be helpful in some cases, it is questionable whether their use is routinely productive for consumers of reports who are legal professionals. Attorneys and judges characteristically do not obtain training that would allow them to accurately understand at least a fair proportion of relevant articles, such as those that include inferential statistics. I know many very bright legal professionals, and if they had undergone relevant educational experiences, they could certainly have learned to understand very well empirical and theoretical matters often contained in such articles. However, such educational experiences are very rarely part of the training of legal professionals. On the other hand, U. S. Supreme Court decisions (*Daubert v. Merrell Dow Pharmaceuticals*, 1993; *General Electric v. Joiner*, 1997) referred to reliance on peer-reviewed scientific data and the importance of expert opinion needing to demonstrate how it relied on scientific evidence.

It is noteworthy that there are differences between state court systems in terms of reliance on *Daubert* versus other criteria for acceptance of expert opinion. Evaluators should be aware of the criteria relied upon where they practice. It will be interesting to see if further consensus develops about the use of references to peer-reviewed articles in evaluation reports.

Perhaps obviously, adherence to ethics and guidelines helps practitioners do high-quality work and stay out of trouble. As noted by a number of authorities on ethics and risk management (e.g., Koocher & Keith-Spiegel, 2008; Woody, 2013), proactive thinking about ethical matters assists an appropriately defensive mindset. Those types of cognitive habits can be especially valuable in the child custody evaluation field. Woody (2013) also referred to the benefits of having a warrior mindset, which actually is not at all aggressive but emphasizes the development of high-level skills, reliance on an appropriate knowledge base, sound judgment, and the exercise of prudence.

An important aspect of maintaining impartiality as a custody evaluator includes avoiding inappropriate advocacy (Benjamin et al., 2009; Zimmerman & Hess, 2009). Evaluators can appropriately function by having the child's best interest as the central focus. There is a risk of evaluators engaging in inappropriate advocacy by veering into becoming overly emotionally involved in terms of favoring one parent over another, or of becoming an ally of one attorney versus another. In other circumstances, it may be tempting for an evaluator to inject counseling into the evaluative process in the expectation that it will do some good for the family, but such behavior greatly risks violating an ethical prohibition about being in multiple roles (e.g., APA (2002) Ethics Code Section 3.05).

There have been numerous statements earlier in this book about the benefits of regularly carrying out procedures such as analyzing evidence for and against parental assertions (and/or evaluator-generated hypotheses) (Chapter 2), and those aimed at facilitating deliberative judgment instead of intuition (Chapter 3). In addition, especially for evaluators in group practices or working for organizations, the development of and adherence to formalized procedures regarding steps in the custody evaluation process can be a productive form of risk management (Benjamin et al., 2009; McGarrah, 2009).

The current summary highlights important factors of ethics, guidelines, and risk management considerations and is best considered as an initial step or springboard for evaluators to delve more thoroughly into such essential matters. Evaluators may wish to consider relatively general books on ethics and risk management in mental health matters by Bersoff (2008), Koocher and Keith-Spiegel (2008), and Woody (2013). Also, a book on ethics and risk management specific to the child custody field was authored by Benjamin and Gollan (2003).

IMPROVING PRACTICE

As described in the early chapters of this book, there had been numerous criticisms of child custody evaluation, and some, though not all have had a good deal of accuracy. A main goal of this book has been to advance the custody evaluation field through enhanced empiricism combined with high-level deliberative judgment about the evaluative information that is gathered in each case.

There also needs to be a social mechanism that promotes and perhaps even requires high levels of competency. The APA and AFCC promote good practice through mandatory ethics and aspirational guidelines, and also publish journals that potentially are outlets for relevant articles that might help to advance the field. The Professional Academy of Custody Evaluators does not actively function to facilitate advancements in the field. The American Board of Professional Psychology (ABPP) certifies general forensic psychologists but not those interested and active only in the forensic child and family area. In order to pursue ABPP forensic certification, a psychologist would need to become proficient in numerous other areas, including competence to stand trial, workers compensation, and personal injury. In response to my inquiry about this matter, ABPP responded that individuals interested in any type of specialty board would need to establish their own organization to do so. An alternate potential way to promote and require a higher level of competency would be if interested and motivated individuals would try to work with their state psychological associations to initiate improved requirements for practice based on statutes or court rules. For example, California has a number of relatively stringent court rules that appear likely to have promoted good practice.

Such possible social mechanisms would likely be focused on training, appropriate certification, maintenance of relevant skills, and balanced procedures to process complaints. Other potentially very useful procedures would require specific record-keeping about cases by custody evaluators. In particular, a common area of skepticism about evaluators is that, if they are hired by one party or attorney, they are simply going to issue a recommendation in favor of whomever hired them (Hagen, 1997). Although a large proportion of evaluations are carried out such that the evaluator is the court's witness, in other cases an evaluator may be an expert retained by one side, even if it is through a court Order. In order to provide data about evaluator objectivity, when the evaluator has been retained by one party, it potentially would be highly productive to require evaluators to keep records about the proportion of cases in which recommendations were made in the favor of the parent who retained them. Of course, there is a moral and ethical imperative that evaluators carry out their work with a primary focus on what is in the child's best psychological interest, no matter who hired them. Somewhat similarly, it may be useful for each evaluator to keep count of the proportion of time they are the court's witness versus a retained expert for one side.

Early Neutral Evaluations

A main drawback to full custody evaluations is the expense and time typically required to complete them. Therefore, as an effort to improve custody evaluations at a systemic level, other briefer and less expensive evaluation models have been proposed, such as early neutral evaluations. For example, in a Minnesota jurisdiction (Pearson, 2006), a male/female team of early neutral evaluators initially just hears each party present their positions about custody and parenting time for two to three hours, and they do not gather any information directly. After that session, the evaluation team either presents opinions and explores settlement possibilities with parents and attorneys, or they may decide to directly collect very limited additional information within one month, such as interviewing children and conducting parent-child observations. If the evaluation team collects additional information, they later meet with parents and attorneys to offer feedback and examine settlement possibilities. If no settlement emerges, a full custody evaluation may then be recommended.

Pearson (2006) described that if the case includes challenging features such as possible mental illness, substance misuse, domestic violence, or child abuse, and early neutral evaluation may not be appropriate. Somewhat similarly, in collaborative law practice, in which mental health professionals sometimes serve as advisors to family law attorneys about parenting plans, there are concerns that full evaluations may be needed when such challenging case factors are present (Lande, 2011).

It is noteworthy that articles on early neutral evaluation (Pearson, 2006; Terzuoli, 2010) and collaborative law (Lande, 2011) did not focus at all on the quality of evaluative procedures or the level of cognitive processing regarding the information that is collected. Instead, primary areas of focus were program features and objectives of arriving at quicker and less expensive settlements.

Those objectives are generally very positive ones given the strain on families of lengthy litigation and related expenses. At the same time, brief evaluative processes have a potential risk of missing crucial information relevant to children's best interest. Clearly, there is a trade-off in potential quality and accuracy between quicker, relatively inexpensive evaluations and full ones; each has their strengths and drawbacks. Overall, at least in jurisdictions where I have practiced, the custody evaluation field appears to have evolved in the last decade such that the most frequent referrals for full evaluations are for highly challenging cases that did not reach settlement after numerous attempts by parties' attorneys and alternative dispute resolution methods.

CONCLUSIONS

It is important to consider developments in the custody evaluation field within the context of some of the most thoughtful and compelling criticisms, such as those made by Emery et al. (2005). They described that major flaws included the use of tests specifically designed for custody evaluation that had no demonstrated validity, and that there was a lack of empirical support for the concept of parental alienation. Those authors maintained that the use of a number of well-established psychological tests was questionable because they did not have relevance for child custody matters, and that there were insufficient empirical data on important questions such as overnight visits for very young children. Also, Emery et al. argued that alternatives, such as the ALI approximation rule, were superior to a system that relied on custody evaluation.

In considering these criticisms, a look at positive developments in the field is warranted. Even prior to the Emery et al. (2005) article, there were advancements in part through the research of Johnston and her colleagues that were associated with the alienated child reformulation (Kelly and Johnston, 2001) of the parental alienation syndrome. Specifically, the child custody field now has evidence that a complex number of factors can contribute to a child resisting contact with a parent, and yet there is also evidence that some such cases largely result from a campaign by one parent to have a child develop an unrealistically negative attitude toward the other.

Another positive development in the field is the expansion of scientific data on some psychological tests used in custody evaluation, as summarized in Chapters 8 through 10. The use of measures such as the MMPI-2 and PAI to assess possible psychopathology is highly relevant for custody evaluation, both because of consistent research evidence that shows parental psychological dysfunction to have a negative impact on children of divorce, and the fact that many state statutes include the mental health functioning of parents in the best interest criteria. Also, much of the contents of the PCRI and PSI are directly relevant for parent-child interaction, a core area of focus for custody evaluation, and there have been research efforts toward at least clarifying the potential utility of these instruments within the child custody context.

There has been considerable focus on the controversy about overnight visits for very young children, in large part through a series of articles in *Family Court Review* (Prof. Emery is the Associate Editor) in 2011 and 2012, and the AFCC Annual Conference in 2012. Although the controversy continues, and there are no answers clearly applicable for every family, there is greater clarity about relevant concepts and research findings. Potentially, an overview of research evidence gives indications about what specific family and circumstantial factors need to be most strongly considered when custody evaluators or others address these emotionally-laden concerns.

Although the ALI (2002) made a noble effort to improve the experiences of children and families of divorce when it proposed the approximation rule, an examination of its specific characteristics revealed that it has significant flaws. An especially major problem was its assumption that parents would be likely to agree on what had been the pattern of past caretaking; clearly, research focused on child custody matters and from entirely different realms of study demonstrated that such parental agreement is seldom going to occur, thereby knocking out much of the foundation of the approximation rule concept.

In the almost two decades since I had been struck by the all too limited empirical foundations for custody evaluation practice, and started my attempts to contribute toward the advancement of the field, there also have been other steps forward, as can be seen in many of the references included here. Of particular importance and direct applicability is the advancement in the methodology of interviewing children so that they are more likely to give accurate and thorough reporting of their experiences. It is noteworthy that, since the publication of the Emery et al. (2005) article, Prof. Otto, one of the authors of the Emery et al. article, stated in a conference presentation that he sometimes conducts custody evaluations (Oldham & Otto, 2008). In addition, Prof. O'Donohue, a repeated critic of child custody evaluation and the other author of the Emery et al. article, recently coauthored a book on conducting empirically-based child custody evaluation (Tolle & O'Donohue, 2013).

However, as in many important and complex endeavors, numerous challenges and problems remain in the child custody evaluation field. As described in prior chapters, recent survey research indicates that significant proportions of evaluators are still using psychological measures that are not applicable and valid for custody evaluation. A number of evaluators continue to hold an overly simplistic, all or nothing view of child alienation. I believe that too few evaluators are sufficiently familiar with accumulated research evidence on children of divorce, and some appear to have inadequate motivation to work toward significant improvements in the quality of their work. The cognitive processing carried out by evaluators, including analyses of data that are collected, is an area that needs greater focus.

As noted at the beginning of this book, it is not enough to espouse an ideal, such as improving outcomes for children of divorce, and merely speak of its importance. No matter what the endeavor, it takes a great deal of gritty, sustained effort by multiple individuals to make progress toward that ideal. In this field, individuals need to acquire a great deal of scholarly and professional knowledge. Also, evaluators need to combine that knowledge with experience gained in the trenches of practice. Obviously, there is a lot of work to do to help children of separation and divorce who are at heightened risk for a whole range of life problems.

Let's keep working to move the field forward.

REFERENCES

Abidin, R. R. (1995). *Parenting Stress Index: Professional manual* (3rd ed.). Odessa, FL: Psychological Assessment Resources.

Abidin, R. R. (2012). *PSI-4 professional manual.* Lutz, FL: Psychological Assessment Resources.

Abidin, R. R., Austin, W. G., & Flens, J. R. (2013). The forensic uses and limitations of the Parenting Stress Index. In R. P Archer & E. M. A. Wheeler (Eds.), *Forensic uses of clinical assessment instruments* (pp. 346–379). New York: Routledge.

Achenbach, T. M. (1991). *Integrative guide for the 1991 CBCL/4–18, YSR, and TRF profiles.* Burlington, VT: University of Vermont.

Achenbach, T. M, & Rescorla, L. A. (2000). *Manual for the ASEBA preschool forms and profiles.* Burlington, VT: University of Vermont.

Achenbach, T. M., & Rescorla L. A. (2001). *Manual for the ASEBA school-age forms and profiles.* Burlington, VT: University of Vermont.

Achenbach, T. M. & Rescorla, L. A. (2013). The Achenbach system of empirically based assessment (ASEBA): Applications in forensic contexts. In R. P. Archer & E. M. A. Wheeler (Eds.), *Forensic uses of clinical assessment instruments* (pp. 311–345). New York: Routledge.

Ackerman, M. J. (1995). *Clinician's guide to child custody evaluations.* Hoboken, NJ: Wiley.

Ackerman, M. A., & Pritzl, T. B. (2011). Child custody evaluation practices: A 20-year follow-up. *Family Court Review, 49,* 618–628.

Allen, D. W. & Brinig, M. F. (2005). *Bargaining in the shadow of joint custody.* University of Iowa Legal Studies Research Paper No. 05-25. Retrieved from SSRN: http://ssrn.com/abstract=820104.

Allen, S. M., & Hawkins, A. J. (1999). Maternal gatekeeping: Mothers' beliefs and behaviors that inhibit greater father involvement in family work. *Journal of Marriage and the Family, 61,* 199–212.

Amato, P. (1993). Children's adjustment to divorce: Theories, hypotheses and empirical support. *Journal of Marriage and the Family, 55,* 23–28.

Amato, P. (2001). Children of divorce in the 1990s: An update of the Amato and Keith (1991) meta-analysis. *Journal of Family Psychology, 15,* 355–370.

Amato, P., & Gilbreth, J. G. (1999). Nonresident fathers and children's well-being: A meta-analysis. *Journal of Marriage and the Family, 61,* 557–573.

Amato, P., & Keith, B. (1991). Parental divorce and the well-being of children: A meta-analysis. *Psychological Bulletin, 110,* 26–46.

Ambady, N., & Rosenthal, R. (1992). Thin slices of expressive behavior as predictors of interpersonal consequences: A meta-analysis. *Psychological Bulletin, 111,* 256–274.

American Academy of Child and Adolescent Psychiatry. (1997). Practice parameters for child custody evaluation. *Journal of the American Academy of Child and Adolescent Psychiatry, 36* (10 Supplement), 57S–68S.

American Academy of Psychiatry and Law. (2005). Ethical guidelines for the practice of forensic psychiatry. Retrieved from www.aapl.org/ethics.htm

American Educational Research Association, American Psychological Association, & National Council on Measurement in Education. (1999). *Standards for educational and psychological testing.* Washington DC: American Educational Research Association.

American Psychological Association. (2002). Ethical principles of psychologists and code of conduct. *American Psychologist, 57,* 1060–1073.

American Psychological Association. (2010). Guidelines for child custody evaluations in family law proceedings. *American Psychologist, 65,* 863–867.

American Psychological Association. (2013). Specialty guidelines for forensic psychology. *American Psychologist, 68,* 7–19.

American Psychological Association, Ethics Committee. (2001). Report of the Ethics Committee, 2000. *American Psychologist, 56,* 680–688.

American Psychological Association, Ethics Committee. (2013). Report of the Ethics Committee. *American Psychologist, 68,* 370–379.

Anastasi, A. & Urbina, S. (1997). *Psychological testing* (7th ed.). Upper Saddle River, NJ: Prentice Hall.

Anderson, E. R., & Greene, S. M. (2013). Beyond divorce: Research on children in repartnered and remarried families. *Family Court Review, 51,* 119–130.

Appel, A. E., & Holden, G. W. (1998). The co-occurrence of spouse and physical abuse: A review and appraisal. *Journal of Family Psychology,* 12, 578–599.

Archer, J. (2000). Sex differences in aggression between heterosexual partners: A meta-analytic review. *Psychological Bulletin, 126,* 651–680.

Archer, J. (2002). Sex differences in physically aggressive acts between heterosexual partners: A meta-analytic review. *Aggression and Violent Behavior, 7,* 213–351.

Arkowitz, H., & Lilienfeld, S. O. (2013, March 19). Is divorce bad for children? *Scientific American.* Retrieved from www.scientificamerican.com/article.cm?id=is-divorce-bad-for-children

Association of Family and Conciliation Courts (AFCC). (2006). *Model standards of practice for child custody evaluation.* Madison, WI: AFCC.

Association of Family and Conciliation Courts (AFCC). (2010). *Planning for shared parenting: A guide for parents living apart.* Madison, WI: AFCC.

Austin, W. G. (2002). Guidelines for utilizing collateral sources of information in child custody evaluations. *Family Court Review, 40,* 177–184.

Austin, W. G. (2008a). Relocation, research, and forensic evaluation, Part I: The effects of residential mobility on children of divorce. *Family Court Review, 46,* 137–150.

Austin, W. G. (2008b). Relocation, research, and forensic evaluation, Part II: Research in support of the relocation risk assessment model. *Family Court Review, 46,* 347–365.

Austin, W. G. & Drozd, L. M. (2013). Judge's bench book for application of the integrated framework for the assessment of intimate partner violence in child custody disputes. *Journal of Child Custody, 10,* 99–119.

Austin, W. G., Fieldstone, L., & Pruett, M. K. (2013). Bench book for assessing parental gatekeeping in parenting disputes: Understanding the dynamics of gate closing and opening for the best interest of children. *Journal of Child Custody, 10,* 1–16.

Austin, W. G., Pruett, M. K., Kirkpatrick, H. D., Flens, J. R., & Gould, J. W. (2013). Parental gatekeeping and child custody/child access evaluations, Part I: Conceptual framework, research, and application. *Family Court Review, 51,* 485–501.

Azar, S. T., Lauretti, A. F., & Loding, B. V. (1998). The evaluation of parental fitness and termination of parental rights cases: A functional-contextual perspective. *Clinical Child & Family Psychology Review, 1,* 77–100.

Babcock, J. C., Jacobson, N. S., Gottman, J. M., & Yerington, T. P. (2000). Attachment, emotional regulation, and of the function of marital violence: Differences between secure, preoccupied, and dismissing violent and nonviolent husbands. *Journal of Family Violence, 15,* 391–409.

Baer, R. A., & Miller, J. (2002). Underreporting of psychopathology on the MMPI-2: A meta-analysis. *Psychological Assessment, 14,* 16–26.

Bagby, R. M., Nicholson, R. A., Buis, T., Radovanovic, H., & Fidler, B. J. (1999). Defensive responding on the MMPI-2 in family custody and access evaluations. *Psychological Assessment, 11,* 24–28.

Baker, A. J. L. (2005a). Long-term effects of parental alienation on the children: A qualitative research study. *American Journal of Family Therapy, 33,* 289–302.

Baker, A. J. L. (2005b). Parental alienation strategies: A qualitative study of adults who experienced parental alienation as a child. *American Journal of Forensic Psychology, 23,* 41–63.

Baker, A. J. L., & Darnall, D. (2006). Behaviors and strategies employed in parental alienation: A survey of parental experiences. *Journal of Divorce and Remarriage, 45,* 97–124.

Bartlett, K. T. (2002). U. S. custody law and trends in the context of the ALI Principles of the Law Family Dissolution. *Virginia Journal of Social Policy and the Law, 10,* 5–53.

Bathurst, K., Gottfried, A.W., & Gottfried, A. D. (1997). Normative data for the MMPI-2 in child custody litigation. *Psychological Assessment, 9,* 205–211.

Baumrind, D. (1966). Effect of authoritative parental control on child behavior. *Child Development, 37,* 887–907.

Baumrind, D. (1972). An exploratory study of socialization effects on black children: Some black-white comparisons. *Child Development, 43,* 261–267.

Bauserman, R. (2002). Child adjustment in joint-custody versus soul-custody arrangements: A meta-analytic review. *Journal of Family Psychology, 16,* 91–102.

Bavolek, S. J. (1984). *Handbook for the Adult-Adolescent Parenting Inventory.* Park City, UT: Family Development Resources.

Beavers, W. R., & Hampson, R. B. (1990). *Successful families: Assessment and intervention.* New York: Norton.

Beck, C. J. A., Sales, B. D., & Emery, R. E. (2004). Research on the impact of family mediation. In J. Folberg, A. L. Milne, & P. Salem (Eds.), *Divorce and family mediation* (pp. 447–482). New York: Guilford.

Benjamin, G. J. H., & Gollan, J. K. (2003). *Family evaluation in custody litigation: Reducing risks of ethical infractions and malpractice.* Washington, DC: American Psychological Association.

Benjamin, G. J. H., Ally, G., & Gollan, J. (2009). Navigating through the minefield with positive practices to prevent complaints. *Professional Psychology: Research and Practice, 40,* 546–548.

Ben-Porath, Y., & Flens, J. R. (2012). Butcher and Williams's (this issue) critique of the MMPI-2-RF is slanted and misleading. *Journal of Child Custody, 9,* 223–232.

Bernet, W. (2008). Parental alienation disorder and DSM-5. *American Journal of Family Therapy, 36,* 349–366.

Bernstein, G. & Triger, Z. (2012). Over-parenting. *University of California Davis Law Review, 44,* 1221–1279.

Bersoff, D. N. (2008). *Ethical conflicts in psychology* (4th ed.). Washington, DC: American Psychological Association.

Best Interest of the Child, 750 Illinois Compiled Statutes (ILCS) 5/602 (2007).

Bettencourt, B. A. & Miller, N. (1996). Gender differences in aggression as a function of provocation: A meta-analysis. *Psychological Bulletin, 119,* 422–447.

Booth, A., & Amato, P. (1991). Divorce and psychological stress. *Journal of Health and Social Behavior, 32,* 396–407.

Bornstein, M. H. (2002). Parenting infants. In M. H. Bornstein (Ed.), *Handbook of Parenting* (2nd ed.) (Vol. 1, 3–43). New York: Psychology Press.

Bousha, D. M. & Twentyman, C. T. (1984). Mother-child interaction style in abuse, neglect, and control groups: Naturalistic observations in the home. *Journal of Abnormal Psychology, 93,* 106–114.

Bow, J. N. (2010). Use of third party information in child custody evaluations. *Behavioral Sciences and the Law, 28,* 511–521.

Bow, J. N., Gottlieb, M. C., Gould-Saltmann, D., & Hendershot, L. (2011). Partners in the process: How attorneys prepare their clients for custody evaluations and litigation. *Family Court Review, 49,* 750–759.

Bow, J. N., & Quinnell, F. A. (2001). Psychologists' current practices and procedures in child custody evaluations: Five years after American Psychological Association Guidelines. *Professional Psychology: Research and Practice, 32,* 261–268.

Bow, J. N., & Quinnell, F. A. (2004). Critique of child custody evaluations by the legal profession. *Family Court Review, 42,* 115–127.

Braver, S. L., Ellman, I. M., & Fabricius, W. V. (2003). Relocation of children after divorce and children's best interest: New evidence and legal considerations. *Journal of Family Psychology, 17,* 206–219.

Braver, S. L., Ellman, I. M., Votruba, A. M., & Fabricius, W. V. (2011). Lay judgments about child custody after divorce. *Psychology, Public Policy, and Law, 17,* 212–240.

Bricklin, B. (1984). *Bricklin Perceptual Scales.* Furlong, PA: Village Publishing.

Bricklin, B. (1989). *Perception-Of-Relationships-Test.* Furlong, PA: Village Publishing.

Bricklin, B. (1995). *The custody evaluation handbook: Research-based solutions and applications.* New York: Brunner/Mazel.

Brodzinsky, D. M. (1993.) On the use and misuse of psychological testing in child custody evaluations. *Professional Psychology: Research and Practice, 24,* 213–219.

Brown, D.A. (2011). The use of supplementary techniques and forensic interviews with children. In M. E. Lamb, D. J. La Rooy, L. C. Malloy, & C. Katz (Eds.),

Children's testimony: A handbook of psychological research and forensic practice (pp. 217–250). Chichester, West Sussex, UK: Wiley-Blackwell.

Bruck, M. (2009). Human figure drawings and children's recall of touching. *Journal of Experimental Psychology: Applied, 15*, 361–374.

Bruck, M., & Melnyk, L. (2004). Individual differences in children's suggestibility: A review and synthesis. *Applied Cognitive Psychology, 18*, 947–996.

Buchanan, C. M., Maccoby, E. E. & Dornbusch, S. M. (1996). *Adolescents after divorce.* Cambridge, MA: Harvard University Press.

Budd, K. S., Clark, J., & Connell, M. A. (2011). *Evaluation of parenting capacity in child protection.* New York: Oxford University Press.

Butcher, J. N. (Ed.). (2006). *MMPI-2: A practitioner's guide.* Washington, DC: American Psychological Association.

Butcher, J. N., Graham, J. R., & Ben-Porath, Y. (1995). Methodological problems and issues in MMPI, MMPI-2, and MMPI-A research. *Psychological Assessment, 7*, 320–329.

Butcher, J. N., Graham, J. R., Ben-Porath, Y., Tellegen, A., Dahlstrom, W. G., & Kaemmer, B. (2001). *Minnesota Multiphasic Personality Inventory-2 (MMPI-2) manual* (2nd ed). Minneapolis, MN: University Of Minnesota Press.

Butcher, J. N., & Williams, C. L. (2012). Problems with using the MMPI-2-RF in forensic evaluations: A clarification to Ellis. *Journal of Child Custody, 9*, 217–222.

Butcher, J. N., Williams, C. L., Graham, J. R., Archer, R. P., Tellegen, A., Ben-Porath, Y., & Kaemmer, B. (1992). *Minnesota Multiphasic Personality Inventory – Adolescent: Manual for administration, scoring and interpretation.* Minneapolis, MN: University of Minnesota Press.

Caldwell, B., & Bradley, R. (1984). *Home Observation for the Measurement of the Environment.* New York: Dorsey Press.

Carlson, J. F. (1995). Test review of Perception-Of-Relationships-Test. In J. C. Conoley & J. C. Impara (Eds.), *The twelfth mental measurements yearbook.* Retrieved from http://marketplace.unl.edu/buros/

Carr, G. D., Moretti, M. M., & Cue, B. J. H. (2005). Evaluating parenting capacity: Validity problems with the MMPI-2, PAI, CAPI, and ratings of child adjustment. *Professional Psychology: Research and Practice, 36*, 188–196.

Cashel, M. L., Rogers, R., Sewall, K., & Martin-Cannici, C. (1995). The Personality Assessment Inventory (PAI) and the detection of defensiveness. *Assessment, 2*, 333–342.

Ceci, S. J., & Bruck M. (1995). *Jeopardy in the courtroom: A scientific analysis of children's testimony.* Washington, DC: American Psychological Association.

Ceci, S. J., & Friedman, R. D. (2000). The suggestibility of children: Scientific research and legal implications. *Cornell Law Review, 86*, 34–108.

Ceci, S. J., Huffman, M. L. C., Smith, E., & Loftus, E. F. (1994). Repeatedly thinking about a non-event: Source misattributions among preschoolers. *Consciousness and Cognition, 3*, 388–407.

Centers for Disease Control and Prevention. (2012). *Fact sheets – alcohol use and health.* Retrieved from www.cdc.gov/alcohol/fact-sheets/alcohol-use.htm.

Cerezo, M. A., D'Ocon, K., & Dolz, L. (1996). Mother-child interactive patterns in abusive families versus nonabusive families: An observational study. *Child Abuse and Neglect, 20*, 573–587.

Chao, R. K. (1994). Beyond parental control and authoritarian parenting style: Understanding Chinese parenting through the cultural notion of training. *Child Development, 65*, 1111–1119.

Chase, K. J., O'Leary, K, D., & Heyman, R. E. (2001). Categorizing partner-violent men within the reactive-proactive typology model. *Journal of Consulting and Clinical Psychology, 69*, 567–572.

Chassin, L., Pitts, S. C., DeLucia, C., & Todd, M. (1999). A longitudinal study of children of alcoholics: Predicting young adults substance use disorders, anxiety, and depression. *Journal of Abnormal Psychology, 108*, 106–119.

Clishman, M. R. & Wilson R. F. (2008). American Law Institute's Principles of the law of family dissolution, eight years after adoption: Guiding principles or obligatory footnote. *Family Law Quarterly, 42*, 573–618.

Cloutier, R. & Jacques, C. (1997). Evolution of residential custody arrangements in separated families: A longitudinal study. *Journal of Divorce and Remarriage, 28*, 17–33.

Coffman, J. K., Guerin, D. W., & Gottfried, A. W. (2006). Reliability and validity of the Parent-Child Relationship Inventory (PCRI): Evidence from a longitudinal cross-informant investigation. *Psychological Assessment, 18*, 209–214.

Cohen, J. (1992). A power primer. *Psychological Bulletin, 112*, 155–159.

Conger, J. (1995). Test review of Perception-Of-Relationships-Test. In J. C. Conoley & J. C. Impara (Eds.), *The twelfth mental measurements yearbook*. Retrieved from http://marketplace.unl.edu/buros/

Conners, C. K. (2008). *Conners 3rd Edition manual*. Toronto, Ontario: Multi-Health Systems.

Craig, R. J. (2013). The Millon Clinical Multiaxial Inventory – III: Use in forensic settings. In R. P Archer & E. M. A. Wheeler (Eds.), *Forensic uses of clinical assessment instruments* (pp. 175–201). New York: Routledge.

Crippen, G. L., & Stuhlman, S. M. (2001–2002). Minnesota's alternatives to primary caretaker placements: Too much of a good thing? *William Mitchell Law Review, 28*, 677–695.

Csikszentmihalyi, M., & Larson, R. (1987). Validity and reliability of the experience-sampling method. *Journal of Nervous and Mental Disease, 175*, 526–536.

Cummings, E. M., & Davies, P. (1994). *Children and the marital conflict: The impact of family dispute and the resolution*. New York: Guilford.

Darling, N., & Steinberg, L. (1993). Parenting style as context: An integrative model. *Psychological Bulletin, 113*, 487–496.

Daubert v. Merrell Dow Pharmaceuticals, Inc., 509 U. S. 579 (1993).

Davidson, M. M. (in press). Test review of Conflict Tactics Scales. In J. F. Carlson, K. F. Geisinger, & J. L. Jonson (Eds.), *The nineteenth mental measurements yearbook*. Retrieved from http://marketplace.unl.edu/buros/

Davies, G. M., Wescott, H. L. & Horan, N. (2000). The impact of questioning style on the content of investigative interviews with suspected child abuse victims. *Psychology,*

Crime & Law, 6, 81–97.

Davies, P. T., & Cummings, E. M. (1994). Marital conflict and child adjustment: An emotional security hypothesis. *Psychological Bulletin, 116,* 387–411.

DePanfilis, D., & Dubowitz, H. (2005). Family Connections: a program for preventing child neglect. *Child Maltreatment, 10,* 108–123.

Depner, C. E., Cannata, K. V., & Simon, M. B. (1992). Building a uniform statistical reporting system: A snapshot of California Family Court services. *Family and Conciliation Courts Review, 37,* 273–296.

Devine, P. G. (1989). Stereotypes and prejudice: Their automatic and controlled components. *Journal of Personality and Social Psychology, 56,* 5–18.

Dietrich-MacLean, G., & Walden, T. (1988). Distinguishing teaching interactions of physically abusive from nonabusive parent-child dyads. *Child Abuse and Neglect, 12,* 469–479.

DiFranza, J. R., & Lew, R. A. (1996). Morbidity and mortality in children associated with the use of tobacco products by other people. *Pediatrics, 97,* 560–568.

Doherty, W. J., & Allen, W. (1994). Family functioning and parental smoking as predictors of adolescent cigarette use: A six-year prospective study. *Journal of Family Psychology, 8,* 347–353.

Dolan, M. J., & Hynan, D. J. (in press). Fighting over bedtime stories: An empirical study of the risks of valuing quantity over quality in child custody decisions. *Law and Psychology Review.* Prepublication version at http://ssrn.com/abstract = 2253061.

Downey, D. B., Ainsworth-Darnell, J. W., & Dufur, M. J. (1998). Sex of parenting and children's well-being in single-parent households. *Journal of Marriage and the Family, 60,* 878–893.

Drozd, L. M. (2008). DVCC protocol. *Journal of Child Custody: Research, Issues, and Practices, 4,* 19–31.

Drozd, L. M., Olesen, N. W. & Saini, M. A. (2013). *Parenting plan and child custody evaluations: Using decision trees to increase evaluator competence and avoid preventable errors.* Sarasota, FL: Professional Resource Press.

Duggan, W. D. (2007). Rock-paper-scissors: Playing the odds with the law of child relocation. *Family Court Review, 45,* 193–213.

Eagly, A. H., Ashmore, R. D., Makhijani, M. G., & Longo, L. C. (1991). What is beautiful is good, but…: A meta-analytic review of research on the physical attractiveness stereotype. *Psychological Bulletin, 110,* 109–128.

Eagly, A. H., & Steffen, V. J. (1986). Gender and aggressive behavior: A meta-analytic review of the social psychological literature. *Psychological Bulletin, 100,* 309–330.

Edens, S. D., Hart, S. D., Johnson, D. W., Johnson, J. K., & Olver, M. E. (2000). Use of the Personality Assessment Inventory to assess psychopathy in offender populations. *Psychological Assessment, 12,* 132–139.

Eaton, N. R., Keyes, K. M., Krueger, R. F., Balsis, S., Skodol, A. E., Markon, K. E., Grant, D. F., & Hasin, D. S. (2012). An invariant dimensional liability model of gender differences in mental disorder prevalence: Evidence from a national sample. *Journal of Abnormal Psychology, 121,* 132–139.

In re Marriage of Eckert, 119 Ill. 2d. 316, 116 Ill. Dec. 220, 518 N.E.2d 1041 (1988).

Egeland, B., Erickson, M. L., Butcher, J. N. & Ben-Porath, Y. (1991). MMPI-2 profiles of women at risk for child abuse. *Journal of Personality Assessment, 57,* 254–263.

Einhorn, H. J., & Hogarth, R. M. (1978). Confidence in judgment: Persistence of the illusion of validity. *Psychological Review, 85,* 395–416.

Ellis, D. (2008). Divorce and the family court: What can be done about domestic violence? *Family Court Review, 46,* 531–536.

Elrod, L. D., & Dale, M. D. (2008–2009). Paradigm shifts and pendulum swings in child custody: The interests of children in the balance. *Family Law Quarterly, 42,* 381–418.

Emery, R. E. (1988). *Marriage, divorce, and children's adjustment.* Thousand Oaks, CA: Sage.

Emery, R. E. (2012.). *Renegotiating family relationships: Divorce, child custody, and mediation* (2nd ed.). New York: Guilford.

Emery, R. E., Otto, R. K., & O'Donohue, W. T. (2005). A critical assessment of child custody evaluations: Limited science and a flawed system. *Psychological Science in the Public Interest, 6,* 1–29.

Epstein, N. B., Baldwin, L. M., & Bishop, D. S. (1983). The McMaster family assessment device. *Journal of Marital and Family Therapy, 9,* 171–180.

Erickson, S. K., Lilienfeld, S. O., & Vitacco, M. J. (2007). A critical examination of the suitability and limitations of psychological tests in family court. *Family Court Review, 45,* 157–174.

Exner, J. E. (2002). *The Rorschach, a comprehensive system: Basic foundations and principles of interpretation.* (4th ed). Hoboken, NJ: Wiley.

Ezzo, F. R., Pinsoneault, T. B., & Evans, T. B. (2007). A comparison of MMPI-2 profiles between child maltreatment cases and two types of custody cases. *Journal of Forensic Psychology Practice, 7,* 29–42.

Fabricius, W. V., & Hall, J. A. (2000). Young adults' perspectives on divorce: Living arrangements. *Family and Conciliation Courts Review, 38,* 446–461.

Fabricius, W. V., & Luecken, L. J. (2007). Postdivorce living arrangements, parental conflict, and long-term physical health correlates for children of divorce. *Journal of Family Psychology, 21,* 195–205.

Fabricius, W. V., Sokol, K. R., Diaz, P., & Braver, S. L. (2012). Parenting time, parent conflict, parent-child relationships, and children's physical health. In K. Kuehnle & L. Drozd (Eds.), *Parenting plan evaluations: Applied research for the family court* (pp. 188–213). New York: Oxford University Press.

Faller, K. C. (2002). *Understanding and assessing child sexual maltreatment* (2nd ed.). Thousand Oaks, CA: Sage.

Fisher, L. (2008). *Rock, paper, scissors: Game theory in everyday life.* New York: Basic Books.

Fivush, R., & Shukat, J. R. (1995). Content, consistency and coherence of early biographical recall. In M. S. Zaragoza, J. R. Graham, G. C. N. Hall, & Y. S. Ben-Porath (Eds.), *Memory and testimony in the child witness* (pp. 5–23). Thousand Oaks, CA: Sage.

Flanagan, R. (2005). Test review of Achenbach System of Empirically Based Assessment. In R. A. Spies & B. S. Plake (Eds.), *The sixteenth mental measurement yearbook.*

Retrieved from http://marketplace.unl.edu/buros/

Flens, J. R. (2005). The responsible use of psychological testing in child custody evaluations: Selection of tests. In J. R. Flens & L. Drozd (Eds.), *Psychological testing in child custody evaluations* (pp. 3–30). New York: Haworth Press.

Fomby, P., & Cherlin, A. J. (2007). Family instability and child well-being. *American Sociological Review, 72,* 181–204.

Forbes, C., Vuchinich, S., & Kneedler, B. (2001). Assessing families with the Family Problem Solving Code. In P. K. Kerig & K. M. Lindahl (Eds.), *Family observational coding systems* (pp. 59–75). Mahweh, NJ: Lawrence Erlbaum.

Fuhrmann, G. S. W., & Zibbell, R. A. (2012). *Evaluation for child custody.* New York: Oxford University Press.

Gallant, W, A., Gorey, K. M., Gallant, M. D., Perry, J. L., & Ryan, K. (1998). The association of personality characteristics with parenting problems among alcoholic couples. *American Journal of Drug & Alcohol Abuse, 24,* 119–129.

Garb, H. N. (1998). *Studying the clinician: Judgment research and psychological assessment.* Washington, D.C.: American Psychological Association.

Garb, H. N., Wood, J. M., Lilienfeld, S. O., & Nezworski, M. T. (2002). Effective use of projective techniques in clinical practice: Let the data help with selection and interpretation. *Professional Psychology: Research and Practice, 33,* 454–463.

Garcia, F., & Gracia, E. (2009). It is always authoritative the optimum parenting style? *Adolescence, 44,* 101–131.

Gardner, R. A. (1992). *The parental alienation syndrome: A guidebook for mental health and legal professionals.* Cresskill, NJ: Creative Therapeutics.

Garven, S., Wood, J. M., Malpass, R. S., & Shaw III, J. S. (1998). More than suggestion: The effect of interviewing techniques from the McMartin Preschool case. *Journal of Applied Psychology, 83,* 347–359.

Gaudin, J. N., Polansky, N. A., Kilpatrick, A. C., & Shilton, P. (1996). Family functioning in neglectful families. *Child Abuse and Neglect, 20,* 363–377.

Gawande, A. (2009). *The checklist manifesto: How to get things right.* New York: Picador.

General Electric Co. v. Joiner, 522 U. S. 136 (1997).

Gerard, A. B. (1994). *Parent-Child Relationship Inventory (PCRI) manual.* Los Angeles: Western Psychological Services.

Gilbert, D. T., & Osborne, R. E. (1989). Thinking backward: Some curable and incurable consequences of cognitive busyness. *Journal of Personality and Social Psychology, 57,* 940–949.

Gilch Pesantez, J. R. (2001). Test-retest reliability and construct validity: The Bricklin Perceptual Scales. *Dissertation Abstracts International: Section B: Sciences and Engineering, 61*(9–B), 4982.

Goldstein, J., Freud, A., & Solnit, A. J. (1973). *Beyond the best interest of the child.* New York: Free Press.

Goodman, J. S., Quas, J. A., & Ogle, C. M. (2010). Child maltreatment and memory. *Annual Review of Psychology, 61,* 325–351.

Gottlieb, L. J. (2012). *The parental alienation syndrome: A family therapy and collaborative systems approach to amelioration.* Springfield, IL: Charles C Thomas.

Gould, J. W., & Martindale, D. A. (2007). *The art and science of child custody evaluations.* New York: Guilford.

Gould, J. W., & Stahl, P. M. (2001). Never paint by the numbers. *Family Court Review, 39,* 372–376.

Graham, J. R. (2006). *MMPI-2: Assessing personality and psychopathology* (4th ed.). New York: Oxford University Press.

Graham, J. R. (2012). *MMPI-2: Assessing personality and psychopathology* (5th ed.). New York: Oxford University Press.

Grant, B. F., Hasin, D. S., Stinson, S. S., Dawson, D. A., Chou, S. P., Ruan, W. J., & Pickering, R. P. (2004). Prevalence, correlates, and disability of personality disorders in the United States: Results from the national epidemiologic survey on alcohol and related conditions. *Journal of Clinical Psychiatry, 65,* 948–958.

Greene, R. L. (2000). *The MMPI-2: An interpretive manual* (2nd ed.). Boston, MA: Allyn & Bacon.

Greene, R. L. (2011). *The MMPI-2/MMPI-2-RF: An interpretive manual* (3rd ed.). Boston, MA: Allyn & Bacon.

Grisso, T. (2003). (with Borum, R., Edens, J. F., Moye, J., & Otto, R. K.) *Evaluating competencies: Forensic assessments and instruments* (2nd ed.). New York: Kluwer Academic/Plenum Publishers.

Grisso, T. (2005). Commentary on "Empirical and ethical problems with custody recommendations": What now? *Family Court Review, 43,* 223–228.

Grisso, T. (2010). Guidance for improving forensic reports: A review of common errors. *Open Access Journal of Forensic Psychology, 2,* 102–115.

Grove, W. M., Barden, R. C., Garb, H. N., & Lilienfeld, S. O. (2002). Failure of Rorschach-Comprehensive-System-based testimony to be admissible under The *Daubert-Joiner-Kumho standard. Psychology, Public Policy, and Law,* 8, 216–234.

Grove, W. M., Zald, D. H., Lebow, B. S., Snitz, B. E., & Nelson, C. (2000). Clinical versus mechanical prediction: A meta-analysis. *Psychological Assessment, 12,* 19–30.

Gunnoe, M. L., & Braver, S. L. (2001). The effects of joint legal custody on mothers, fathers, and children controlling for factors that predispose a sole maternal versus joint legal award. *Law and Human Behavior, 25,* 25–43.

Hagen, M. A. (1997). *Whores of the court: The fraud of psychiatric testimony and the rape of American justice.* New York: Regan.

Hagen, M. A. & Castagna, N. (2001). The real numbers: Psychological testing in custody evaluations. *Professional Psychology: Research and Practice, 32,* 269–271.

Handel, R., Archer, R., Elkins, D., Mason, J., & Simonds-Bisbee, E. (2011). Psychometric properties of the Minnesota Multiphasic Personality Inventory-Adolescent (MMPI-A) Clinical, Content, and Supplementary scales in a forensic sample. *Journal of Personality Assessment, 93,* 566–581.

Hart, S. N. (1989). Test review of the Child Abuse Potential Inventory, Form VI. In J. C. Conoley & J. J. Kramer (Eds.), *The tenth mental measurements yearbook.* Retrieved from http://marketplace.unl.edu/buros/

Hayne, H. (2004). Infant memory development: Implications for childhood amnesia. *Developmental Review, 24,* 33–73.

Heinze, M. C., & Grisso, T. (1996). Reviews of instruments assessing parenting competencies used in child custody evaluations. *Behavioral Sciences and the Law*, *14*, 293–313.

Hershkowitz, I. (2009). Socioemotional factors in child sexual abuse investigations. *Child Maltreatment*, *14*, 172–181.

Hershkowitz, I. (2011). Rapport building in investigative interviews of children. In M. E. Lamb, D. J. La Rooy, L. C. Malloy, & C. Katz (Eds.), *Children's testimony: A handbook of psychological research and forensic practice* (pp. 109–128). Chichester, West Sussex, UK: Wiley-Blackwell.

Hetherington, E. M. & Clingempeel, G. W. (1992) (with Anderson, E. R., Deal, J. E., Hagan, M. S., Hollier, E. A., & Lindner, M. S.). Coping with marital transitions: A family systems perspective. *Monographs of the Society for Research in Child Development*, *57*(2–3), 1–242.

Hetherington, E. M., Bridges, M. & Insabella, G. M. (1998). What matters? What does not?: Five perspectives on the association between marital transitions and children's adjustment. *American Psychologist*, *53*, 167–184.

Hodges, W. F. (1986). *Interventions for children of divorce: Custody, access, and psychotherapy*. Hoboken, NJ: Wiley

Holtzworth-Munroe, A., & Stuart, G. L. (1994). Typologies of male batterers: Three subtypes and of the differences among them. *Psychological Bulletin*, *116*, 476–497.

Hutcheson, G. D., Baxter, J. S., Telfer, K., & Warden, D. (1995). Child witness statement quality: Question type and errors of omission. *Law and Human Behavior*, *19*, 631–648.

Hynan, D. J. (1998). Interviewing children in custody evaluations. *Family and Conciliation Courts Review*, *36*, 466–478.

Hynan, D. J. (2002). Child health and safety factors in custody evaluations. *Journal of Forensic Psychology Practice*, *2*, 73–80.

Hynan, D. J. (2003a). Forensic child evaluations. In L. VandeCreek & T. L. Jackson (Eds.), *Innovations in clinical practice: Focus on children and families* (pp. 63–81). Sarasota, FL: Professional Resources Press.

Hynan, D. J. (2003b). Parent-child observations in custody evaluations. *Family Court Review*, *41*, 214–223.

Hynan, D. J. (2004). Unsupported gender differences on some personality disorder scales of the Millon Clinical Multiaxial Inventory-III. *Professional Psychology: Research and Practice*, *35*, 105–110.

Hynan, D. J. (2012). Young children, attachment security, and parenting schedules. *Family Court Review*, *50*, 471–480.

Hynan, D. J. (2013a). Assessing parenting in child custody evaluation: Use of the Parent-Child Relationship Inventory. *Open Access Journal of Forensic Psychology*, *5*, 182–198.

Hynan, D. J. (2013b). Use of the Personality Assessment Inventory in child custody evaluation. *Open Access Journal of Forensic Psychology*, *5*, 120–133.

In re Marriage of Collingbourne, 204 Ill. 2d 498, 274 Ill. Dec. 440, 791 N.E.2d 532 (2003).

Jacobo, M. C., Blais, M. A., Baity, M. R., & Harley, R. (2007). Concurrent validity of the Personality Assessment Inventory Borderline Scales in patients seeking dialectical behavior therapy. *Journal of Personality Assessment, 88*, 74–80.

Jaffe, P. G., Baker, L. L., & Cunningham, A. J. (2004). *Protecting children from domestic violence: Strategies for community interventions.* New York: Guilford.

Jaffe, P. G., Johnston, J. R., Crooks, C. V., & Bala, N. (2008). Custody disputes involving allegations of domestic violence: Toward a differentiated approach to parenting plans. *Family Court Review, 46*, 500–523.

Johnson, J. G., Cohen, P., Chen, H., Kasen, S., & Brook, S. (2006). Parenting behaviors associated with risk for offspring personality disorder during adulthood. *Archives of General Psychiatry, 63*, 579–587.

Johnson, M. P. (1995). Patriarchal terrorism and common couple violence: Two forms of violence against women. *Journal of Marriage and the Family, 57*, 283–294.

Johnson, M. P. (2006). Conflict and control: Gender symmetry and asymmetry and domestic violence. *Violence Against Women, 12*, 1003–1018.

Johnston, J. R. (1993). Children of divorce who refuse visitation. In J. H. Bray & C. Depner (Eds.), *Nonresidential parenting: New vistas in family living* (pp. 109–135). Newbury Park, CA: Sage.

Johnston, J. R. (2003). Parental alignments and rejection: An empirical study of alienation in children of divorce. *Journal of the American Academy of Psychiatry and the Law, 31*, 58–70.

Johnston, J. R., & Campbell, L. E. G. (1988). *Impasses of divorce: The dynamics and resolution of family conflict.* New York: Free Press.

Johnston, J. R., Lee, S., Olesen, N. W., & Walters, M. G. (2005). Allegations and substantiations of abuse in custody-disputing families. *Family Court Review, 43*, 283–294.

Johnston, J. R., Walters, M. G., & Olesen, N. W. (2005a). The psychological functioning of alienated children in custody disputing families: An exploratory study. *American Journal of Forensic Psychology, 23*, 39–64.

Johnston, J. R., Walters, M. G., & Olesen, N. W. (2005b). Is it alienating parenting, role reversal or child abuse? A study of children's rejection of a parent in child custody disputes. *Journal of Emotional Abuse, 5*, 191–218.

Joint Custody, 750 Illinois Compiled Statutes (ILCS) 5/602.1 (2010).

Jouriles, E. N., Norwood, W. D., McDonald, R., Vincent, J. P., & Mahoney, A. (1996). Physical violence and other forms of marital aggression: Links with children's behavior problems. *Journal of Family Psychology, 10*, 223–234.

Kahan, D. M., Braman, D., Cohen, G. L., Gastil, J., & Slovic, P. (2010). Who fears the HPV vaccine, who doesn't, and why? An experimental study of the mechanism of cultural cognition. *Law and the Human Behavior, 34*, 501–516.

Kahn, F. I., Welch, T. L., & Zillmer, E. A. (1993). MMPI-2 profiles of battered women in transition. *Journal of Personality Assessment, 60*, 100–111.

Kahneman, D. (2003a). A perspective on judgment and choice: Mapping bounded rationality. *American Psychologist, 58*, 697–720.

Kahneman, D. (2003b). Experiences of collaborative research. *American Psychologist, 58*, 723–730.

Kahneman, D. (2011). *Thinking, fast and slow*. New York: Farrar, Straus & Giroux.

Kahneman, D., & Klein, G. (2009). Conditions for intuitive expertise: A failure to disagree. *American Psychologist, 64*, 515–526.

Karelaia, N., & Hogarth, R. M. (2008). Determinants of linear judgment: A meta-analysis of lens model studies. *Psychological Bulletin, 134*, 404–426.

Keller, P. S., El-Sheikh, M., Keiley, M., & Laio, P. (2009). Longitudinal relations between marital aggression and alcohol problems. *Psychology of Addictive Behaviors, 23*, 2–13.

Kelly, J. B. (2012). Risk and protective factors associated with child and adolescent adjustment following separation and divorce: Social science applications. In K. Kuehnle & L. Drozd (Eds.), *Parenting plan evaluations: Applied research for the family court* (pp. 49–84). New York: Oxford University Press.

Kelly, J. B., & Johnson, M. P. (2008). Differentiating types of intimate partner violence: Research update and implications for interventions. *Family Court Review, 46*, 476–499.

Kelly, J. B., & Johnston, J. R. (2001). The alienated child: A reformulation of the parental alienation syndrome. *Family Court Review, 39*, 249–266.

Kelly, J. B., & Lamb, M. E. (2000). Using child development research to make appropriate custody and access decisions. *Family & Conciliation Courts Review, 38*, 297–311.

Kelly, J. B., & Lamb, M. E. (2003). Developmental issues in relocation cases involving young children: Whether, when, and how? *Journal of Family Psychology, 17*, 193–205.

Kelly, R. F., & Ramsey, S. H. (2009). Child custody evaluations: The need for systems-level outcome assessments. *Family Court Review, 47*, 286–303.

Kelly, R. F., & Ward, S. L. (2002). Allocating custodial responsibilities at divorce: Social science research and the American Law Institute's approximation rule. *Family Court Review, 40*, 350–370.

Kerig, P. K. (2001). Introduction and overview: Conceptual issues in family observational research. In P. K. Kerig & K. M. Lindahl (Eds.), *Family observational coding systems: Resources for systemic research* (pp. 1–22). Mahwah, NJ: Lawrence Erlbaum.

Khan, F., Welch, T., & Zillmer, E. A. (1993). MMPI-2 profiles of battered women in transition. *Journal of Personality Assessment, 60*, 100–111.

Kirkland, K., & Kirkland, K. L. (2001). Frequency of child custody evaluation complaints and related disciplinary action: A survey of the association of state and provincial psychology boards. *Professional Psychology: Research and Practice, 32*, 171–174.

Koocher, G. P., & Keith-Spiegel, P. (2008). *Ethics in psychology and the mental health professions: Standards and cases*. New York: Oxford University Press.

Korkman, J., Santtila, P., Drzewiecki, T., & Sandnabba, N. K. (2008). Failing to keep it simple: Language use in child sexual abuse interviews with three 8-year-old children. *Psychology, Crime & Law, 14*, 41–60.

Krauss, D. A., & Sales, B. D. (2000). Legal standards, expertise, and experts in the resolution of contested child custody cases. *Psychology, Public Policy, and Law, 6*, 843–879.

Krishnakumar, A., & Buehler, C. (2000). Interparental conflict and parenting behavior: A meta-analytic review. *Family Relations, 49,* 25–44.

Kropp, P. R., Hart, S. D., Webster, C. D., & Eaves, D. (1999). *Spousal assault risk assessment guide.* Toronto, Ontario, Canada: Multi-Health Systems.

Kruger, J., Windschitl, P. D., Burrus, J., Fessel, F., & Chambers, J. R. (2008). The rational side of egocentrism in social comparisons. *Journal of Experimental Social Psychology, 44,* 220–232.

Kuehnle, K. (1996). *Assessing allegations of child sexual abuse.* Sarasota, FL: Professional Resource Press.

Kuehnle, K., & Kirkpatrick, H. D. (2005). Evaluating allegations of child sexual abuse within complex child custody cases. In K. Kuehnle & L. Drozd (Eds.), *Child custody litigation: Allegations of child sexual abuse* (pp. 3–39). New York: Haworth.

Kumho Tire Co. v. Carmichael, 526 U. S. 137 (1999).

Lahey, B. B., Conger, R. D., Atkeson, B. M., & Treiber, F. A. (1984). Parenting behavior and emotional status of physically abusive mothers. *Journal of Consulting and Clinical Psychology, 52,* 1062–1071.

Lamb, M. E. (2007). The "approximation rule": Another proposed reform that misses the target. *Child Development Perspectives, 1,* 35–36.

Lamb, M. E., Hershkowitz, I., Orbach, Y., & Esplin, P. W. (2008). *Tell me what happened.* Hoboken, NJ: Wiley.

Lamb, M. E., & Kelly, J. B. (2001). Using the empirical literature to guide the development of parenting plans: A rejoinder to Solomon and Biringen. *Family Court Review, 39,* 365–371.

Lamb, M. E., Sternberg, K. J., Orbach, Y., Esplin, P. W., & Mitchell, S. (2002). Is ongoing feedback necessary to maintain the quality of investigative interviews with allegedly abused children? *Applied Developmental Science, 6,* 35–41.

Lamb, M. E., Sternberg, K. J., Orbach, Y., Esplin, P. W., Stewart, H., & Mitchell, S. (2003). Age differences in young children's responses to open-ended invitations in the course of forensic interviews. *Journal of Consulting and Clinical Psychology, 71,* 926–934.

Landauer, T. K., & Dumais, S. T. (1997). A solution to Plato's problem: The latent semantic analysis theory of acquisition, induction, and representation of knowledge. *Psychological Review, 104,* 211–240.

Lande, J. (2011). An empirical analysis of collaborative practice. *Family Court Review, 49,* 257–281.

Langer, F. (2011). Using the NEO Personality Inventory in child custody evaluations: a practitioner's perspective. *Journal of Child Custody, 8,* 323–344.

Lansford, J. E. (2009). Parental divorce and children's adjustment. *Perspectives on Psychological Science, 4,* 140–152.

La Rooy, D., Katz, C., Malloy, L. C., & Lamb, M. E. (2010). Do we need to rethink guidance on repeated interviews? *Psychology, Public Policy, and Law, 16,* 373–392.

La Rooy, D., Malloy, L. C., & Lamb, M. E. (2011). The development of memory in childhood. In M. E. Lamb, La Rooy, D. J., Malloy, L. C., & Katz, C. (Eds.), *Children's testimony: A handbook of psychological research and forensic practice* (pp. 49–68). Chichester, West Sussex, UK: Wiley-Blackwell.

Laursen, B. (1995). Conflict and social interaction in adolescent relationships. *Journal of Research on Adolescence, 5,* 55–70.

Levy, R. L. (2006). Custody law and the ALI's Principles: A little history, a little policy, and some very tentative judgments. In R. F. Wilson (Ed.), *Reconceiving the family: Critique on the American Law Institute's Principles of the Law of Family Dissolution* (pp. 67–91). New York: Cambridge University Press.

Lindahl, K. M., & Malik, N. M. (1996). *System for Coding Interactions and Family Functioning (SCIFF).* Unpublished manuscript, University of Miami, Miami, FL.

Lindahl, K. M., & Malik, N. M. (1999). Marital conflict, family processes, and boys' externalizing behavior in Hispanic American and European American families. *Journal of Clinical Child Psychology, 28,* 12–24.

London, K., & Nunez, N. (2002). Examining the efficacy of truth/lie discussions in predicting and increasing the veracity of children's reports. *Journal of Experimental Child Psychology, 83,* 131–147.

Lovasi, G. S., Diez Roux, A. V., Hoffman, E. A., Kawut, S. M., Jacobs, D. R., & Barr, R. G. (2010). Association of environmental tobacco smoke exposure in childhood with early emphysema in adulthood among nonsmokers. *American Journal of Epidemiology, 171*(1), 54–62.

Lowry, L. R. (2004). Evaluative mediation. In J. Folberg, A. L. Milne, & P. Salem (Eds.), *Divorce and family mediation: Models, techniques, and applications* (pp. 72–91). New York: Guilford.

Ludolph, P. S. (2012). The special issue on attachment: Overreaching theory and data. *Family Court Review, 50,* 486–495.

Ludolph, P. S. & Bow, J. N. (2012). Complex alienation dynamics and very young children. *Journal of Child Custody, 9,* 153–178.

Luftman, V. H., Veltkamp, L. J., Clark, J. J., Lannacone, S., & Snooks, H. (2005). Practice guidelines in child custody evaluations for licensed clinical social workers. *Clinical Social Work Journal, 33,* 327–357.

Lyon, T. D., & Dorado, J. (2008). Truth induction in young maltreated children: The effects of oath-taking and reassurance on true and false disclosures. *Child Abuse and Neglect, 32,* 738–748.

Maccoby, E. E., & Martin, J. A. (1983). Socialization in the context of the family: Parent-child interaction. In P. H. Mussen, (Series Ed.) & E. M. Hetherington (Vol. Ed.), *Handbook of child psychology* (4th ed.) (Vol. 4, pp. 1–101). Hoboken, NJ: Wiley.

Maccoby, E. E., & Mnookin, R. W. (1992). *Dividing the child: Social and legal dilemmas of custody.* Cambridge, MA: Harvard University Press.

Maddux, J. A., Biller, B. A., Berry, E. J., Michalowski, S. B., & D'Urso, A. V. (2013). Categorization of abuse criteria by expert ratings and the elusive diagnosis of abuse. *Open Access Journal of Forensic Psychology, 5,* 182–193.

Main, M., Hesse, E., & Hesse, S. (2011). Attachment theory and research: Overview with suggested applications to child custody. *Family Court Review, 49,* 426–463.

Marchant, G. J., & Paulson, S. E. (1998). Test review of the Parent-Child Relationship Inventory. In J. C. Impara & P. S. Plake (Eds.), *The thirteenth mental measurement yearbook.* Retrieved from the Buros Institute's Test Reviews Online website: http: www.buros.org.

Martindale, D. M., & Gould, J. W. (2013). Deconstructing custody evaluation reports. *Journal of the American Academy of Matrimonial Lawyers, 25*, 357-374. Retrieved from www.aaml.org/sites/default/files/MAT210_2.pdf

Martindale, D. A., Tippins, T. M., Ben-Porath, Y. S., Wittman, J. K., & Austin, W. G. (2012). Assessment instruments selection should be guided by validity analysis not professional plebiscite: Response to a flawed survey. *Family Court Review, 50*, 502-507.

McCain, R. A. (2004). *Game theory: A non-technical introduction to the analysis of strategy.* Mason, OH: Thomson South-Western.

McCann, J. T., Flens, J. R., Campagna, V., Collman, P., Lazzaro, T., & Connor, E. (2001). The MCMI-III in child custody evaluations: A normative study. *Journal of Forensic Psychology Practice, 1*, 27–44.

McDonald, R., Jouriles, E. N., Briggs-Gowan, M. J., Rosenfield, D., & Carter, A. S. (2007). Violence toward a family member, angry adult conflict, and child adjustment difficulties: Relations in families with 1- to 3-year-old children. *Journal of Family Psychology, 21*, 176–184.

McGarrah, N. A. (2009). Walking with care through the minefields: The roles of training, competent, collaboration, and support. *Professional Psychology: Research and Practice, 40*, 544–546.

McIntosh, J. E., & Prinz, R. J. (1993). The incidence of alleged sexual abuse in 603 family court cases. *Law and Human Behavior, 17*, 95–101.

McIntosh, J. E., & Smyth, B. (2012). Shared-time parenting: An evidence-based matrix for evaluating risk. In K. Kuehnle & L. Drozd (Eds.), *Parenting plan evaluations: Applied research for the family court* (pp. 155–187). New York: Oxford University Press.

McIntosh, J. E., Smyth, B., & Kelaher, M. (2010). *Parenting arrangements post-separation: Patterns and outcomes, Pt. II: Relationships between overnight care patterns and psycho-emotional development in infants and young children.* North Carlton, Australia: Family Transitions.

McIntosh, J. E., Smyth, B., Wells, Y., & Long, C. (2010). *Parenting arrangements post-separation, Pt. I: A longitudinal study of school-age children in high-conflict divorce.* North Carlton, Australia: Family Transitions.

McIntosh, J. E., Wells, Y. D., Smyth, B. M., & Long, C. M. (2008). Child-focused and child-inclusive divorce mediation: Comparative outcomes from a prospective study of postseparation adjustment. *Family Court Review, 46*, 105–124.

McKay, J. M., Pickens, J., & Stewart, K. L. (1996). Inventoried and observed stress in parent-child interactions. *Current Psychology, 15*, 232–234.

McKenzie, S. J., Klein, K. R., Epstein, Letter L. H., & McCurley, J. (1993). Effects of setting and number of observations on generalizability of parent-child interactions in childhood obesity treatment. *Journal of Psychopathology and Behavioral Assessment, 15*, 129–139.

Medoff, D. (1999). MMPI-2 validity scales in child custody evaluations: Clinical versus statistical significance. *Behavioral Science and the Law, 17*, 409–411.

Melton, G. B. (1989). Test review of the Child Abuse Potential Inventory, Form VI. In J. C. Conoley & J. J. Kramer (Eds.), *The tenth mental measurements yearbook.* Retrieved from http://marketplace.unl.edu/buros/

Melton, G. B., Petrila, J., Poythress, N. G., & Slobogin, C. (2007). *Psychological evaluations for the courts: A handbook for mental health professionals andlawyers* (3rd ed.). New York: Guilford.

Meyer, G. J. (1997). Assessing reliability: Critical corrections for a critical examination of the Rorschach Comprehensive System. *Psychological Assessment, 9,* 480–489.

Meyer, G. J., Hilsenroth, M. J., Baxter, D., Exner, J. E., Fowler, J. C., Piers, C. C., & Resnick, J. (2002). An examination of interrater reliability for scoring the Rorschach Comprehensive System in eight data sets. *Journal of Personality Assessment, 78,* 219–274.

Millon, T. (1994). *Millon Clinical Multiaxial Inventory-III manual.* Minneapolis, MN: National Computer Systems.

Millon, T., Davis, R., & Millon, C. (1997). *The Millon Clinical Multiaxial Inventory–III manual* (2nd ed.). Minneapolis, MN: National Computer Systems.

Millon, T. (2009). (with Millon, C., Davis, R., & Grossman, S.) *Millon Clinical Multiaxial Inventory–III manual* (4th ed.). Bloomington, MN: NCS Pearson.

Milne, A. L., Folberg, J, & Salem, P. (2004). The evolution of divorce and family mediation: An overview. In J. Folberg, A. L. Milne, & P. Salem (Eds.), *Divorce and family mediation: Models, techniques, and applications* (pp. 3–28). New York: Guilford.

Milner, J. S. (1986). *Child Abuse Potential Inventory: Manual* (2nd ed.). DeKalb, IL: Psytec.

Milner, J. S. (1989). Additional cross-validation of the Child Abuse Potential Inventory. *Psychological Assessment, 1,* 219–223.

Minnesota Laws, 518.17(1) (A) (13) (2004).

Mnookin, R. H., & Kornhauser, L. (1979). Bargaining in the shadow of the law: The case of divorce. *Yale Law Journal, 88,* 950–997.

Morey, L. C. (2007). *Personality Assessment Inventory: Professional manual* (2nd ed.). Lutz, FL: Psychological Assessment Resources.

National Conference of Commissioners on Uniform State Laws. (1979). *Uniform marriage and divorce act.* St. Paul, MN: West.

Newcomb, M. D. & Bentler, P. M. (1989). Substance use and abuse among children and teenagers. *American Psychologist, 44,* 242–248.

Newmark, L., Harrell, A., & Salem, P. (1995). Domestic violence and empowerment in custody and visitation cases. *Family and Conciliation Courts Review, 33,* 30–62.

Nichols-Hadeed, C., Cerulli, C., Kaukeinen, K., Rhodes, K. V., & Campbell, J. (2012). Assessing danger: What judges need to know. *Family Court Review, 50,* 150–158.

Oldershaw, L., Walters G. C., & Hall, D. K. (1989). A behavioral approach to the classification of different types of physically abusive mothers. *Merrill-Palmer Quarterly, 35,* 255–279.

Oldham, S. S. & Otto, R. K. (2008, May). *The utility of psychological testing in custody evaluation contexts.* Paper presented at the Joint Conference of the ABA Section of Family Law and the American Psychological Association, 2008 Spring CLE Conference, Chicago, IL.

Oliver, P. H., Guerin, D. W., & Coffman, J. K. (2009). Big five parental personality traits, parenting behaviors, and adolescent behavior problems: A mediation model. *Personality and Individual Differences, 47,* 405–414.

Osborne, L. A., & Reed, P. (2010). Stress and self-perceived parenting behaviors of parents of children with autistic spectrum conditions. *Research in Autism Spectrum Disorders, 4,* 405–414.

Otto, R. K., & Edens, J. F. (2003). Parenting capacity. In Grisso, T. (with Borum, R., Edens, J. F., Moye, J., & Otto, R. K.), *Evaluating competencies: Forensic assessments and instruments* (2nd ed.) (pp. 229–308). New York: Kluwer Academic/Plenum Publishers.

Patterson, G. R. (1982). *Coercive family process.* Eugene, OR: Castalia.

Paulhus, D. L. (1984). Two-component models of socially desirable responding. *Journal of Personality and Social Psychology, 46,* 598–609.

Peacock, W. W. (2009). MMPI-2 personality profiles of heterosexual female perpetrators of domestic violence. *Dissertation Abstracts International: Section B: The Sciences and Engineering, 70*(3-B), 1954.

Pearson, Y. (2006). (with Bankovics, G., Baumann, M., Darcy, N., DeVries, S., Goetz, J. & Kowalsky, G.). Early neutral evaluations: Applications to custody and parenting time cases program development and implementation in Hennepin County, Minnesota. *Family Court Review, 44,* 672–682.

Pence, E., & Paymar, M. (1993). *Education groups for men who batter: The Duluth model.* New York: Springer.

Peskind, S. N. (2014). *Divorce in Illinois: The legal process, your rights, and what to expect.* Omaha, NE: Addicus Books.

Pickar, D. B., & Kahn, J. J. (2011). Settlement-focused parenting plan consultations: An evaluative mediation alternative to child custody evaluations. *Family Court Review, 49,* 59–71.

Pickar, D. B., & Kaufman, R. L. (2013). The child custody evaluation report: Toward an integrated model of practice. *Journal of Child Custody, 10,* 17–53.

Pikula v. Pikula, 374 N.W. 2nd 705 (Minn. 1985).

Pinsoneault, T. B., & Ezzo, F. R. (2012). A comparison of MMPI-2-RF between child maltreatment and non-maltreatment custody cases. *Journal of Forensic Psychology Practice, 12,* 227–237.

Poole, D. A., & Lamb, M. E. (1998). *Investigative interviews of children: A guide for helping professionals.* Washington, DC: American Psychological Association.

Poole, D. A., & White, L. T. (1991). Effects of question repetition on the eyewitness testimony of children and adults. *Developmental Psychology, 23,* 975–986.

Poole, D. A., & White, L. T. (1993). Two years later: Effects of question repetition and retention interval on the eyewitness testimony of children and adults. *Developmental Psychology, 29,* 844–853.

Pope, K. S., Butcher, J. N., & Seelen, J. (2000). *The MMPI, MMPI-2, & MMPI-A in court* (2nd ed). Washington, DC: American Psychological Association.

Pope, K. S., Butcher, J. N., & Seelen, J. (2006). *The MMPI, MMPI-2, & MMPI-A in court* (3rd ed). Washington, DC: American Psychological Association.

Posthuma, A. B., & Harper, J. F. (1988). Comparison of MMPI-2 responses of child custody and personal injury litigants. *Professional Psychology: Research and Practice, 29,* 437–443.

Pruett, M. K., Arthur, L. A., & Ebling, R. (2007). The hand that rocks the cradle: Maternal gatekeeping after divorce. *Pace Law Review, 27,* 709–739.

Pruett, M. K., & Barker, C. (2009). Joint custody: A judicious choice for families – but how, when, and why? In R. M. Galatzer-Levy, L. Krause, & J. Galatzer-Levy (Eds.), *The scientific basis of child custody decisions* (2nd ed.) (pp. 417–462.), Hoboken, NJ: Wiley.

Pruett, M. K., Ebling, R., & Insabella, G. (2004). Critical aspects of parenting plans for young children: Injecting data into the debate about overnights. *Family Court Review, 42*, 39–59.

Pruett, M. K., Insabella, G., & Gustafson, K. (2005). The Collaborative Divorce Project: A court-based intervention for separating parents with young children. *Family Court Review, 43*, 38–51.

Pruett, K., & Pruett, M. K. (2009). *Partnership parenting.* Cambridge, MA: Da Capo Press.

Quas, J. A., Goodman, G. S., Bidrose, S., Pipe, M., Craw, S., & Ablin, D. S. (1999). Emotion and memory: Children's long-term remembering, forgetting, and suggestibility. *Journal of Experimental Child Psychology, 72*, 235–270.

Quas, J. A., Thompson, W. C., & Clarke-Stewart, A. (2005). Do jurors know what isn't so about child witnesses? *Law and Human Behavior, 29*, 425–456.

Quinell, F. A. & Bow, J. A. (2001). Psychological tests used in child custody evaluations. *Behavioral Sciences & the Law, 19*, 491–501.

Quinsey, V. L., & Lalumiere, M. (2001). *Assessment of sexual offenders against children (APSAC study guides)* (2nd ed.). Thousand Oaks, CA: Sage.

Riggs, S. A. (2005). Is the Approximation Rule in the child's best interest? A critique from the perspective of attachment theory. *Family Court Review, 43*, 481–493.

Roberts, K. P., Brubacher, S. P., Powell, M. B., & Price, H. L. (2011). Practice narratives. In M. E. Lamb, D. J. LaRooy, L. C. Malloy, & C. Katz (Eds.), *Children's testimony: A handbook of psychological research and forensic practice* (pp. 129–146). Chichester, West Sussex, UK: Wiley-Blackwell.

Roberts, K. P., Lamb, M. E., & Sternberg, K. J. (2004). The effects of rapport-building style on children's reports of a staged event. *Applied Cognitive Psychology, 18*, 189–202.

Rogers, R., Salekin, R. T., & Sewell, K. W. (1999). Validation of the Millon Clinical Multiaxial Inventory for Axis II disorders: Does it meet the Daubert standard? *Law and Human Behavior, 23*, 425–443.

Rorbaugh, J. B. (2008). *A comprehensive guide to child custody evaluations: Mental health and legal perspectives.* New York: Springer.

Ross, M. & Sicoly, F. (1979). Egocentric biases in availability and attribution. *Journal of Personality and Social Psychology, 37*, 322–336.

Sachsenmaier, S. J. (2005). Complex child custody evaluations: Evaluating the alleged incestuous parent. In K. Kuehnle & L. Drozd (Eds.), *Child custody litigation: Allegations of child sexual abuse* (pp. 57–97). New York: Haworth.

Saini, M., Johnston, J. R., Fidler, B. J., & Bala, N. (2012). Empirical studies of alienation. In K. Kuehnle & L.Drozd (Eds.), *Parenting plan evaluations: Applied research for the family court* (pp. 399–441). New York: Oxford University Press.

Saini, M., Mishna, F., Barnes, J., & Polak, S. (2013). Parenting online: An exploration of virtual parenting time in the context of separation and divorce. *Journal of Child Custody, 10*, 120–140.

Sanbonmatsu, D. M., & Fazio, R. H. (1990). The role of attitudes in memory-based decision-making. *Journal of Personality and Social Psychology, 59*, 614–622.

Sanfey, A. G. (2007, October 26). Social decision-making: Insights from game theory and neuroscience. *Science, 318*, 598–602.

Schleuderer, C., & Campagna, V. (2004). Assessing substance abuse questions in child custody evaluations. *Family Court Review, 42*, 375–383.

Schutz, B. M., Dixon, E. B., Lindenberger, J. C., & Ruther, N. J. (1989). *Solomon's sword: A practical guide to conducting child custody evaluations.* San Francisco, CA: Jossey-Bass.

Scott, E. S. (1992). Pluralism, parental preference, and child custody. *California Law Review, 80*, 615–672.

Scott, R. L., Flowers, J. V., Bulnes, A., Olmsted, E., & Carbajal-Madrid, P. (2009). English-speaking and Spanish-speaking domestic violence perpetrators: An MMPI-2 assessment. *Journal of Interpersonal Violence, 24*, 1859–1874.

Sederberg, P. B., Howard, M. W., & Kahana, M. J. (2008). A context-based theory of recency and contiguity and free recall. *Psychological Review, 115*, 893–912.

Sedlak, A. J., Mettenberg, J., Basena, M., Petta, I., McPherson, K., Greene, A. & Li, S. (2010). *Fourth national incidence study of child abuse and neglect (NIS–4): Report to Congress, executive summary.* Washington, DC: U.S. Department of Health and Human Services, Administration for Children and Families.

Shaffer, M. B. (1992). Test review of the Bricklin Perceptual Scales. In J. J. Kramer & J. C. Conoley (Eds.), *The eleventh mental measurements yearbook.* Retrieved from http://marketplace.unl.edu/buros/

Shelton, K. H., & Harold, G. T. (2008). Interparental conflict, negative parenting, and children's adjustment: Bridging links between parents' depression and children's psychological distress. *Journal of Family Psychology, 22*, 712–724.

Sher, K. J., Walitzer, K. S., Wood, P. K., & Brent, E. E. (1991). Characteristics of children of alcoholics: Putative risk factors, substance use and abuse, and psychopathology. *Journal of Abnormal Psychology, 100*, 427–448.

Shienvold, A. (2004). Hybrid processes. In J. Folberg, A. L. Milne, & P. Salem (Eds.), *Divorce and family mediation: Models, techniques, and applications* (pp. 112–128). New York: Guilford.

Siegel, J. C. (1996). Traditional MMPI-2 validity indicators and initial presentation in custody evaluations. *American Journal of Forensic Psychology, 14*, 55–63.

Siegel, J. C., Bow, J. N., & Gottlieb, M. C. (2012). The MMPI-2 in high conflict child custody cases. *American Journal of Forensic Psychology, 30*, 21–34.

Siegel, J. C., & Langford, J. S. (1998). MMPI-2 validity scales and suspected parental alienation syndrome. *American Journal of Forensic Psychology, 16*, 5–14.

Singer, J., Hoppe, C. F., Lee, S. M., Olesen, N. W., & Walters, M. G. (2008). Child custody litigants: Rorschach data from a large sample. In C. B. Gacono & F. B. Evans (with N. Kaser-Boyd & L. A. Gacono) (Eds.), *The handbook of forensic Rorschach assessment* (pp. 445–466). New York: Routledge.

Sloman, S. A. (1996). The empirical case for two systems of reasoning. *Psychological Bulletin, 119*, 3–22.

Solomon, J., & George, C. (1999). The development of attachment in separated and divorced families: Effects of overnight visitation, parent, and couple variables. *Attachment and Human Development, 1*, 1–33.

Sroufe, L. A., Egeland, B., Carlson, E., & Collins, W. A. (2005). *The development of the person: The Minnesota study of risk and adaptation from birth to adulthood.* New York: Guilford.

Sroufe, L. A., & McIntosh, J. (2011). Divorce and attachment relationships: The longitudinal journey. *Family Court Review, 49,* 464–473.

Stahl, P. M. (1994). *Conducting child custody evaluations: A comprehensive guide.* Thousand Oaks, CA: Sage.

Stahl, P. M. (2011). *Conducting child custody evaluations: From basic to complex issues.* Los Angeles, CA: Sage.

Stahl, P. M. (2013). Emerging issues in relocation cases. *Journal of the American Association of Matrimonial Lawyers, 25,* 425–451. Retrieved from www.aaml.org/sites/default/files/MAT206_2. pdf

Standridge, J. B., Adams, S. M., & Zotos, A. P. (2010, March 1). Urine drug screening: A valuable office procedure. *American Family Physician, 81,* 635–640. Retrieved from www.aafp.org/afp/2010/0301/p365/html

Stanovich, K. E., & West, R. F. (2002). Individual differences in reasoning: Implications for the rationality debate. In T. Gilovich, D. Griffin, & D. Kahneman (Eds.), *Heuristics and biases* (pp. 421–440). New York: Cambridge University Press.

Steinberg, L., Lamborn, S., Dornbusch, S., & Darling, N. (1992). Impact of parenting practices on adolescence achievement: Authoritative parenting, school involvement, and encouragement to succeed. *Child Development, 63,* 1266–1281.

Steinberg, L., & Silk, J. S. (2002). Parenting adolescents. In M. H. Bornstein (Ed.), *Handbook of parenting* (2nd ed.) (Vol. 1, pp. 103–134). New York: Psychology Press.

Stinson, J. N., Dawson, D. A., Goldstein, R. B., Chou, S. P., Huang, B., Smith, S. M., Ruan, W. J., Pulay, A. J., Saha, T. D., Pickering, R. P., & Grant, B. F. (2008). Prevalence, correlates, disability, and comorbidity of DSM-IV narcissistic personality disorder: Results from the Wave 2 National Epidemiologic Surveyon Alcohol And Related Conditions. *Journal of Clinical Psychiatry, 69,* 1033–1045.

Straus, M. A. (1979). Measuring intrafamily conflict and violence: The Conflict Tactics Scales. *Journal of Marriage and the Family, 41,* 75–88.

Straus, M. A., Hamby, S. L., Boney-McCoy, S., & Sugarman, D. B. (1996). The revised Conflict Tactics Scales (CTS2): Development and preliminary psychometric data. *Journal of Family Issues, 17,* 283–316.

Straus, M. A., Hamby, S. L., & Warren, W. L. (2003). *The Conflict Tactics Scales handbook.* Los Angeles, CA: Western Psychological Services.

Stricker, G., & Trierweiler, S. J. (1995). The local clinical scientist: A bridge between science and practice. *American Psychologist, 50,* 995–1002.

Strong, D. R., Greene, R. L., Hoppe, C., Johnston, T., & Olesen, N. (1999). Taxometric analysis of impression management and self-deception on the MMPI-2 in child-custody litigants. *Journal of Personality Assessment, 73,* 1–18.

Sullivan, M., Ward, P., & Deutsch, R. M. (2010). Overcoming barriers family camp. *Family Court Review, 48,* 116–135.

Sweeney, M. M. (2010). Remarriage and stepfamilies: Strategic sites for family scholarship in the 21st century. *Journal of Marriage and Family, 72,* 667–684.

Talwar, V., Lee, K., Bala, N., & Lindsay, R. C. L. (2002). Children's conceptual knowledge of lying and its relation to their actual behaviors: Implications for court. *Law and Human Behavior, 26,* 395–415.

Talwar, V., Lee, K., Bala, N., & Lindsay, R. C. L. (2004). Children's lie-telling to conceal a parent's transgression: Legal implications. *Law and Human Behavior, 28,* 411–435.

Terzuoli, M. (2010). Relying on the unreliable: How a court rule could alleviate the problems inherent in the neutral mental health evaluation process in child custody cases. *Family Court Review, 48,* 571–582.

Thoennes, N., & Tjaden, P. G. (1990). The extent, nature, and validity of sexual abuse allegations in custody/visitation disputes. *Child Abuse & Neglect, 14,* 151–163.

Thomas, J. T., Hecht, S. S., Luo, X., Ming, X., Ahluwalia, J. S., & Carmella, S. C. (2014). Thirdhand tobacco smoke: A tobacco-specific lung carcinogen on surfaces in smokers' homes. *Nicotine & Tobacco Research, 16*(1), 26–32.

Thomas, S. S. (2004, January 8). *Family Law Section Council's proposed re-write of the Illinois Custody Act.* Memorandum to the Board of Governors, Illinois State Bar Association.

Time poll, home (2009, October 26). *Time, 174*(16), 32.

Tippins, T. M., & Wittman, J. P. (2005). Empirical and ethical problems with custody recommendations: A call for clinical humility and judicial vigilance. *Family Court Review, 43,* 193–222.

Tobin, N. L., Seals, R. W., & Vincent, J. P. (2011). Response patterns on the Parent-Child Relationship Inventory in a simulated child custody evaluation. *Journal of Child Custody, 8,* 284–300.

Tolle, L. W., & O'Donohue, W. T. (2012). *Improving the quality of child custody evaluations.* New York: Springer.

Tornello, S. A., Emery, R., Rowen, J., Potter, D., Ocker, B., & Xu, Y. (2013). Overnight custody arrangements, attachment, and adjustment among very young children. *Journal of Marriage and Family, 75,* 871–885.

Tschann, J. M., Johnston, J. R., Kline, M., & Wallerstein, J. M. (1989). Family process and children's functioning during divorce. *Journal of Marriage and the Family, 51,* 431–444.

Tversky, A., & Kahneman, D. (1974). Judgment under uncertainty: Heuristics and biases. *Science, 185,* 1124–1131.

U. S. National Library of Medicine, National Institutes of Health. (2013). *Toxicology screen.* Retrieved from www.nlm.nih.gov/medlineplus/ency/article/003578.htm

Vacca, J. J. (in press). Test review of Conflict Tactics Scales. In J. F. Carlson, K. F. Geisinger, & J. L. Jonson (Eds.), *The nineteenth mental measurements yearbook.* Retrieved from http://marketplace.unl.edu/buros/

Ver Steegh, N., & Dalton, C. (2008). Report from the Wingspread Conference on domestic violence and family courts. *Family Court Review, 46,* 454–476.

Vesga-Lopez, O., Schneier, F. R., Wang, S. Heimberg, R. G., Liu, S., Hasin, D. S., & Blanco, C. (2008). Gender differences in generalized anxiety disorder: Results from the National Epidemiologic Survey on Alcohol and Related Conditons (NESARC). *Journal of Clinical Psychiatry, 69,* 1606–1616.

Visitation, 750 Illinois Compiled Statutes (ILCS) 5/607 (2013).

Vuchinich, S., Angelelli, J., & Gatherum, A. (1996). Context and development in family problem solving with preadolescent children. *Child Development, 67,* 1276–1288.

Walker, L. E. (1984). *The battered woman syndrome.* New York: Springer.

Walker, L. E., & Shapiro, D. L. (2010). Parental alienation disorder: Why label children with mental diagnoses? *Journal of Child Custody, 7,* 266–286.

Wallerstein, J. S., & Kelly, J. B. (1976). The effects of parental divorce: Experiences of the child in later latency. *American Journal of Orthopsychiatry, 46*(2), 256–269.

Warshak, R. A. (2007). Punching the parenting timeclock: The approximation rule, social science, and baseball bats kids. *Family Court Review, 45,* 600–612.

Warshak, R. A. (2010). Family Bridges: Using insights from social science to reconnect parents and alienated children. *Family Court Review, 48,* 48–80.

Warshak, R. A. (2011). Parenting by the clock: The best-interest-of-the-child standard, judicial discretion, and the American Law Institute's "approximation rule." *University of Baltimore Law Review, 41,* 83–164.

Waters, E., & McIntosh, J. (2011). Are we asking the right questions about attachment? *Family Court Review, 49,* 474–482.

Waters, E., Merrick, S., Treboux, D., Crowell, J., & Albersheim, L. (2000). Attachment security in infancy and early adulthood: A twenty-year longitudinal study. *Child Development, 71,* 684–689.

Weiner, I. B. (2013). The Rorschach inkblot method. In R. P Archer & E. M. A. Wheeler (Eds.), *Forensic uses of clinical assessment instruments* (pp. 202–229). New York: Routledge.

Weinfield, N. S., Ogawa, J. R., & Egeland, B. (2002). Predictability of observed mother-child interaction from preschool to middle school in a high-risk sample. *Child Development, 73,* 528–543.

Weitzman, S. (2000). *Not to people like us: Hidden abuse in upscale marriages.* New York: Basic Books.

Wilson, R. F. (Ed.). (2006). *Reconceiving the family: Critique of the American Law Institute's Principles of the Law of Family Dissolution.* New York: Cambridge University Press.

Wilson, S. R., Rack, J. J., Shi, X., & Norris, A. M. (2008). Comparing physically abusive, neglectful, and non-maltreating parents during interactions with their children: A meta-analysis of observational studies. *Child Abuse and Neglect, 29,* 897–911.

Winickoff, J. P., Friebely, J., Tanski, S. E., Sherrod, C., Matt, G. E., Hovell, M. E., & McMillen, R. C. (2009). Beliefs about the health effects of "thirdhand" smoke and home smoking bans. *Pediatrics, 123*(1), e74-e79. Retrieved from http://pediatrics.aappublications.org/content/123/1/e74

Wolman, R., & Pomerance, R. (2012). Telepresence technology in divorce and separation. *Open Access Journal of Forensic Psychology, 4,* 51–68.

Wood, J. M., Nezworski, M. T., & Stejskal, W. J. (1996). The comprehensive system for the Rorschach: A critical examination. *Psychological Science, 7,* 3–10.

Woody, R. H. (2000). Child custody: *Practice standards, ethical issues, and legal safeguards for mental health professionals.* Sarasota, FL: Professional Resource Press.

Woody, R. H. (2013). *Legal self-defense for mental health practitioners: Quality care and risk management strategies.* New York: Springer Publishing Co.

World Health Organization, World Mental Health Survey Initiative. (2007). *National comorbidity survey (NCS) and national comorbidity survey replication (NCS-R).* Retrieved from http://www.hcp.med.harvard.edu.ncs/

Young, K. R., & Weed, N. C. (2006). Assessing alcohol- and drug-abusing clients with the MMPI-2. In J. N. Butcher (Ed.), *MMPI-2: A practitioner's guide* (pp. 361–379). Washington, DC: American Psychological Association.

Zimmerman, J., & Hess, A. K. (2009). Navigating through the divorce and child custody minefield. *Professional Psychology: Research and Practice, 40,* 540–544.

INDEX